Women of the Gobi

About the Author

Kate James was born in Melbourne in 1972 and lived in South India from 1980 to 1987 before returning to Australia. She has worked as a journalist for religious, country and suburban newspapers, and is currently a freelance editor, mostly on travel guidebooks.

Women of the Gobi

Journeys on the Silk Road

PLUTO PRESS AUSTRALIA

First published in 2006 by
Pluto Press Australia
PO Box 617
North Melbourne Victoria 3051
www.plutoaustralia.com

Copyright © Katherine James 2006

Cover Design by Peter Long
Edited by Stephanie Holt
Typeset by J&M Typesetting
Printed and bound by Griffin Press

All rights reserved. No part of this book may be reprinted or reproduced or utilised in any from or by any electronic, mechanical or other means, now known or hereafter invented, including photocopying and recording or in any information storage or retrieval system, without permission in writing from the publisher.

James, Kate (Katherine Muriel), 1972- .
    Women of the Gobi : journeys on the silk road.

    ISBN 9781864033298.
    ISBN 1 86403 329 0.

    1. James, Kate (Katherine Muriel), 1972-   - Travel. 2. Women travelers - Gobi Desert (Mongolia and China) - Biography. 3. Women missionaries - Gobi Desert (Mongolia and China) - Biography. 4. Australians - Gobi Desert (Mongolia and China) - Travel. 5. Gobi Desert (Mongolia and China) - Description and travel. I. Title.

915.1046

Every effort has been made by the author and publisher to contact holders of copyright to obtain permission to reproduce copyright material. However, if any permissions have been inadvertently overlooked or were unobtainable, apologies are offered, and should the rightful party contact the publisher all due credit with necessary and reasonable arrangements will be made at the first opportunity.

To my brother, Jack

Acknowledgments

Special thanks, firstly, to the very generous Trio of Valerie Griffiths, Patricia East and Marion Myers.

In Australia, thanks to Tony Moore, Sarah Crisp and Brendan O'Dwyer at Pluto Press; editor Stephanie Holt; cartographer Julie Sheridan; David Marks for the author photo; Presbyterian archivists Christine Palmer and Judith Kilmartin; Estelle Bannister and everyone else who responded to my letter in *New Life*; Tracey Yuan Tao and Evelyn Chen at Red Crane; Kathy Caddy at the Bible College of Victoria; and Anthony Garnaut, for language tips and other good advice. Thanks also to Gerald Murnane, for feedback and for teaching that profoundly influenced my writing for the better.

In China thanks to everyone who helped me, especially Wang Bao Long, Ma Jian Sheng, Liu Yi, Niu Xiao Jun, 'James and Ange' and Dan Washburn. In England, thanks to Catharine, Andy and Ben McEwan, for sharing their home; Charlotte Hails at Overseas Missionary Fellowship, for retrieving archived photos; and Peter Meadow, Bible Society Librarian at Cambridge University Library, for permission to quote from material in the society's archives.

Finally, thanks to Jack, for joining me, and Alex and Isaac, for letting him go; to the rest of my family, for their wholehearted support; and to Chris, with love, for help in a thousand big and small ways, and for assuming I could do it.

Early photos reproduced by courtesy of the Overseas Missionary Fellowship. Extracts from Hodder & Stoughton books, as listed in the bibliography, reproduced with the permisson of Hodder & Stoughton, UK.

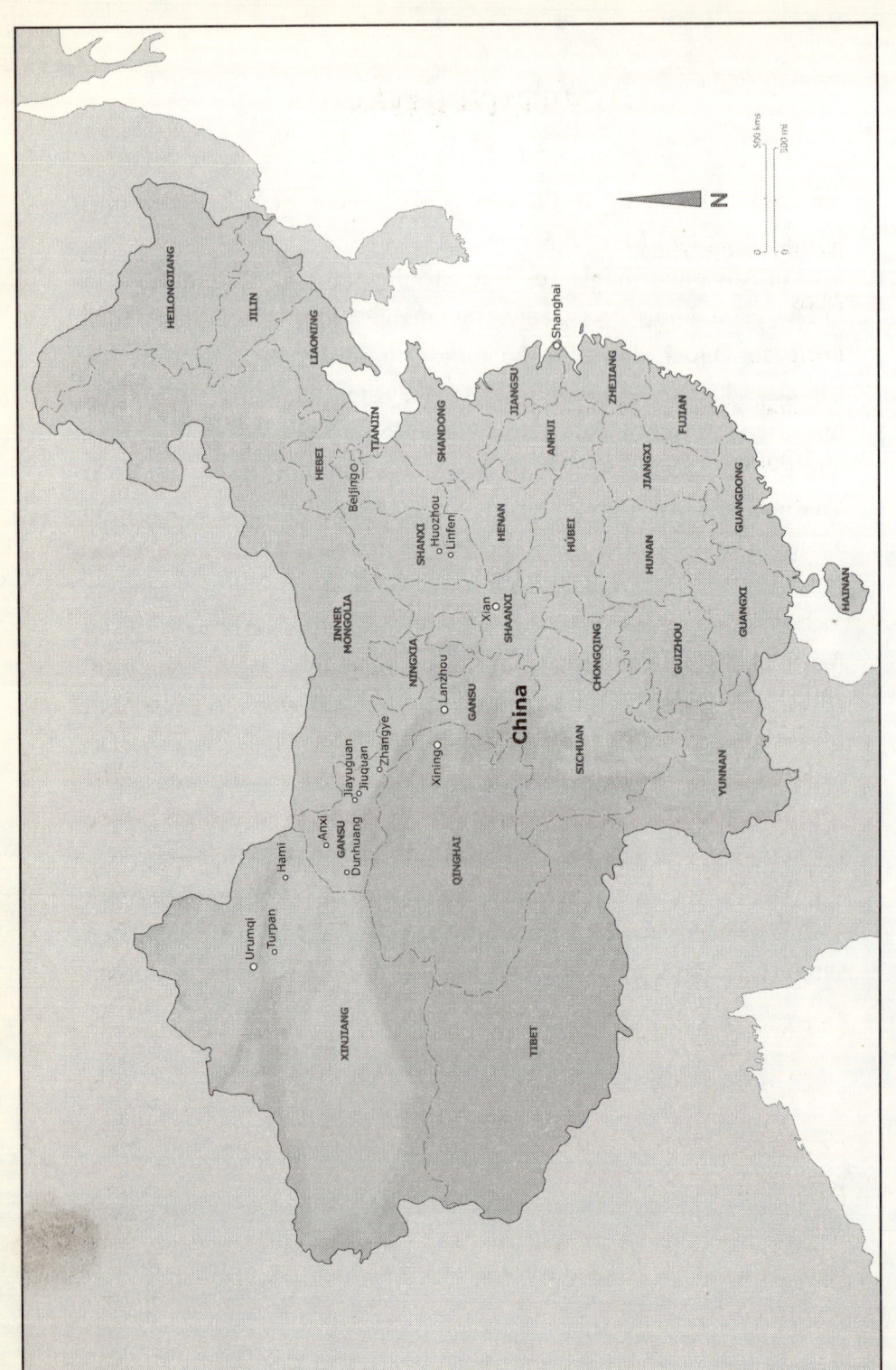

Contents

Acknowledgments	vii
Map	viii
Prologue Ooty	1
Chapter One Melbourne	16
Chapter Two Huozhou	30
Chapter Three Xi'an	50
Chapter Four Topsy	67
Chapter Five Xining	77
Chapter Six Somewhere north of Xining	89
Chapter Seven Zhangye	107
Chapter Eight Jiayuguan	118
Chapter Nine Into the Gobi	136
Chapter Ten Dunhuang	151
Chapter Eleven Hami	170
Chapter Twelve Turpan	190
Chapter Thirteen The Mountain of God	215
Chapter Fourteen England	238
Epilogue Shanghai	255
Bibliography	260

Prologue

Ooty

When I was eight years old I made cubbies in the woodshed among the stored belongings of dead and near-dead missionaries. I would wedge myself between tin trunks and use a horse blanket as a roof for an imaginary fort; then I would read Famous Five books and write letters to my grandparents in Australia. I could hear Ardu the goat bleating outside, and Raju chopping wood.

Dear Grandpa,
How are you? I am fine. The curries are very hot.

My mother helped manage a missionary guesthouse called Montauban, in Ooty, a town surrounded by eucalyptus trees in the Nilgiri hills of south India, where it drizzled a lot. We had moved there from Melbourne, so it wasn't a big change. My father was a history teacher at Hebron, an international boarding school in Ooty.

Every morning he and my brother Jack and I would walk there from Montauban, where we lived, skirting the dirty puddles that formed in potholes on the road.

My mother said the missionaries would come to Montauban and unpack their trunks when it got too hot for them on The Plains. The trunks were full of cardigans and tweed skirts and woollen blankets. I took 'The Plains' to mean the rest of India, below our hills, where the air was hot and dry. I imagined The Plains were like the watercolour painting on the wall in the dining room, which showed a man leading a bullock cart piled with bundles. He wore a turban and a blank expression, and the landscape behind him was flat and yellow.

Some of the missionaries had been holidaying at Montauban every year for forty or fifty years. My mother said they came from an era when people went to the mission field expecting to die there. Next to the turbaned man on the dining-room wall was a black-and-white photo, taken in the 1950s, of missionaries gathered on the Montauban veranda. They all looked serious, and there were lots of horn-rimmed glasses. By 1980, the year my family arrived in India, only a handful of the people in the photo were still alive. They were all women.

Almost every missionary woman could tell a story about walking to the front of the church and dedicating her life to God, after a particularly stirring sermon. These women had grown up in nominally Christian countries at a time when church attendance was high, but they had all been through some kind of conversion experience that had taken them beyond the Sunday-morning, insurance-against-hell Christianity that most people believed in, however loosely. The women had become so enthusiastic about serving the Lord that they had signed up with a mission organisation and boarded a ship for India, where they were apprenticed to a senior missionary. They learned a local language and helped set up some worthy project or other in a hot, dusty backwater, and they stayed put. They nursed, or ran agricultural programs, or taught orphans. And once a year they came to Montauban to speak English and use proper cutlery, or that's what my mother said.

I was a little scared of the old missionary women. They smelled of 4711 cologne and mothballs and body odour. They were even older than my Australian Nana, who wore slacks and cried at the airport and put Minties in my hand luggage. On Indian streets and trains, old women pinched my cheek and called me sweetie-baba. 'So cute, isn't it?' they said. But the missionaries didn't think I was cute. They only noticed Jack and me when we accidentally flouted decades of Montauban tradition.

The first time this happened, my family and a Miss Wills were eating dinner in our flat. It was a quiet time – she was the only guest – so the dining room had been closed up and the curtains and rugs hung out on the lawn to try to get rid of the boiled-beef smell. When we finished eating, my father read a Bible passage and prayed, and Jack excused himself from the table and stood up. He was a polite six-year-old. But Miss Wills was apoplectic. 'Sit, sit, sit!' she said. 'The Master hasn't risen yet!'

My father was only the default Master. Bert, the long-time manager, was away administering an orphanage in Karnataka. Bert had his fingers in a lot of pies.

But dining-room ritual went this way, and always had, at least as far back as Miss Wills could remember. At six o'clock Raju would stand on the veranda and whack a hanging piece of metal (erroneously referred to as 'the bell') with a soup ladle or other handy object. This indicated to everyone on the property that the meal was about to start. People stood behind their seats until the Master – Bert, or my father, or at a pinch my mother – said grace and sat down. Master ladled out the soup, and Raju and the other young Indian men who worked at Montauban passed the bowls around the table. The men kept ready-tied turbans on pegs behind the dining-room door and wore them at a rakish angle. The Senior Missionary Lady – whoever had spent most years on the mission field – sat on the right of the Master and was in charge of the teapot. After the meal, Bible reading and prayer, everyone had to remain seated until the Master stood up.

After dinner, when most people retired to the communal living room to read or sing light opera tunes around the piano or play fiercely contested board games, the Senior Missionary Lady always claimed the seat closest to the fire. In the years we spent at Montauban in the 1980s, I learned to love Gilbert and Sullivan, and playing Scrabble, and I still do.

'And *where*, pray tell, are the fish knives?' one of the missionaries asked at dinner one night. My mother liked that one. She quoted it a lot.

When we moved to India my mother was only 32, with dyed-blonde curls and an open laugh, and the dourness of the missionary ladies wore her patience at times. But whenever she complained, she would pause afterwards – as she would pause if you asked her about the women now – and tell you how hard they worked all year round and how important Montauban and its traditions were for them, and how, really, we could learn a lot from them. She said they were tough old birds.

My mother's ability to be utterly committed to something and still laugh at its ridiculous aspects helps explain why I was 26 years old before I walked away from Christianity. My parents set an example that made me believe I could be a decent and intelligent person, that I could have integrity *and* a sense of humour, while dedicating myself to Jesus and the community of believers. It's not their fault I fell short in the faith department.

Prologue

Late in 1981, when my family had been in India for nearly two years, Bert was driving back to Ooty from his orphanage in Karnataka and stopped at a bank somewhere on the way home to withdraw a few thousand rupees for a land deal. He didn't make it back to Ooty. The next day his car was found on the side of the road somewhere outside Mysore. His body was nearby. Nobody told me exactly how he was killed.

The old generation of missionaries almost disappeared over the next couple of years. New missionaries arrived, often with children who trampled on the flowerbeds. They didn't come to Montauban to be Western, like the older missionaries – they were pretty much Western all the time. For them, Montauban was just a convenient place to stay when they visited their children at Hebron School.

Routines were relaxed in the following years, due in no small part to my mother's subversive influence. The Montauban domestic staff were told they could take their turbans home, and quite possibly they took that to mean they could take the fish knives too, which would account for their disappearance. One of my mother's lasting legacies was the dining room. She tore down the orange polyester curtains, took the overnight train to Bangalore to buy massive lengths of a pale fabric with an Art Nouveau print, and had the whole room painted in pastels.

One day in 1985, just after Easter, an English hippy came to Montauban. Jack was climbing the cypress tree and saw her wandering up the driveway. I don't know how she got there; Montauban was up a quiet back street, and we weren't in the Lonely Planet. There may have been a guesthouse policy about only taking Christian workers, but I can't imagine that my mother had the heart to turn the girl away.

The hippy was wearing a sari petticoat, which she had mistaken for a skirt, and a tight t-shirt, and no bra. She had a string of jasmine flowers in her hair and – horror of horrors – a red mark on her forehead. 'Yeah, I went to the temple near the market, the priest put this on me,' she said cheerily. 'It was wild.' She was on some kind of spiritual quest, she told my mother. Finding herself. There was no one else staying at Montauban, so she didn't meet anyone except my family and Raju, who kept offering her hot-water bottles and cups of tea, which is more than he'd ever done for me. She ate with us that night and, as a nice counter-balance to her temple experience, she got to hear me recite Bible verses after dinner. I was preparing for the Scripture Union inter-school memory-verse competition, where I would compete against other thirteen-year-olds from English Medium schools in the Nilgiri hills. I was practising hard because there was no way I was going to lose to those girls from St Hilda's College again. That year we were memorising verses from the book of Revelation.

> And when he had taken the book, the four beasts and four and twenty elders fell down before the Lamb, having every one of them harps, and golden vials full of odours, which are the prayers of saints. And they sung a new song, saying, Thou art worthy to take the book, and to open the seals thereof; for thou wast slain, and hast redeemed us to God by thy blood out of every kindred, and tongue, and people, and nation.

I don't remember being concerned about the hippy's presence at memory-verse practice, but I heard my mother laughing about it later, telling someone the hippy girl had looked a bit overwhelmed.

Between 1980 and 1987 my family lived at both Montauban and Hebron School, going back and forth every couple of years. My mother and father spent a year at the school as dormitory parents to about twenty little boys, giving my mother the chance to paint complicated murals on the dormitory walls ('I thought I'd do a jungle scene for the standard five boys and Asterix and Obelix for standard six').

Prologue

Twice a year we went on holiday to Goa or Kovalam or some other beach where travellers congregated and where the 1960s were still alive. My father would unbutton his shirt and have an Ayuravedic massage and listen to Bob Dylan. By my early teens I would ignore my family and wander the beaches in my sarong, stopping to drink lemon tea alone in thatched cafes and gaze at sexy young backpackers who also sat alone in cafes, bathed in the light of glorious Arabian Sea sunsets, with a guidebook and a bottle of beer on the table in front of them. I knew I would probably end up being some kind of missionary when I grew up, but in my fantasies I was a golden-skinned hippy.

In 1987 we moved back to Melbourne. I was fifteen years old.

I visited Montauban about fifteen years later. I had taken a few weeks off work and was heading up to Goa to swim in the ocean and lie on the sand and eat fish curry and get clothes made cheaply. I was embarrassed to admit this to our family friends in India, who were all busy doing useful things. My mother's friend Kathy, an Anglo-Indian woman who then managed Montauban, was very friendly. She pointed out my mother's curtains and refused to let me pay my bill, but I suspected she was wondering what I was doing there. I intimated that the travel was connected to my job as a guidebook editor, which wasn't true.

The truth was that I had turned out more like a hippy than a missionary.

Deep down, I wasn't sure if this was a good thing or not. On the one hand, I wasn't a cultural imperialist, forcing my beliefs onto people with millennia-old traditions of their own. On the other hand, how many dying lepers had I washed today?

I spent a few days walking around the muddy streets of Ooty and breathing the cold, thin air. The legless beggar still sat in front of

Chellaram's department store and the goats were still clustered around the Gandhi statue and the autorickshaws still strained up the hills with their badly tuned engines that spewed out familiar-smelling fumes, and I felt the elation of coming home. I recognised it as the same happiness I felt every time I returned to Melbourne.

The last day I spent in Ooty was a Saturday. I had planned my visit to avoid being there on a Sunday. I didn't want to go to church, but people would talk if I didn't go. I didn't want to talk to people about my faith, or lack of it.

Saturday started with toast and tea in the Montauban dining room. The sunlight dappled the walls. In place of the long formal table I remembered, there was a collection of small, cafe-style tables, only one of which was set for breakfast. I recognised the silver toast-racks of my childhood. I sat with the one other visitor, an American who introduced herself as Winnie and told me about her job with a missionary organisation called Interserve, visiting the organisation's workers all over India to check how they were managing and how Interserve could help them. She was in Ooty to visit Interserve workers' children who were boarding at Hebron School.

I took to Winnie. She didn't ask me what I was doing in India. We talked about the sameness of mission guesthouses around the subcontinent, down to the dusty biographies on the bookshelves. She mentioned books by Cable and French, and was surprised I hadn't heard of them. She said they travelled through the Gobi desert on mule carts and visited harems and isolated Tibetan monasteries and made brave escapes from bloodthirsty brigands. 'One of the feminist presses reissued one of their books a few years ago,' she said, as if that might jog my memory. 'You should track down their books, you'd like them.'

I pulled my notebook out of my daypack and wrote down the names Mildred Cable and Francesca French.

Later in the day I caught a bus to the train that took me up the

Prologue

southwest coast of India to Goa, where I mostly read novels on Benaulim beach. Around me, sunburned Europeans talked about rave parties and haggled over prices with women who carried baskets of fruit along the sand.

The books weren't hard to hunt down on eBay. Attributed to Mildred Cable and Francesca French, they seemed to have been mainly written by Mildred but polished by Francesca. I discovered that a third woman, Francesca's sister Evangeline, or 'Eva', also travelled with them. The first book I read was called *Something Happened*, an account the women described as their 'spiritual biography'.

The three women and their lives felt familiar and interesting to me right from the start. They didn't sound like prigs or battleaxes or any of those words that usually apply to Victorian missionary women. Their conversion stories were the kind that I had grown up hearing in church and reading at bedtime, but the honest, funny way they told them drew me in.

Eva's story was told first. She grew up in a literary household in cosmopolitan Geneva, where she had been a defiant child, and a 'fervent Nihilist, incipient Communist and embryonic Bolshevist' teenager. She hated the provincial English life forced on her in her late teens after the family moved to Portsmouth, and her miserable moods made her whole family unhappy. Mildred later wrote of Eva:

> For a young lady to hold strong opinions, to be revolutionary in outlook and unusual in small ways was sufficient to bring her under suspicion. Misery and depression closed in upon her like a dense fog ... the things which occupied her mind could never be ventilated in provincial society, and the conversation of the tea-party bored her to tears.

A turning point came at a local church. The way Mildred told Eva's story reminded me of the missionary women in India.

> An evangelistic mission was being held and the pulpit was occupied by an elderly man who, after the singing of a gospel hymn, began with utter simplicity to speak on an incident in the life of Christ. As [Eva] sat in that pew, the preacher, the choir and the congregation suddenly ceased to exist for her, and she was alone with Christ. As the vision broke upon her she fell at His feet and begged forgiveness for all the sin and rebellion of the past... then and there she accepted salvation and staked her all on the fact that Christ has died for her... In this moment of illumination she saw that above chaos there was a plan, and in that plan a place for her.

She told everyone at home about it. Almost immediately she had her heart set on going to China, and she was accepted by the China Inland Mission. She sailed out in 1893, when she was 22 years old.

As missions go, the CIM was in many ways a radical, forward-thinking organisation. It was founded in 1865 by Hudson Taylor, a young missionary who was frustrated with the way other missionaries huddled together in expatriate ghettoes in China's big cities. Taylor accepted candidates from many countries and backgrounds as long as they had a basic Protestant faith. All its members had to learn fluent Mandarin or Cantonese, and they lived and dressed like locals. The mission lobbied for years against the British government's opium trade in China.

Eva spent eight years as an itinerant missionary in Shanxi province, and saw many of her friends killed in the 1900 Boxer Uprising, before she was joined by Mildred Cable. Mildred was the studious daughter of a Guilford draper. She made a Christian commitment in her teens and read books about martyrs for pleasure, and she was still a schoolgirl when she contacted the CIM. Over the next few years she did extensive medical training – under a respectable woman doctor, of course – and in 1901 she sailed out to meet Eva.

When Eva first saw Mildred step off the cart she thought the CIM was mad to send a 'frail child' into such a harsh place, even though Mildred, at 22, was the same age that Eva was when she first came to China eight years earlier. Eva soon changed her mind about Mildred. In the town of Huozhou the pair founded a school for girls and an opium refuge for women. When Eva was amused, the corners of her mouth twitched slightly, but Mildred laughed loud and often.

Francesca French was quieter than her older sister, and thought of herself as cultivated and sensitive. Her own Christian conversion experience came just a few days before Eva's, but, unlike Eva, she didn't share it loudly with the rest of the family. Francesca had gone walking in the evening to escape Eva's tears and shouting, and started to feel only God could change her sister's terrible unhappiness and its effect on the family. '[Francesca] was profoundly conscious that she had no right of access to God, unless the act of reconciliation had taken place…By an act of faith she flung herself on grace, and found herself on the breast of God.'

After Eva went to China, Francesca was the obvious choice to care for their ageing mother, and she did it with good grace. But when their mother died in 1908, 34-year-old Francesca joined Eva and Mildred, who made a concerted effort to let her into their close friendship.

Mildred had decided that 'if [her friendship with Eva] reveals an exclusive element it will bring unhappiness to both, but if there be nothing of the kind, the relationship between the three of us might develop into something better than we have yet known'. She was right. The three women were obviously a happy team, working together at the church and school in Huozhou for another fifteen years. They didn't style themselves as the Trio, but that's what everyone in the CIM called them. The Chinese Christians they lived among called them 'our three-in-one teachers'.

In 1922, the women told their Chinese church pastor that they were going to leave Huozhou and travel thousands of miles into China's northwest to evangelise along the Silk Road routes. These were areas populated mainly by Uyghur Muslims, Eurasian-featured people who were descended from Turkic tribes and were almost unknown by China's majority Han Chinese, let alone Western missionaries. Pastor Wang cried at the news. He had already started looking at plots of land he could buy so the teachers could be buried in Huozhou.

Pastor Wang's tears were not the only negative reaction. 'Some wrote, saying in more or less parliamentary language, that there were no fools like old fools,' Mildred wrote. But they went, and with the eventual blessing of the CIM.

Reading this, I felt as if there was a whole undercurrent of struggle between the women and the male CIM leadership in this story that wasn't explicitly stated. I was glad the women got their way. I liked the idea of them digging their heels in against what I imagined were dour, bearded men who weren't used to women answering back.

There were three routes the Trio could have taken to get across China. They could have ridden camels through Inner Mongolia or taken a boat trip up the Yellow River or, travelled on a mule cart along the main road through the ancient Chinese capital of Xi'an. Mildred voted for camels, Francesca for the boat, and Eva for the mule cart.

Then Eva broke her wrist. While she recovered, their move was held up by a couple of months, and the changed weather conditions meant that the southern, mule-cart route that Eva wanted became the only option. Mildred noted in a good-humoured way that while she could hardly have broken her wrist on purpose, it did seem that Eva always got her own way.

The mules were loaded up and old friends were embraced and the women set off. A handyman cook called Brother Chen and a series of different cart drivers travelled with them. It took more than a year, but in late 1923 they arrived at their new base, the town of Jiuquan, at the western end of the Great Wall.

Just beyond Jiuquan was Jiayuguan, the military fort that symbolised the far western reaches of China. The Chinese called Jiayuguan 'the mouth', and anywhere to the west of the fort was 'outside the mouth'. Beyond the fort were the deserts of the Gobi and the wilds of Central Asia. Here exiles and prisoners were spat out, through the fort's Traveller's Gate, into the barren desert.

The fort at Jiayuguan would be the starting point of the Trio's thirteen years of journeys back and forth along the section of the Silk Road that extends across this remote corner of China. The most famous Cable and French book, *The Gobi Desert*, begins with them passing through the mouth of the fort.

> One evening before sunset our carts clattered noisily through the echoing arch, plunged through the awkward double gates, swung aside to avoid the spirit mound, pulled up a short steep ascent and drew up on the level plain just where the great stone tablet stood which bore the inscription: 'Earth's greatest Barrier.' The two friendly soldiers were there to see us off. 'Look here, Lady,' one of them said excitedly, 'you cannot start without throwing a stone at our old wall.'
>
> They led us to where a portion of the brick facing of the fortress wall had been broken away, leaving a rough hollow, and nearby lay a large heap of small stones.
>
> 'It is the custom that every traveller as he goes outside the wall, should throw a stone at the fortress. If the stone rebounds

he will come back safe and sound, but if not ... ' he left the doom unuttered. We each picked up a few small stones and threw them. Rebounding from the wall they skipped back with a sharp sound, and the two boys grinned with pleasure.

'What a strange noise,' I said. 'It is like the cheeping of chicks.'

'That is the echo of this spot,' they said proudly. 'It is lucky to have heard it. Your journey will be prosperous.'

As the sun was now nearing the horizon the carter shouted, 'We must be off,' and the soldier boys saluted and said, 'We shall meet again.' Then they quickly turned and re-entered the fortress, for the trumpet was calling all men to barracks. The gate swung to, and we heard them shoot the heavy bar. We were irrevocably launched on the long trek.

After I read this, following the journey in the Trio's books and hand-drawn maps just didn't seem enough. I wanted to get up and see it for myself. I wanted to throw my own rock against the wall of Jiayuguan fort. That passage – the sound of the cheeping rocks rebounding from the wall – convinced me to follow Mildred, Francesca and Eva along the Silk Road. That was well before I had read the rest of their books, and before I even knew exactly where their route lay. 'China, Mongolia, the 'stans, that general area,' I would tell people. I borrowed coffee-table books about China from the library and looked at the desert. In the Melbourne winter, I couldn't imagine how it would feel to walk on a sand dune in the bright sun.

As I started telling people about my plans, I emphasised different parts of the story, depending on who I was talking to.

'They were amazing women, so independent, they had all these colourful adventures in dangerous parts of Central Asia where no Western women had travelled before,' I said to my work colleagues, educated young women who had travelled in Asia and bought statues of the Buddha that sat next to their computers. They thought Eastern religions were colourful and peaceful and exotic, but I remembered an incident in another workplace when a new girl shocked my colleagues by pinning a Bible verse onto the cubicle wall above her desk ('And surely I am with you always, even to the end of the age'). 'Oh my God, if she starts Bible-bashing us I'm going to tell Human Resources,' one of them said. So I played down the missionary aspect. I explained that the Trio had a tolerant attitude towards other religions, and that they wrote about visiting monasteries and having dialogues with Buddhist priests. I said they did a lot of good work in educating Chinese girls. I suggested that, like nuns in the Middle Ages, they had taken on the only vocation that gave women opportunities and freedom from traditional family life. I wanted to tell them, and perhaps convince myself, that there were reasons apart from old-fashioned Christianity for the Trio to have committed themselves to China.

I told the teacher in my Mandarin class that I wanted to learn more about Chinese culture.

I told my grandmother I was writing a missionary biography. I said I was going to find out if they were any Christians in northwest China today, and if there was any memory of the Trio left there.

I told my politically conservative father that I was going to see what communism was really like, and I promised him that I would not believe any propaganda that tour guides might try to feed me. I told him that long before his favourite author, George Orwell, was writing about the awful bureaucracy and ultimate moral failure of communism, Eva French had abandoned her drawing-room Bolshevism and dreams of a proletarian utopia in favour of a humane, small-scale and spiritual approach to dealing with people's problems.

I confided to my brother that, for a change, I would be travelling with a purpose.

Jack looked confused. 'How will you get a porpoise through Customs?' he said.

Chapter One

Melbourne

It was summertime in the mid-1920s. The Trio's cart reached the inn at about five in the morning, when the sky was still dark. The three women, their cart driver and their fellow evangelists, Elder and Mrs Liu, had been travelling through the Gobi desert overnight to avoid the daytime heat. The oasis inn was the only settlement for miles around, and it couldn't be found on any official maps.

The owner heard them coming. He got up and prepared two rooms by sweeping the rubbish left by previous guests into the corners. Using dried pieces of desert scrub for kindling, he made a fire and put a pot of water on it. His son pumped a set of bellows on the flames.

Francesca gave a bag of flour to the owner, and he asked if they preferred their noodles watery or stodgy. He mixed some dough, stretched it and chopped it into noodles, and threw them into the water. Then he prepared the table by putting out a bowl of salt. 'This is a concession to style, for, as a matter of fact, the *mien* has been boiled in such brackish water that no further salt will be needed,' Mildred wrote.

After checking on the mules, the travellers went to bed. The sun was coming up. Their rooms had no windows. Light came from a lamp – a wick of cotton in a bowl of linseed oil – set on a niche in the wall. The bowl was cracked, and the oil dripped in a slick down the wall.

The sleeping platform, called a 'kang', was made of mud bricks that were heated from underneath with burned manure. The heat was more welcome than the acrid smoke. The roof was hung with matting that had grown fungus over the years. When the wind blew, the guests were showered with what Mildred called 'unpleasant particles'.

In spite of the smoke and fungus and fleas, the women were full and exhausted and they slept well. Hours later, Mildred was woken by flies crawling on her face and a shaft of sunlight shining through a gap in the matting. She could hear the owner and his wife shouting at each other. She laughed, remembering the name of the establishment: the Inn of Peace and Happiness.

Fifteen years later, the Trio stayed in one of the best hotels in my hometown, Melbourne. They enjoyed the starched sheets and fluffy carpets. But the women went to bed hungry because they couldn't get a meal in the late evening. 'We found the cafeteria closed for the night, the lounge tea over, and no possibility of a meal of any kind,' Mildred wrote, adding, 'We viewed the prospect of a hungry bedtime in a magnificent hotel with the same equanimity as we had so often done in rude Gobi conditions.'

It was 1946. Mildred, Eva and Francesca were in Melbourne doing the same things they had done for thirteen years on northwest China's Silk Road trading routes – talking about Jesus and selling books. In China they had sold Bibles in a range of Central Asian languages, but by this time they were offering autographed copies of bestselling accounts of their own adventures. They were famous enough to have been sent on a promotional tour, a year-long trip around the British dominions, financed by the British and Foreign Bible Society.

As the Trio discovered, eating outside prescribed hours in Melbourne was only for bohemians. By most accounts the city was extraordinarily insular, ordered and conservative in the 1940s and '50s, at least for the middle classes. Mildred noticed that people were mainly interested in their own backyards. In her reports about the Trio's travels she would give picturesque, Chinese-sounding names to the towns she visited, and she called Melbourne the City of Homes. 'Unlike some other towns where amusements and gaiety fill every spare moment, the citizens of Melbourne make home their chief pride.'

I imagined that respectable Melbourne would have reminded the Trio of the kind of stifling atmosphere they left behind in England when they first started new lives in China. They even noted that the suburbs of Melbourne had familiar English names: Kew, Richmond, Malvern ...

I noticed that too. After my family returned to Melbourne from India, I travelled from Bayswater to Canterbury on the train every morning to get to school, where I listened to the girls talking about what happened on *Neighbours* the night before. I memorised the name of each station along the way; I could recite them all now. I didn't want to lose my bearings. Every afternoon I took the train home (Blackburn, Nunawading, Mitcham, Ringwood, Heathmont) and I looked out the window at the backs of red-brick houses. My mother picked me up at the station and when I got home I watched television, but I didn't watch *Neighbours*. I watched *Monkey*.

When I first started researching the Trio's journeys, the television series *Monkey* was my main point of reference about northwest

China. Filmed in Japan in the late 1970s, the show was based on Wu Cheng'en's 16th-century epic, *Journey to the West*, which was inspired in turn by the real 7th-century journeys of pilgrim priest Xuan Zang. *Monkey* followed the adventures of a priest called Tripitaka who travelled from China to India to bring back Buddhist scriptures. Accompanying him were pig spirit Pigsy, fish spirit Sandy and 'Great Sage and Equal of Heaven' Monkey, who had been kicked out of heaven for stealing the Jade Emperor's peaches.

Monkey was dubbed by English actors with pantomime Chinese accents. Tripitaka, inexplicably, was played by a gorgeous actress in a bald wig. There were cheesy gold-cardboard costumes and rickety sets and disco music and puns (Pigsy: 'All these people, I am their idol!' Monkey: 'Bone idle!'). Best of all were the fights. Everyone was always fighting, in spite of Tripitaka's wet exhortations to nonviolence. Tripitaka was a bit of a stiff. Each episode ended with a voice-over, where the narrator would espouse a piece of Buddhist philosophy, and a theme tune, with lyrics about finding your own utopia.

After the episode finished, I was back in Melbourne in a small house on a quarter-acre block in the outer suburbs. In India I had walked everywhere and my friends from all around the world all lived in the same compound as me, but in the suburbs there was nothing within walking distance except the houses of strangers, and everyone was white. I told the girls at school that I wouldn't be in Melbourne for long. I would go to university, maybe get married, and then I would go back to India as some kind of missionary or teacher or aid worker. It hadn't occurred to me that Christianity might be stifling me. I thought it was just the isolation that came with living in the suburbs of a big city. Like Eva, I wanted to escape a restrictive environment.

I think it's clear that by leaving England the Trio did escape. They were energetic and independent, and there was little they could have done in England, either as spinsters or mothers, that would have given them the scope for adventure and autonomy offered by missionary life in China. It's a common enough assumption now that heading to the mission field was once an excuse for single, respectable women to see the world. In the introduction to the Virago Travellers 1984 reprint of *The Gobi Desert*, Marina Warner asked 'Is it possible that the missionary work served Mildred and the French sisters, and the other women like them, as a pretext to escape from the stultifying "feminine" lives Guilford and Portsmouth held out to them?'

To which the answer, I think, is yes, absolutely, and no, not at all. The more I read, the more it was clear that these women were for real. The Bible and their understanding of God's nature seemed to genuinely inform everything they did. Pilgrims they talked to in the wilds of northwest China might never meet another Christian, and the women knew they had a responsibility to represent the faith. They called themselves 'Christ's ambassadors'.

They also experienced danger that went beyond adventure. Eva's friends died violently in the Boxer Uprising of 1900, and she barely escaped with her own life. They were all captured by a rebel general who gave his officers random orders to kill while Mildred was dressing his gunshot wounds. They were trapped in sandstorms, huddled against camels and barely able to breathe. I don't think their sole motivation, even unconsciously, was to escape traditional gender roles.

Mildred spelled out the dangers the day after she arrived in Melbourne, when she preached the Sunday-morning sermon at the Scots Presbyterian Church. She spoke against living an ordinary life, against getting into a rut and paying lip service to Christianity. 'It is very difficult in the parts in which I have lived to be a nominal Christian,' she said. 'To be a Christian involves persecution, suffering and maybe death, and a man does not die for that in which he does not believe.' This was the first in a series of talks that attracted thousands of listeners.

Church-going, home-loving Melbourne embraced the Trio. They had almost been mobbed when they arrived on the *Australia Star*. Mildred wrote:

> Crowds of people had assembled to meet the boat and among them were camera-men and reporters ... and as a result of a brief interview on deck all that there was to know about us, together with the best picture we ever had taken, appeared that evening in the Melbourne papers.

The Trio met the governor and premier of Victoria and the Archbishop of Melbourne. They made radio broadcasts, preached at church services, and addressed women's groups and missionary candidates.

I tried to think of someone who would make that sort of impression on my home town today. The only person I could think of was the Dalai Lama.

I had booked my tickets to China and organised an itinerary that would take me to most of the towns the Trio described in their books, and I had made plans to write my own book. Jack had announced that he would join me part way through my trip, and we had arranged to meet at Jiayuguan fort. I had an iBook laptop computer full of notes about each town, and I had learned some Mandarin; I could say 'My name is Kate and this is my little brother, Jack.'

But I wasn't sure yet that I really knew the Trio very well. It seemed suddenly urgent that I make some kind of connection with them, that I should fall in step with them before I left for China. I decided to visit a church where Mildred had preached, and I took a twenty-minute tram trip from my flat to Collins Street, in Melbourne's central business district.

The woman behind the desk in the vestry at Scots Presbyterian Church had a tag that said 'Jean' pinned to her blouse. She didn't recognise the names French and Cable. I told her the women had attracted an overflowing congregation to the church. 'There were more than a thousand when the queen came out in the fifties,' Jean said.

There was only one other person in the church, a young man who sat in one of the pews. He wore shorts and ate a sandwich, and if he was praying, he was doing it very discreetly.

I looked around, unsure of what I was looking for. The church was how non-churchgoers imagine a church to be, with high ceilings, arches, stained glass and carved, dark wood. It was a lot grander than the weatherboard barns and red-brick halls my low-church evangelical family had always attended. It felt very empty.

Next door to the church, outside the Presbyterian administrative building, a sandwich board chained to the railings of the front steps advertised free English classes for Asian students and migrants. I knew a woman who taught one of these classes. She gave a weekly hour-long lesson to an elderly Chinese couple who had been in Australia for a couple of years. After the class they would have tea and biscuits together, and then another woman would run a half-hour Bible study for the couple. They were not Christians, but they would sit and listen to the Bible class. This was the pay-off for the free English lessons.

If I was going to make a connection with the Trio, I decided, people might be better than places. Of the hundreds of people who saw the Trio in Melbourne, I thought, someone must still be alive and able to remember them.

It's not difficult to contact older evangelical Christians in Australia. They all read *New Life*, a newspaper that runs news and reviews, obituaries, missionary newsletters, and reprinted columns about family values by conservative American commentators like Charles Colson and James Dobson. When I was nineteen years old, it became the first publication that ever paid me to write and edit.

'It's important you realise what kind of paper we are,' the editor had said, when I approached him looking for work. He looked at my nose ring and tie-dyed skirt. 'We're not for the agonising evangelical.'

I kept my agony to myself and reported on church meetings and visits from overseas church leaders. I once interviewed a Chinese woman who represented a publishing house that printed Bibles in China. Just a few years earlier, Bibles had to be smuggled to Chinese Christians, and we had been told that anyone in China in possession of a Bible could be executed. But Mrs Wang – a member of the Three Self Patriotic Movement, the only officially sanctioned Protestant organisation in China – said Christians were absolutely free to read the Bible and worship in China.

'There is no persecution of Christians,' she said. I wrote it down. When I showed the editor my interview, he smiled, then sighed. 'No persecution if you're in a Three Self church,' he said. He ran a short version of the interview, but in the same issue published a report from the Religious Liberties Commission about pastors from underground churches in China being thrown into jail and tortured.

I thought *New Life* would be the best place to track down people who saw the Trio in 1946. I wrote a letter to the paper, asking people to contact me if they had memories of the tour. After it was published, I received a few letters and phone calls, and one invitation. Estelle Bannister called me up from a few suburbs away and asked me to come around.

Estelle was small, with a round face and white hair in a bun, like a cartoon of a grandmother. Her unit was decorated with souvenirs from her overseas travels. A framed photograph on the wall showed her riding an elephant. In 1946 she was a seventeen-year-old art student, and her memories of the time were all visual.

'Mildred Cable looked like a priest,' she told me. 'She wore black and had a big cross around her neck. She leaned very seriously on the pulpit.'

Estelle stood up to act out Mildred. She put her fist on her hip in a deliberate way, stuck her chin forward and glared over the top of her glasses. She looked authoritative and quite transformed. I saw Mildred for a moment, and I couldn't help smiling. I had my connection.

'Francesca looked like a lady,' Estelle said, as she sat back down at the kitchen table. 'She would rave on about the desert, the mountains, she made it sound beautiful.'

Estelle said Eva was quiet, and seemed tired. 'But you could see that they looked after each other.'

Estelle had saved newspaper cuttings about the Trio's visit, and had photocopied them for me. She had read all their books. Inspired at least partly by the physical and moral courage of the Trio, Estelle and her daughter had travelled around China with a tour group in the late 1990s. She had been disappointed that she didn't meet any Christians. 'The guide told me there were no Christians in China,' she said. 'I told him, "Listen, I'm here and I'm a Christian."'

She showed me photographs of her trip. In one of them, she and her daughter stood in the desert in front of a statue of a monkey wearing a tunic and carrying a fan. 'That's near Turpan,' she said. 'I think it's a character from a Chinese story.'

I knew where Turpan was – it was one of the final stops on my itinerary. The Trio had travelled through the town many times, and had written about its colourful market and intense heat and oversized poisonous insects. But this was the first I knew of Monkey's connection to Turpan. I found myself smiling again.

When I was putting my notebook away, Estelle said 'I have a surprise for you.' She said her friend Susan had some facsimile copies

Melbourne

of a booklet written by Mildred Cable. It was called *A Parable of Jade*. When Estelle told Susan about my impending visit, Susan told Estelle to find out if I was a real Christian. If I was, she would send me a copy of the booklet. 'She wanted me to wait and see if you were the real deal,' Estelle said.

I thanked her. I knew I should say something else, but I didn't. I drove home with a familiar sick feeling. My car smelled of stale takeaway food. I remembered feeling this way all through my early twenties, when I'd pretended, and even wanted, to be a real Christian, in the years before I broke down and told my family that I couldn't be like them. The whole time I was scared I'd be found out. Now I'd passed as that girl without really meaning to. I felt as if I'd stolen something from Estelle, and it was only a matter of time before she found out.

The Trio might have been serious-minded and celibate old missionaries, but they were concerned about their clothes. I found this a comfort in the week before I left Australia, while I was packing and repacking and wondering which jeans would suit me best in the Gobi desert.

In China the Trio wore the same long skirt and crossover top that their neighbours wore. Eva always wore grey, Mildred wore blue and Francesca wore brown. But their letters to friends show that every time they went back to England they worried about looking frumpy when they arrived, and they argued about what was fashionable. In a letter from Shangai just before they sailed to England in 1926, Eva wrote:

> At this particular juncture, Mildred began to reveal those peculiarly trying traits in her character which only seem to come to the surface when dressmaking or millinery demand attention.

Nothing would satisfy her but a dress, the bodice of which reached the rim of her chin, whilst the skirt nearly touched the floor! As authorities on matters of fashion, she would quote people who, to our certain knowledge, had bought their last dress eight years previously!

Eva and Francesca came from a well-off family, and had been well-dressed young women. When Eva first visited the China Inland Mission training home where she would spend two years before going to China, the staff hinted that her dress was too smart for a missionary candidate. She went home and determinedly made a dowdy, shapeless dress. When she was finished, she and Francesca agreed that any missionary would be proud to wear it.

Eva was willing to put up with a lot, even ugly clothes, if it would help her get to China. Later she admitted that she masked her naturally outspoken, adventurous personality at this stage because she thought it might jeopardise her chances of being accepted as a missionary. In the training home she tried to be neat and quiet. She wondered if she would ever be good enough after the housekeeper reacted to her poor attempts at hospital corners: 'My dear, what would the Chinese say to a bed made like that?'

When she reached China, Eva let go of the submissive persona and started showing signs of the girl she had been, the six-year-old who had to be bribed by nuns (with chocolate) to climb down from the roof of the Belgian convent where she went to school. Years later, Mildred wrote to friends about Eva clambering over a rotting bridge across a ravine in Tibet. Mildred and Francesca refused to follow her and called her back. 'We hope that you may some day see a picture of EFF balancing herself in mid-air on a trembling pine log, and appreciate the feelings of her companions as they watched her return, smiling and complacent.'

The photo hasn't survived, but I kept that picture in my head for a long time.

I thought about the three women so often that I began to dream about them. In my imagination, their different personalities had become quite distinct. Mildred was the most intense, but also the most cheerful. Little things gave her a lot of joy. She was the chief writer and preacher, and the other two called her 'our star'. Eva was brave and restless and didn't suffer fools gladly. Francesca was quiet and capable and secretly wrote poetry.

Their characters were described in a 1964 biography written by a friend, Bible Society secretary William Platt. 'Mildred, actually the youngest, was certainly the "father figure", Francesca was mother to them all, and Eva, the eldest in years, was puckish, utterly frank, always unpredictable, sometimes mischievous, quite unsentimental – the "naughty boy" of the family.'

The Trio's Chinese friends gave them Chinese names: Mildred was "Kai All Brave", Francesca was "Feng Precious Pearl" and Eva was "Feng Polished Jade".

A few nights before I left Melbourne I was lying in bed reading Mildred and Francesca's book for potential missionaries, *Ambassadors for Christ*. My boyfriend was playing on his Game Boy. He leaned over and read over my shoulder, 'to make my fullest contribution to the uplift of a heathen people...' He emphasised the word 'heathen'.

'What?' I said. I shut the book before he could read any more.

'Well, you know,' he said. My boyfriend has never been to church.

'It's not how someone would use the word heathen now; it just meant not Christian,' I said. 'Don't just look at a word like heathen and use that to dismiss everything they said and did.'

'You can't just sweep that stuff under the carpet,' he said. He killed a few more monsters and I pretended to read for a few minutes.

'Did they do anything shitty?' he said.

'What?'

'Did they only help people if they converted? Did they help open up trade routes to get opium into the country? Did they tell Chinese people they had to act like middle-class English people?'

My boyfriend's favourite quote about missionaries is attributed to King Kamehameha of Hawaii, who is supposed to have told Robert Louis Stephenson: 'When the missionaries came we had the land and they had the Bibles. They told us to bow our heads and pray, and when we looked up they had the land and we had the Bibles.'

'No, they didn't do any of that stuff,' I said. 'They hated what opium was doing to people and they blamed the English government and traders for bringing it into China. They spent most of their time educating girls and running an opium refuge for women. They wore Chinese clothes and they spoke fluent Mandarin and they made a huge deal about following local customs and how important it was for Chinese Christians to have their own leaders and make the faith their own.'

The next day my boyfriend gave me two presents. One was Arthur Waley's 1942 translation of Wu Cheng'en's *Journey to the West*, which is simply called *Monkey*. Then he gave me a bright-red Game Boy with a Scrabble cartridge. I could play Scrabble against any of five pixellated characters. The Easy character was a tattooed young woman who wore a confused expression, and Mr Hard was a bald man who disconcertingly raised his eyebrows up and down while considering his next move. Along with *The Gobi Desert* and *Monkey*, the Scrabble family would be my constant companions for the next few months.

Chapter Two

Huozhou

The strange fact is that the world goes on against all reasonable odds. A hundred years, and even unimaginable evil is just called history.
 Monkey Series 1, 'What Monkey Calls the Dog-Woman'

In every youth hostel in the world you can find a resident bore who has been travelling for too many years. It's usually a middle-aged male with a ponytail. Sometimes you get two of them, and they talk over each other, both of them determined to be the top bore. It's like watching two walruses fight on the Discovery Channel.

The bore in Beijing was Belgian. He was king of the courtyard at the Far East International Hostel. Young backpackers sat around his table, soaking up his wisdom and buying him beers. I heard snatches of advice and expertise on my trips between the dormitory and the toilet.

'What Mao didn't understand about the Chinese character was …'

'The difference between us and the Chinese is …'

'The only places worth seeing in China are …'

The courtyard conversations took on a more relaxed tone when he wasn't there.

'… and that's why you have to get drunk before you go out.'

'… so the music wasn't so good but the drinks were cheap.'

I spent more time in that courtyard than I should have. Beijing had looked huge and unfriendly from the taxi window on the way from the airport, and in the few days I spent there I couldn't work out how to launch myself into it. I had a bad introduction to the city with my first taxi driver, who had initially agreed to a 50 yuan fee, but when we arrived at the hostel and I gave him a 100 yuan note he had only given back 20 yuan. When I'd insisted on my change, he had shaken his head, pulled my backpack off the back seat and thrown it in the dust on the ground, and driven away.

The hostel was in an old compound in an area made up of narrow backstreets. Its architecture was everything I expected from China. Stone lions guarded the narrow entrance, the latticed window frames were painted dark red, and the paved courtyard was hung with lanterns. I saw almost nothing like it again. It would be concrete all the way from here on. Later I read that these backstreet areas were known as *hutong*, and that most of them were slated to be demolished before Beijing hosted the Olympic games in 2008.

I didn't talk much to other travellers in those first few days. Instead, I drank a few Tsing Tao beers, at what I later discovered to be about three times the usual price, and wrote in my notebook. Culture shock is a bit like the runs, I wrote. No matter how well prepared you are, it can hit you any time.

Unfortunately, I had a bit of both.

On my third and last day in Beijing, a guy with a floppy fringe brought his beer over to my table, put his feet up on a chair and introduced himself as Michael. I had seen him talking to two blonde Swedish girls earlier in the day. He was hitting on both of them in what seemed to be a high-risk, double-or-nothing gamble.

Michael turned out to be second-generation Chinese Canadian, or possibly Canadian Chinese. He had been travelling around the south for months, overstaying his visa. He didn't know where to go next, so he asked about my plans and I told him about the Trio and how I was heading towards the northwestern deserts of Xinjiang province. I said I wanted to meet the Uyghurs, the Turkic Muslim people of the far northwest that the Trio had written about.

'The who?' he said. 'What are you talking about?'

I told him there were about eight million Uyghurs in and around Xinjiang. 'They seem to have a pretty hard time of it,' I said. 'They can't get good jobs because they're not atheists so they can't join the Communist Party, and the government puts all these restrictions on their children hearing religious teaching, and it sounds like the government's using the threat of Muslim terrorism as an excuse to throw them in jail if they start advocating Uyghur separatism.'

I had come across stories about the Uyghur nationalist movement time and time again while I researched the provinces the Trio travelled through. Websites with names like 'Uyghur World' described a culture that seemed more Middle Eastern than Chinese, and many of them raged against persecution of Uyghurs by the Chinese government.

Michael looked almost animated. 'Wow,' he said.

He paused and took a swig of beer. 'How would you like someone to come with you who speaks a bit of Chinese?' he said. 'I think it would be really interesting for me.'

I started to stutter something about already having a train ticket for Linfen and leaving that night. Michael shrugged. He didn't mention travelling with me again.

'So these women you're researching, they were Christians?' he asked. 'Someone told me a story about Christians, it happened here in Beijing just a few days ago.'

This was Michael's story. A pastor from South Korea was in China, visiting Christians. He was on the subway, speaking on his mobile phone about his plans to talk to an unregistered group of believers. He thought he was safe because he was speaking Korean, but a woman on the subway understood Korean, overheard him and used her own mobile phone to report him. The authorities picked up the pastor at the next station. They confiscated his laptop computer and found all the email addresses on it. All his foreign contacts in China were deported. Michael didn't know what happened to the pastor's Chinese contacts.

I got the impression this was at least a third-hand story.

As Michael and I ate fried rice in the hostel's cafe, overlooking the alley, people rode past on pushbikes and motorbikes with trays attached to the back. The trays were loaded with vegetables, or sand, or crates of beer, or a jumble of computer parts, or someone's grandma. An old man in a blue Mao suit and cap hobbled back and forth with a cane. A Pekinese ran around his feet. 'He's got that whole quaint-old-Chinaman look going on,' I said. 'Maybe he's been planted here by the tourist authorities to provide local colour.'

'Do you think they would do that?' Michael said seriously.

The taxi driver who took me to the train station that night smiled a lot, and he switched on his meter before I even asked. He pointed out landmarks along the way, and laughed in a good-natured way when I tried to speak Mandarin. In the ID photo on the dashboard he looked serious, even worried. At the station he got out and lifted my pack onto my back, even though he was holding up a row of taxis behind him.

Inside Beijing West station I bought baozi, steamed bread that I hoped would contain pork but turned out to be hiding cold cabbage. What looked like drinking yogurt turned out to be warm soymilk. I ate and drank standing up in a crowded waiting hall, with my pack still strapped to me, while an instrumental version of the *Titanic* theme, Celine Dion's 'My Heart Will Go On', played over the speaker system. All the seats were taken, and the train wasn't due for another hour. Every man in the room seemed to be smoking.

The destination printed on my ticket was Linfen, a town of approximately one million people in central Shanxi province. I couldn't be sure of Linfen's size, because Chinese population figures always differed wildly from source to source, but it was big enough to have a university, and I had exchanged emails with one of the university's administrative staff, a guy who spoke a little English and called himself Paul. He had offered to meet me at the train station and take me on a local bus to Huozhou, the small town where the Trio had worked for more than twenty years before they loaded up the mule cart and headed towards the Gobi.

I was glad to be putting Beijing behind me and travelling the same route that the Trio would have taken, towards the town that they loved. I imagined that visiting a small town with a Chinese guide would be easier than negotiating the streets of Beijing on my own, where I had done nothing more adventurous than catching taxis between the hostel and Tiananmen Square.

A girl of about my age came up behind me and pulled at my jacket. She spoke fast Mandarin, almost none of which I could understand. I thought she was telling me off. I pulled a worried face and said, '*Bu mingbai*' – I don't understand – but she pulled me after her towards her group of friends. They were moving their bags off a seat so I could sit down with them. One of them held out an open rubbish bag for the plastic baozi wrapper and empty cup I had been clutching for the last half hour.

Like most people in Beijing, the girls were dressed in a neat, clean version of casual clothes. One of them wore a hooded sweatshirt just like mine. The only scruffy-looking people I had seen in Beijing were some thin young men who were gawking at the sights in Tiananmen Square. They wore dusty, greasy suits that screamed 'up from the country'.

One of the young women spoke slowly enough for me to understand some of her questions about where I was from and which train I was catching. 'Ah, Aodaliya,' she said. 'Very beautiful. Big.' She held out her arms to indicate the size of Australia. She and her friends were catching a different train, she said. We waved and smiled like old friends when my train arrived.

On the train I shared a compartment with a family. The daughter looked about twelve years old. She wore jeans, and a pink sweatshirt that had the words PLAY BOG printed on it in the same font that *Playboy* magazine uses. She whined about having to sleep on the top bunk, and her mother seemed to be explaining that Grandma couldn't be expected to climb up there. Grandma pretended not to hear the conversation. She looked out the window and slurped tea from a vacuum flask. I couldn't catch why the daughter didn't want the top bunk. I suspected it was because the loudspeakers were up there, and she didn't want to bear the full brunt of the instrumental version of Lionel Ritchie's 'Hello'.

When I passed by the next compartment on the way to the toilet, I saw a man wearing pyjamas and hooked up to an IV drip. He had a suit jacket draped over his shoulders. He looked straight at me, his face drawn and sad. Friends sat around him, playing cards and drinking tea and talking loudly.

At 10 p.m. the music stopped and most of the lights turned off. The family went to sleep, but I sat up late looking out of the window, although there was little to see in the dark. Hours later we reached Shanxi province and passed straight through the town of Pingyao.

When Eva French first came to China, in the years before she was a third of a Trio, she described Pingyao as 'the place I keep my boxes'.

Eva used Pingyao as her base from 1893 to 1900, but she didn't spend much time there. She spent those years riding a donkey from village to village, staying with Chinese Christians, preaching, improving her Mandarin and listening to women talk about their lives. Early on she travelled with a Chinese woman, an old gossip who knew everyone for miles around, but before too long Eva knew everyone too.

Eva believed she was liked and appreciated by the locals. But early in 1900 she started to notice changes in the way she was treated. The villagers didn't greet her quite as effusively as they had. There was a new edge of rudeness in her dealings with everyone from hired workmen to officials. Her Chinese friends told her that a storm was coming. One night she stayed with Mrs Meng, a convert who told her about the Righteous and Harmonious Fists, a group that was threatening to kill foreigners and Christians. Mrs Meng whispered this news to Eva late at night, while they lay on the kang.

A few weeks later Mrs Meng was beheaded in her courtyard. The men who came to kill her granted her last wish to first change into her best dress and say a prayer. Eva only heard about her friend's fate the next year, when the uprising was over.

About 600 Chinese Christians were killed in Shanxi in 1900.

Outside of China, the Righteous and Harmonious Fists are known as 'Boxers', a term coined by a missionary. The movement was grassroots and spontaneous, and in the early days the Boxers were just as opposed to China's ruling Qing dynasty as they were to foreigners. This changed in 1899 when the Empress Dowager Cixi, who controlled the court, became their protector and officially encouraged them.

The Boxers practiced mystical rituals and promised adherents that these drills would make them magically impervious to guns and knives. The empress apparently believed this was true, and she wanted the Boxers on her side.

Like the Boxers, the empress was angry at the way European powers demanded territory, railways and mining concessions. She was still smarting at the aftermath of the mid-19th century opium wars, when China had tried to stop the British from illegally, and lucratively, smuggling opium into the country. China, defeated by British weapons, had been forced to sign a series of humiliating treaties that gave Europeans vastly increased freedom to live and trade in Chinese cities. The same treaties also gave Western missionaries freedom to proselytise.

At the local level, in the villages Eva visited, there was a general mistrust of foreigners. Many people thought foreigners were responsible for the ongoing droughts and harvest failure. Ancestral spirits and feng shui seemed to have been disturbed by railway lines, telegraph poles and church spires. The educational and medical methods that came with Christianity were unfamiliar. Villagers resented the fact that converts stopped paying money towards local temple funds, putting more financial pressure on the rest of village.

Missionaries liked to think they were different from the European traders and diplomats who were exploiting the Chinese. But when push came to shove, everyone knew the missionaries came under the protection of their government representatives, and Chinese Christian converts came under the protection of the missionaries. They were all tainted.

From Eva's point of view, Shanxi residents had no reason to turn against Christians. The missionaries, and in turn the local Christians, had rehabilitated opium addicts, they had taught uneducated peasants to read and write in their own language, and they offered free medical help to the sick. More importantly, they had pointed people to God, who could liberate them from the burden of sin.

But that didn't stop the mob that gathered around the house

where Eva was visiting other young missionary women, in Jiexiu, just south of Pingyao, in June 1900. People shouted 'Kill the foreign devils!' The crowd got bigger and the shouting got louder.

Eva took charge. She was 28, and the most senior missionary present. She told the other women to keep together and not look frightened, and she walked them all briskly through the middle of the mob all the way to the courthouse, where she planned to ask for protection from the town magistrate, the Mandarin. The walk took ten minutes. Nobody touched the women.

The Mandarin obviously didn't want to hurt them, but he had to sound aggressive in front of the mob, so he paced around the courts, shouting that he had orders to kill the women. 'Where are your men?' he said loudly.

After seven years of listening to spoken Mandarin, Eva could pick from his accent that he came from the south, where the Boxers had less influence. Then he passed close to Eva and whispered 'Whatever you do, don't go north.' Shouting again, he told the crowd he was arranging to have the women sent north to Beijing.

After a night in the courthouse, the women were given papers to travel with. The papers ordered the Mandarin of each district on their route to be personally responsible for their safety – or else take personal responsibility for killing them.

The women were given carts, and an escort of soldiers that took them south to the provincial border. One of the soldiers told the women that they had not been attacked on their way to see the Mandarin because each woman had been seen to be carrying an object in the long sleeve of her dress, and word had gone around that these were pistols. In fact, they were carrying their Bibles.

There are just a few copies left, in Christian institutions around the world, of a big black book called *Martyred Missionaries of the China Inland Mission – Perils and Sufferings of Some who Escaped*. Eva was one of the contributors. She wrote about the early part of her party's months-long trek to Shanghai, and she wrote tributes to three English women, friends of hers who were killed early in the uprising.

Before reaching China, I had spent ten days in Germany and England, where I visited a few libraries in search of Trio-related material. I found a copy of *Martyred Missionaries* at a missionary training college in Gloucester, and read about Eva's escape.

En route to Shanghai, Eva and the women from Jiexiu joined up with another group of missionaries. Fifteen or so of them travelled together, including a couple whose two daughters died and had to be buried by the roadside. In every village, people threw rocks and sticks at them. They had to beg for food and water, and they went hungry much of the time. They slept on the ground, or in a single filthy room, or in vermin-infested prison cells. A later account says a man in the party went mad. This isn't mentioned in *Martyred Missionaries*. The editors seem to have excised anything that was not straightforwardly heroic and tragic.

Eva's family in England was told she had almost certainly been killed. For months they waited for more news. One day, Francesca 'was so conscious of peril threatening her sister that she made a note of the date, thinking it not improbable that she had been killed at that time'. Later, after they heard that Eva was safe, Francesca discovered that her premonition came on the day that Eva was closest to death. Her party had been travelling on a country road, and Eva was sitting on the front cart, when a group of Boxers stopped them. One of the men pulled Eva by her hair and threw her onto the ground, holding his sword above her head as if he was about to bring it down. Then he became distracted. Another man had cut open a box kept on the cart, and coins spilled onto the road. The way Eva told it, the man who was ready to kill her couldn't stand the sight of someone getting at the money before him. He rushed towards the box, pushed the other man aside, and ran away with the money.

Eva got up and dusted herself off. She didn't feel so bad. Later she said she felt strangely peaceful when she saw the sword about to fall. This made her feel better about the final moments of all her friends who had recently been killed. She believed God would have given them the same peace.

Turning the pages of *Martyred Missionaries*, I saw a photo of Eva's party after they reached safety in Shanghai. Until then I had only seen photos of the Trio taken in their later years in China, when they had wispy grey hair worn in loose buns, and granny glasses, and comfortable, middle-aged bodies. They clearly didn't bother with corsets.

But this photo showed an Eva I would never have recognised. She was slim, with dark hair pulled back so tight it stretched her face. She looked very sharp and very grim, and she stared directly at me. I thought it was an extraordinary picture. My first reaction was to tear the page out and take it home with me. I looked around the library, and then I looked at the picture again.

Twelve people were posed together. They all wore Chinese robes. There wasn't the smallest sign of happiness in any of them. They were wary and thin. I could hardly look at Mrs Lutley, whose little daughters, Mary and Edith, had died on the road. Her cheeks were hollow and she wasn't looking at the camera, or anywhere else. A Mr Dreyer, who was in the party, wrote: 'It was beautiful to behold the Christian fortitude and submission with which the sorely bereaved parents bore their heavy loss.' I don't think he was a parent himself.

On the way to Linfen, my train passed though Shanxi's capital, Taiyuan. That's where about 45 of Eva's friends and colleagues were beheaded outside the courts, one after another, on a summer's day in June 1900. Among them were Jane Stevens and Mildred Clarke, missionaries from the town of Huozhou, the place I was about to visit, where Eva later settled and would live from 1901 to 1923. The pictures in *Martyred Missionaries* show two pretty women in high-collared dresses. They couldn't have been more than thirty years old.

In the morning, as soon as it was light, I strapped my pack on and stood by the train door. At every station I turned to the smokers around the doorway and asked, 'Is this Linfen?'. I was sure I was going to miss my town. Only random stations seemed to have the town name written in roman script.

Paul was waiting for me at the train-station exit, with his friend Jian. They were in their twenties, and neatly dressed. Paul had a row of pens clipped to his shirt pocket, and he held a zip-up folder. 'James Kate?' he said.

We shook hands and discussed whether I should book into a hotel before we went to Huozhou. I said I needed to find somewhere fairly cheap, around 200 yuan for a night.

Jian said, 'That's not cheap, that's expensive!'

I laughed nervously and tried to cover myself by saying, 'Oh, I've just come from Beijing, I'm still thinking of Beijing prices!' and the men laughed too. Great start, I thought.

Paul hailed a taxi and took me to a concrete tower full of glittering brass fittings. He used his university identification card to negotiate a reduced rate for me, and then we walked to the bus station, where Paul bought my ticket and wouldn't take any money from me.

The other passengers drew the curtains across their windows. I was the only person who wanted to look outside. I wanted to see the road into Huozhou.

Christians had lived in Huozhou since the 1880s, when a Chinese convert called Hsi moved there to set up an opium refuge for men. He claimed that a dream had revealed this was the right place for his treatment centre. He asked the China Inland Mission for women missionaries to teach the local women, and he was sent two young Norwegians, Sophie Reuter and Anna Jakobsen.

Anna turned out to be a disappointment to the CIM and Pastor Hsi. She made the mistake of genuinely believing all people were the same in God's eyes, and she fell in love with a local evangelist called Cheng. They married against the wishes – in fact, the orders – of both Pastor Hsi and the CIM leaders. An American pastor in Taiyuan performed the marriage service, and one of the few guests was Eva French.

We only know Eva was there because someone sent the CIM a list of everyone who attended the wedding. There is no way of knowing whether Eva was reprimanded for her loyalty to her friend.

After the wedding, Anna and Cheng disappear from official CIM history. During the Boxer Uprising they joined one of the many groups of missionaries whose dramatic escapes were told in *Martyred Missionaries*. But the book left out the names of Anna, Cheng and their baby daughter, Mary.

The next missionaries to be sent to Huozhou were Mildred Clarke and Jane Stevens. They were instructed to learn from Anna's mistake and not be too intimate with the locals. The Boxers caught up with them before they had time to settle into the community.

Eva arrived in Huozhou in 1901 with new missionary Mildred Cable. Eva had been sent back to England after the Boxer Uprising, but she doesn't seem to have even considered staying there. She returned to China as soon as she could.

Christians in Huozhou said approvingly that Eva's Mandarin was 'as good as Miss Jakobsen's'. Mildred's wasn't quite as good at first. On one occasion she meant to say she came from a family of six, but she told people she had sixty children.

Mildred liked Eva's itinerant lifestyle, but she reluctantly realised that, as the talented organiser and delegator, she should stay put and run a girls school that had recently been established. She started with 24 students and had 70 by the end of the year. With funding from Westminster Chapel in London, where Mildred was a member, the Trio oversaw the construction of a new set of buildings for the school. In 1910, two years after Francesca had joined them in Huozhou, a church building to seat 600 people was built.

By 1922, the year before the Trio left Huozhou, the school had 150 students. Parents for miles around – some Christians, others not – sacrificed to send their children there. School terms were timed so the girls could go home and help their families during the harvest. Mildred and her Chinese teachers taught the girls how to read and write Chinese characters, as well as giving them lessons in science and astronomy, Chinese and European history, and Confucian ethics and Bible stories. The Trio thought of Confucius as a wise philosopher rather than a religious leader, so they didn't see any clash between teaching him alongside the Bible.

I told Jian I didn't know what had happened to the compound where the Trio lived and where the church and school and medical clinics were located. I said I didn't know if there were any Christians in Huozhou, and I just wanted to see the town. The truth was I didn't want Paul and Jian to think they had failed me if we found no evidence of the Trio in Huozhou.

Jian said he wasn't a Christian, but his mother liked to read the Bible. 'She has trouble remembering the Bible names,' he said. I asked him if there was any danger of persecution for Christians in this part of Shanxi. 'Oh no,' he said, as if he didn't understand why I would even ask. 'Everyone is free in China now.'

From the window, the countryside looked black and ripped apart. It was easy to see this was coal-mining country. The air was warm but the sky was a polluted grey. I thought about news reports I had seen on television at home, about Chinese coal miners dying in accidents.

Mildred once wrote that the area around Huozhou was full of poppy fields, with snow-topped mountains in the background. She said dust from the northwestern deserts sometimes blew this far east. She described the bridge over the Fen River at the entrance to the town, and the metal cow that sat on the bridge. 'To this brazen image is committed the important function of guarding Hwochow from flood, and so successfully does it accomplish its task that dryness and drought are the normal conditions of the countryside!'

We walked over the bridge. I couldn't see the cow. The Fen River was just a trickle of water running through the middle of a wide, sandy bed. On the far side of the bridge, Paul hailed a cab and asked the driver if he knew of any Christian meeting places in town. 'I can take you to some Catholics,' he said.

We took a short ride down a backstreet and got out in a courtyard between three crumbling buildings. One was an eye clinic, judging by the equipment and charts on the wall. Paul spoke to a woman with a cross pinned to her lapel, who told us to sit down and left the room. On the wall, next to an eye chart, was a poster of a blonde Jesus holding a lamb.

The woman came back leading an old man. She said he was 93 years old and had been a Catholic all his life. He was a bit deaf, she explained, but we could write down questions for him. Paul started writing, and the man started talking. In fact, he wouldn't shut up. I only understood the occasional word, but Jian assured me it wasn't relevant.

The old man nodded at me and held his hands together as if he was praying, or giving me an Indian-style *namaste* greeting. He appeared to have plenty more to say, but I could tell that Paul was gently trying to wind up the conversation. Finally we said goodbye and shook hands with the old man and the eye doctor. They stood at the entrance to the clinic and waved as we walked down the street.

Jian said: 'The ladies you are researching, they followed the teachings of Martin Luther King? Not the same as these Catholics.'

The old man had been giving Paul and Jian a lesson in church history. I said yes, the women were Protestants, and that Protestantism had indeed arisen from the writings of Martin Luther. I thought that explaining the difference between the German theological reformer and the American civil rights leader, who also happened to be a reverend, would only complicate things.

Paul said the old man had given him the address of a Protestant church. The man told Paul that Catholics and Protestants in Huozhou didn't talk to each other in the past, but now they were friends.

The Trio never mentioned any Catholics living in Huozhou. One of their fellow CIM missionaries, a rabidly anti-Catholic Scotsman called George Hunter, once caused a scandal in Urumqi by refusing to sit down at the governor's banquet because a Catholic priest had also been invited. The fact that he regularly ate with Muslims and Buddhists didn't seem to concern him. When Mildred and Francesca wrote Hunter's biography, many years later, they said it was ironic that during World War II he had to spend a year in a Chinese jail cell with a Catholic priest.

We walked past shops and stalls and open-air motorbike repairs stands and hundreds of people riding bikes. Paul asked for directions along the way, and we were pointed to a busy street stretching uphill from the squat tower that seemed to mark the centre of town. We walked uphill until Paul pointed to a grey building with Chinese characters carved on the wall. 'This was the old church,' he said. I recognised the characters for 'three' on the wall, and Paul confirmed this was a Three Self Patriotic Movement church.

The church had two doorways, with the characters for Men and Women carved above them. The women's entrance was bricked up; the men's entrance was a wooden door, which I opened. Inside was a laneway and an open door from where we could see into the church. It was full of people. A sermon was being preached. I couldn't understand the language, but I had been to church so often for so many years that I recognised the rhythm of the preacher's words.

Small children playing around the doorway stared at me in disbelief. 'Take a photo!' Jian hissed, and he pushed me into the back of the church. The back half of the congregation turned round, whispering and staring. I hurriedly backed into the laneway. Jian laughed. 'They think you're the Virgin Mary appearing to them!' he said. I was wearing a blue blouse, and a headscarf to cover my night-on-a-train hair. He could have been right.

We stood around in the lane outside the door, while little boys sat on the ground and looked at me. One of them peed on the ground next to me and splashed my shoes.

I heard the congregation reciting together in Mandarin. I wondered if they were saying the Lord's Prayer, which I had heard many times in Indian languages. I realised I was hearing a chant the Trio must have known by heart. Then there were sounds of people standing up and milling around, and we went inside and I looked around the church, at the concrete floor and bare pews. Paul found the pastor and introduced me. The pastor didn't speak any English, but he immediately pulled me to the front of the church and showed me a heavy stone tablet. On it was carved:

Women's Bible School
Erected by the congregation of
Westminster Chapel London
1909

'Westminster Chapel was Mildred's church,' I said to Paul. 'This must be the right place.' When I first saw the church I had wondered if it would provide a connection to the Trio, but this was more than I dared hope for. I ran my fingers over the stone letters, and looked around the church again.

The pastor and his wife talked to Paul and Jian. The pastor said the church was all that was left of the old compound. There were shops and houses on one side, and a Public Security Bureau complex on the other. I knew about the PSB. It was responsible for security and social order, and its staff had more power than the ordinary police. This was where you would be interrogated if you were in trouble with the Communist authorities.

The pastor's wife said her late grandmother had known the three foreign teachers. She called over her mother-in-law, a cheerful woman who said she remembered later missionaries from the 1940s. She said they were well thought of by locals, and that they helped people in World War II, when the Japanese attacked. 'I'm 80!' she said proudly.

The pastor explained that the rest of the compound was destroyed in the 1940s, but church members had salvaged the stone tablet. The church had been abandoned for a while, but now there were three or four thousand Christians in the Huozhou area. I didn't think to ask if he meant both Catholics and Protestants. The pastor's father and grandfather had been Christian pastors here, too. Neither he nor his father had ever had any contact with foreign Christians.

The pastor and a few other men from the church walked us around a side street, behind the Public Security Bureau, and further up the hill, and showed us some abandoned buildings with broken roof tiles and no windows or door frames. This was the foreign teachers' residence, the pastor said. I took some photos.

Jian told me the pastor had invited us back to his house. But somewhere on the walk back to the church, something gave the pastor the willies. 'Someone must have said something to him,' Jian said later. When we sat down on the pews back at the church, we were having trouble getting answers to questions. The pastor spoke in a soft voice. I asked Jian what was going on. 'They might have some legal problem,' he said. Paul and the pastor kept talking, quietly and seriously. I might have imagined it, but the pastor seemed to be gesturing next door, towards the Public Security Bureau.

'I don't want to make trouble for them,' I said to Paul. 'It's enough that I've seen this place and talked to him.' I wanted to ask more questions about Huozhou's Christians and how life had changed for them over the past decades. I wanted to know if he had ever had to make difficult compromises in order for his church to be officially recognised, which is what I'd read about other pastors. But it didn't look as if I would get any answers.

When Paul told them we would go, everyone was friendly again, and they clasped my hands as we said goodbye.

While we were walking back down the hill, Jian said the pastor had originally offered to show us some documents from the time of the three foreign teachers, but later said he would have to get permission from the leader of his church, and he couldn't do that today. I assumed that his leader was someone higher up in the Three Self Patriotic Movement.

Paul, Jian and I stopped at a restaurant on the way to the bus stop. We were given a private room with a table that seemed to be designed for an extended family banquet. The tablecloth didn't appear to have been changed since the last extended family banquet, but the food was very good.

Jian and Paul ordered up a storm after quizzing me and discovering I would eat anything. While we ate three different kinds of dumplings, and meatballs called Lion's Heads that were bubbling in an iron hotpot, an instrumental version of the Carpenters' 'Close to You' played in the background.

Back in Melbourne, my Mandarin teacher, Tracey, had warned me that in China, everyone tries to pay for each other after a shared meal. She had watched relatives almost get into fist fights at the end of a meal. She said that if you really wanted to pay, you did it before the bill came, by pretending you were getting up to go to the toilet.

So at the end of the meal, I did this. I mimed to the woman at the counter that I was paying on the sly, and she thought it was a great joke. She called the waitress over to tell her, and they giggled and passed me the receipt furtively as if the whole thing was a huge conspiracy.

Then I made the mistake of actually going to the toilet. Everyone I knew who had travelled in China had warnings and horrible stories about Chinese toilets. 'I grew up in India, I'll be fine,' I said many times.

Piles of shit were everywhere, in various stages of decay. There was no evidence of running water. The light bulb had blown, which was probably a good thing. The smell was … bad.

The Trio would never have written about toilets. But as I travelled I wondered how they dealt with these things. They would have had to squat over foul pits at oasis inns. What sort of plans and precautions did they have to take when they had their periods? Where did they go to the toilet during those long treks through the flat desert? Did they make the cart driver look the other way?

Back at the hotel in Linfen, after a long bath, I switched through the TV channels and discovered CCTV9, the English-language station. The main news story was about a coal-mining accident in the north of Shanxi. A young woman was interviewed near the scene. Her husband was trapped underground. The woman was smiling and looked calm, but the subtitles under her face told a different story. 'They're saying time is running out for them,' she said. 'This is like a nightmare.'

I blew my nose. Dirty goop came out. Then I fell into a coal-black sleep.

Chapter Three

Xi'an

> What is wisdom? It has little to do with beliefs. These change year by year from person to person. Only one who does not dare give up beliefs because he has no wisdom will insist that others believe as he does. Cleverness learns something, but wisdom gives up some certainty every day.
>
> *Monkey* Series 2, 'What is Wisdom?'

My next stop was the city of Xi'an. 'Because you want to see terracotta warriors,' Jian said when I told him where I was going. It wasn't a question.

The warriors were only discovered in 1974, after peasants found a few pieces of old pottery in an empty field outside Xi'an. Archaeologists and historians descended on the area, and thousands of life-sized terracotta soldiers, horses and weapons were eventually unearthed. They had been buried in the second century BC with

Xi'an

Emperor Qin Shi Huang, presumably to guard him in the afterlife. In the last three decades, tens of thousands of Chinese and foreign tourists have visited the warriors.

The soldiers and their horses were still sleeping peacefully under the ground when the Trio passed through the ancient Chinese capital of Xi'an in 1922. For them, the city was historically significant because its Forest of Steles Museum housed the earliest record of Christianity in China, an engraved stone known as the Nestorian Stele. For me, Xi'an was important as the first major stop on the Trio's cross-China journey and the supposed starting point for Monkey's trip to India.

After our visit to Huozhou, Paul had insisted that he would walk me to my bus the next morning. He was waiting in the hotel foyer at 6 a.m., and he carried my pack to the Linfen bus station. After he bought my ticket he got on the bus with me, found my seat, and ordered out the man who was already sitting there.

Paul and I shook hands. He took a breath and looked straight at me, for the first time, and said in a heartfelt way, 'I'm sorry my English not good.' I reassured him his English was much better than my Chinese, and thanked him. In his first email to me he had signed off with: 'In China we say it is our pleasure to help you'.

I had been telling Paul about my itinerary, and my eventual destination of Urumqi, on the far side of Xinjiang province and the Gobi desert. He understood why I was going to Xi'an – the warriors, of course – but he was clearly a bit perturbed about my subsequent plans to travel all the way across China without an interpreter or porter or guide. I wasn't surprised. Xinjiang and the other northwestern provinces – Qinghai, Tibet, Gansu – seem to be considered the far edges of civilisation by most of the majority Han Chinese. Even before I left Australia, a Chinese-born work colleague had warned me I was 'heading out to the boondocks'.

I comforted myself that attitudes were much the same in the Trio's time. Most of their missionary colleagues and Chinese friends disapproved of their decision to leave Huozhou after more than twenty years and strike out along the Silk Road. 'They were very senior and highly respected women launching out into the wilds,' a CIM historian wrote to me. 'They were accused of boredom and itchy feet, not being prepared to stick it out where they were. They were abandoning their fluent Mandarin and understanding of Chinese women and leadership in the women's work in China to move to the Muslim ethnic minorities of Central Asia.'

Maybe they *were* bored, though it seems unlikely. They certainly thought it was time for the church in Huozhou to become independent of Western Christians and choose its own leaders. Mildred wrote:

> The material was there, and the Chinese Church was supplying young men and women, earnest devoted servants of Jesus Christ who, given the training and granted the blessing of God, could do a work which it would be impossible for the most earnest Westerner to accomplish. Faults they will have, as we, and while of a different order, who shall say that these failings make them in God's sight more unfit for preaching the Gospel than ours have made us?

The Trio also felt the Huozhou school no longer needed them. Well-trained local teachers looked after the younger girls, and the senior classes were empty, because the provincial government had recruited all the older girls to teach in other schools.

The women had been inspired by a 1922 paper produced by the National Christian Conference of China that reported 'the absence of any Christian witness along the Silk Road from Gansu to Urumqi'. Buddhism and Islam had spread along the Silk Road routes in past centuries, the Trio reasoned. Maybe Christianity could do the same. Mildred was 43, Francesca was 48 and Eva was 50 when they started out from Shanxi province on the three-miles-an-hour journey halfway across China towards their new base in northern Gansu.

The Xi'an bus contained only men, most of whom were smoking. From time to time someone would spit on the floor and rub the bolus into the floor with his shoe. The bus filled up, but nobody sat next to me until just before we left. The seats were small and hard, and for the next five hours the man next to me chain-smoked.

I tried to wave the smoke away without causing a scene. It occurred to me that with the loosening of trade restrictions in the past few years, multinational companies had probably started pushing tobacco onto the Chinese in much the same way that the British had encouraged them to smoke opium a hundred years earlier. All my friends at home were giving up smoking, because health regulations had forced smokers out of restaurants, taxis and even music venues; the men of China were probably all that was keeping the tobacco industry in business.

Outside were great stretches of plains, with low mountains on one side. The sky was still grey. We crossed two wide, silted-up riverbeds that were almost dry. 'The rivers are all drying up,' I was told later in Xi'an. 'Even people in their twenties say they remember when the rivers were full.'

Mildred wrote that the Xi'an plain was fertile and beautiful, but the edges of the towns we drove through were confrontingly ugly, with open drains, crumbling roads and mounds of rubbish. The smaller villages were a little more attractive. They had a few shimmering poplar trees around them, and vestiges of older, more graceful architecture. On a roof in one village, I saw a Christian cross.

None of the men on the bus said anything to me. The loudspeakers at the front of the bus blasted that awful Celine Dion song.

About an hour before we reached Xi'an, a young woman in a bright yellow t-shirt got on the bus. The man next to me stood up and squeezed in with some other men so she could sit next to me. She knew a few words of English, and wanted to use them. She asked where I was from. When I told her, she said 'Ah, Aodaliya. Kangaroo.' She put her hands together, miming a kangaroo's paws, and bounced in her seat.

She opened her bag, pulled out a packet of biscuits and offered me one. 'Mmm, de-licious,' she said as we both ate. They weren't delicious at all, but it was probably the only English word she knew to describe food. It was certainly the only one I knew in Mandarin, so I nodded and agreed with her. 'Mmm, *haochi*,' I said.

Paul had written down the Chinese characters for a budget hotel called the Ludao Binguan. I showed the name to taxi drivers when we reached Xi'an, but they laughed and waved me away. I wasn't sure why. Only one man was willing to take me to the hotel. He had a motorbike with an unsteady-looking double seat rigged up on the back, he grinned a lot, and he had a running patter going, none of which I could understand except the words for 'five yuan'. The taxi drivers nudged each other and pointed when they saw me climbing onto the motorbike with my backpack.

I didn't trust the driver. My map placed the hotel just near the bus station, but we twisted and turned through narrow backstreets. Eventually we stopped outside a shiny new hotel with red lanterns hanging outside, and gold lettering on the facade. It didn't look like a budget hotel, and I assumed the driver got a commission for bringing people here. I gave him a ten yuan note and he indicated that he had no change. I gave up on him and walked into the lobby to talk to the reception staff. 'I want to go to Ludao Binguan,' I kept repeating, sounding increasingly shrill. I could feel my face turning red. The receptionist said 'Yes, here,' each time I repeated myself, but I couldn't shake the feeling that I was being scammed. Then I noticed the prices posted above the desk. They were the same as the prices in my guidebook. A man wearing a suit gave me a card with 'Ludao Binguan' printed on it.

'Oh,' I said. The motorbike-taxi driver, who had been watching through the glass doors the whole time, waved at me, still grinning.

Just a few days into my journey and, despite my best intentions, I was in danger of becoming the kind of person who gives foreigners a bad reputation in China.

In the hotel room I lay back on the polyester bedspread and thought about the Trio. They seem to have avoided making scenes, even when they were blatantly being scammed. I remembered a story about them pretending to ignore a fight going on around them. Later, re-reading the Trio's book *A Desert Journal*, I realised that this happened on the same stretch of road I had just travelled.

On their journey from Huozhou to Xi'an, the women had most of their bags stolen. After this they were accompanied, against their wishes, by groups of soldiers sent by the local governor. The soldiers would demand money for having protected them. This started to become expensive, and when they parted with one group, they handed out less money than the previous posse had received.

They were in a crowded marketplace at the time. The soldiers started shouting and demanding more money. Passers-by joined in, loudly taking sides. Mildred wrote about the Trio's reaction:

> Years of experience had taught us that such situations can only successfully be met by the adoption of an attitude of heavy indifference, and thus we sat, like three images of Buddha, expressionless, while our officially appointed defenders called on their protective deities to see to it that our carts were overturned, our baggage stolen, and we ourselves the victims of brigands, in retribution of our miserliness.

The soldiers finally had to give up, and they left the women to continue their journey alone.

My first task in Xi'an was to telephone James and Ange, a young English couple who worked as teachers. Mutual friends had made me promise to look them up. James and Ange were Christians, and outside of work they were making contacts with local Christians and talking about their faith with people they met.

Ange suggested that we go out for dinner that night, and they came to the hotel to meet me. James was neat and dark-haired, but I could see Ange walking down the street from blocks away. She was tall and blonde, as distinctive as the Swedish backpackers in Beijing.

We introduced ourselves and caught a bus towards the Muslim quarter. Rain was pouring heavily when we got off the bus, so to keep dry we ducked down some stairs and through a subway that led to an upmarket shopping centre. It was disorienting, with bright lights, mirrors, perfume smells and ads for brands like Chanel and Yves St Laurent. It could have been anywhere in the world. At the entrance to the centre, a young man in an expensive suit was handing out plastic bags so people could cover their dripping umbrellas. He bowed to each customer.

By the time we emerged, the sky was getting darker and the rain was easing. Children and women approached us, brandishing bright strings of felt animals and other souvenirs for sale. Ange said this was typical Xi'an folk art. One child flew a kite-like string of plastic birds that was silhouetted against the grey sky. The children shouted to each other, and James and Ange chatted fluently with them in Mandarin.

James and Ange had been in Xi'an for six years. James said they liked it. 'Not that we're here to enjoy ourselves,' Ange added.

In the Muslim quarter, restaurateurs were pulling chairs and tables out onto the streets. We walked down a narrow street, past hawker stalls and lanterns hanging outside bright noisy restaurants in brightly painted restored wooden buildings. I could see the dome of the Great Mosque at the end of the street. 'This is the part of Xi'an the government wants people to see,' Ange said.

James and Ange's favourite restaurant was packed with customers. Everyone seemed to be shouting, and waiters zoomed around with precariously laden trays of steaming bowls. The smells were fantastic. James ordered, and then he asked me what I was doing in China.

We had already exchanged emails, but I had been warned by our mutal friends to be cautious. James and Ange believed their emails could be intercepted, so I could not use words like 'missionary' or 'Christian'. Their parents in England screened their emails before forwarding them on to China.

Over noodles and dumplings, I talked about the Trio, and explained that my background gave me a particular interest in them. 'I hope I'll be able to reflect a bit about my ambivalent feelings about missionaries,' I said. James and Ange both nodded.

Later, while we were eating sweet eight-jewel congee, Ange said 'So tell me about your ambivalence.' I think she had been building up the courage to ask.

I mumbled. I said that even the most enlightened missionaries of the Trio's era had underlying attitudes about race and culture that I couldn't like or agree with. I told her I wasn't an evangelical anymore, but I said it had been hard to leave, and I still had a lot of respect for many Christians. They nodded again.

I've found it's a lot easier to say 'I'm not an evangelical' than 'I'm not a Christian.' It implies doubts about the literal truth of the whole Bible, or maybe no longer believing that all non-Christians are going to Hell, while still having faith in a basically Judeo-Christian deity. Not many people will push further.

'So what exactly do you believe?' Ange asked.

I had to think for a moment. I couldn't say 'nothing'. I told them the last stop on my itinerary was Heaven Lake in Xinjiang, where Bogeda Feng, the Mountain of God, overlooks the lake. I joked that it sounded like a good spot to pause for a while and meditate about spiritual things before I went home. I made it sound as if I was half serious.

I didn't know how to tell Ange all the things I *didn't* believe; that I just couldn't swallow Christianity's concrete claims of absolute, physical truth, while at the same time I didn't like the metaphysical, magical side of Christian belief. When one of my friends rejected Christianity in favour of crystals and reiki healing and astral travel ('Because I'm still a very spiritual person') I told her she may as well have stuck with Christianity. Maybe I just wasn't a very spiritual person.

I changed the subject and asked James about his students. I wondered what young Chinese people thought about religion.

James said there had been a rise in religious observance over the past few years, but he thought it was linked to consumerism rather than any kind of spiritual yearning. People paid homage at Buddhist shrines because they thought they could get something out of it, he said. Even young people who said they were atheists would burn incense for something they really wanted. 'It's all tied to money,' he said.

I had seen a report on CCTV9 about graduating students who were desperate to find jobs. It showed one young woman going to a temple to burn incense to a deity who would help her find a good job. She was apologetic when the reporter asked her about this; she was just covering all her bases. The reporter also interviewed an employment consultant who said students were too picky about where they would work. He said there were plenty of good jobs out in the northwestern provinces, but everyone wanted to live in the eastern cities.

James and Ange and I walked past the souvenir sellers clustered around the walls of the Great Mosque. They sold t-shirts, silk scarves and jade cups, miniature terracotta warriors, postcards and bangles, Chairman Mao alarm clocks, army caps and wall hangings. One stall had a sign up in English that said they could paint a wall hanging with your favourite Bible verse in Chinese. 'They know their market,' Ange said. Groups of Americans on package tours to see the terracotta warriors were often led around here, she said.

Mildred Cable had written about Xi'an's impressive city gates and towers. Unlike most Chinese cities, Xi'an still has its four gates, connected by solid walls. I arranged to meet Ange by the south gate two days later, so we could visit the Forest of Steles Museum together and see the Nestorian Stele.

The next day I went on a bus tour to see the terracotta warriors. I kind of felt obliged. The statues were lined up in a pit inside an enormous shed. The entrance fee was extremely high by Chinese standards. Crowds of Chinese and Western tourists filed around the edges of the pit and took photos over each other's heads.

On the way to the warriors, I overheard the following exchange on the tour bus.

Two young Australian men sat on the back seat. I had seen them in the lobby of my hotel. Their names, I later learned, were Brad and Murray. Brad was reading a passage about the terracotta warriors in his guidebook. He looked up and spoke to his friend.

'So we have to pay however many yuan to get on this bus, then we'll have to pay more to get in to see the terracotta warriors, and then we have to pay extra to take photos of them ...'

Murray said: 'Do you have to pay to scratch your arse?'

I met Ange at Xi'an's south gate the following morning. The street leading from the gate to the Forest of Steles Museum was lined with upmarket souvenir shops full of jade, and Ange and I browsed in the shops. I wanted to buy a jade horse for a friend who was born in the Chinese Year of the Horse, but I thought Ange might disapprove. I knew some Christians believed that objects connected to astrology and non-Christian religions carried demons and curses with them.

My parents had never been comfortable with this kind of thinking. But many missionaries we knew in India illustrated their sermons with stories about demon attacks that stopped when Hindu (or animist, or Muslim) images or objects were removed from the homes of converts.

In the Trio's early writings it's made clear that the women believed in literal spirits that could inhabit objects. This would have put them on common ground with growing numbers of Edwardian-era spiritualists back in England, as well as with most Chinese people. *Monkey* is full of matter-of-fact tales about good, bad and indifferent spirits and demons. When Mildred told the story of Huozhou's Pastor Hsi and his wife, she wrote that an image in their house caused some kind of demon to influence Mrs Hsi, taking her over and making her attack her husband. The shrine was destroyed 'and Mrs Hsi was free of the tormenting spirit'.

Nothing like this appeared in the Trio's letters or books after they left Huozhou. It's hard to tell whether their views changed, or if they or their publishers became more circumspect about this kind of thing when their books became more popular with mainstream readers.

Ange wasn't concerned about the astrological symbolism of the jade animals, she just thought they were overpriced. We walked on to the museum.

The Forest of Steles Museum is housed in a Confucian temple, and is packed with thousands of engraved stone tablets dating from as early as the Han Dynasty, which ran from 206 BC to AD 220. The tablet I had come to see, the Nestorian or Da Qin Stele, was carved in AD 781. The Trio had come here to see it on their way across the country.

The tablet is tall and solid, and is mounted on the back of a stone tortoise. It tells the story of how Nestorian Christianity came to China from the west in AD 635, and it records the beliefs of Christians in China. At the top of the tablet, a carved cross rises out of a lotus flower.

Months earlier, Ange had emailed me and asked 'Have you read the J Sutras?' She was referring to Martin Palmer's book *The Jesus Sutras*, but she didn't feel safe using the name 'Jesus' in an email. In the book, Palmer argues that Nestorian Christianity wasn't a heretical sect – as I had read elsewhere – but a legitimate form of Eastern Christianity, and that Chinese Christianity had incorporated aspects of Buddhism, Confucianism and Taoism by the time the stone was carved. The community that Palmer called 'Taoist Christian' was officially vegetarian and nonviolent, treated men and women as equals, and had compiled writings that combined Chinese and Western imagery and ideas.

Christianity flourished in China from the 7th century until the reign of Emperor Wu Zong, who fiercely suppressed both Christians and Buddhists, killing thousands of monks in 845. A few Nestorian communities survived in China – Marco Polo met some in the 12th century – but the churches eventually disappeared. The next round of missionaries to China were Italian Jesuit priests who arrived in 1582. Until workmen dug up the Nestorian Stele in 1625, the Jesuits believed they were the first Christians to reach China.

Ange and I looked at the other tablets. I thought that the Trio, with their fluent Mandarin, would have appreciated these, but the dense strings of characters I couldn't read began to all look the same to me. Mildred had admired an engraving of Confucius in the museum, but I couldn't find it, and my feet had started to ache.

'Have you seen enough?' Ange asked. I felt guilty about leaving so soon, without having taken in more Culture. I felt even worse when I thought about the list in my guidebook of Xi'an's 'must-see' temples and pagodas and museums that I had yet to explore.

'We could go to my local beauty salon and get a facial and massage,' Ange said. I was really beginning to like her. I said that temples and museums were all very well, but I would learn more about modern China in the salon. 'China's famous for its massage, isn't it?' I said. 'It's a cultural experience, right?'

'Sure,' she said, smiling.

When we went outside to hail a taxi, we walked past an old man who sat at the side of the road. A weeping burn down his shin was exposed. He called out to us, asking for money, and we kept walking, not looking at him. When we had passed him, Ange said 'We still don't know what to do about beggars.' She said periodic raids swept them off the street, and advertising campaigns told people not to give them money. She said she had handed coins to beggars when she first arrived in China, and people on the street had ticked her off for encouraging them.

At the salon, we lay on our backs with quilts draped over us, while pretty girls wearing pastel-coloured uniforms and facemasks smeared creams on our cheeks and plucked our eyebrows and occasionally whispered to each other.

I'm sure they were whispering to preserve a relaxing atmosphere. But I started feeling self-conscious and imagining that they were making fun of us. 'Can you believe how huge these women are! Check out their pasty complexions!'

According to Ange, beauty salons were a major new industry in China, and staying slim was hugely important to her female students. 'So they all eat diddly squat,' she said. Over the past couple of years she had seen all sorts of weight-loss pills and potions and contraptions flooding the market. I had already noticed television advertisements for diet pills and breast implants. One commercial showed a group of girls all congratulating their friend for losing weight. The final scene showed her getting married in a big white dress in a Western-looking church.

Ange said one of her Chinese colleagues went on holiday for a fortnight and spent the whole time hooked up to some kind of fat-jiggling machine.

'But I don't think I've ever seen an overweight Chinese woman,' I said.

'Maybe because they're all hooked up to fat-jiggling machines,' Ange said.

We agreed that it's hard for Western women not to feel a bit lumpen and sexless in China, surrounded as they are by petite, beautiful women wearing tight jeans that show off petite, beautiful backsides. I had been told, as if it was gospel, that Chinese Men Are Not Attracted to Western Women, and I wasn't likely to ask any Chinese men if this was true.

'Of course it's different for Western men in China,' I said to Ange. I thought it was different for Western men almost everywhere. They would always be treated as if they were attractive because of what they represented, because of the privileges and money that people assumed they had.

I told Ange about a scene I'd witnessed on the first morning I was in Xi'an. Just a few doors down from my hotel, two pretty Chinese girls were pulling a young backpacker into a shopfront where hairdressing products sat unused on a bench. The girls were giggling and teasing him, and he was resisting and laughing. It all seemed so innocent that they could have been sisters kidding around with an older brother.

I had mentioned this to Brad and Murray, the Australians I met on the bus tour to the terracotta warriors. 'Was that really a brothel, do you think?' I had asked, wide-eyed. They said they'd been propositioned by the same girls. 'Never seen a town with so many knocking shops,' Murray said.

Prostitution is the only thing that seems to have made Mildred Cable lose her temper. She may have learned to sit like an expressionless Buddha when people tried to rip her off, but she wrote about pacing the streets 'in impotent rage [at the] vileness of man' after meeting some prostitutes in a small oasis town.

The girls looked very young, with elaborate clothes and hairstyles, and make-up that made them look out of place in the simple inn where they invited Mildred to join them for tea. She watched them all attend to an older woman, preparing her opium pipe and lighting it for her. The woman claimed the girls were her nieces, but Mildred knew a company of soldiers was about to arrive in the town.

She didn't blame the girls. She said they all came from areas where famine had driven their families to sell them.

> The helpless victims had feared, wept, and then stolidly accepted the sacrifice required of them to save the lives of their parents. 'It is the decree of the gods,' they would say, and there was heroism in the calm under which they hid agony and offered themselves for the sake of others.

I asked Ange about the brothels, how they could be so conspicuous when they were illegal. I was confused about attitudes towards authority in China. Some illicit activities seemed to flourish out in the open, while in other ways people seemed frightened, even paranoid, about following the rules and avoiding trouble.

Ange didn't have any answers. She said it was a confusing time. Things seemed far more relaxed on the surface because of the rise of consumerism and the disappearance of many forms of overt Communist Party propaganda. But occasionally she would see a police van pull up on the street, and a shop or house would be raided, and people would be bundled away and nobody would talk about it. There were street-stall vendors who would call you over with a smile, but they would have a lookout posted down the street, and if anyone with a uniform came by they would pack up their pirated DVDs and disappear in a second. One of Ange's Chinese work colleagues had spoken about his Christian faith in the workplace. He was officially disciplined and sent to re-education classes. Everyone in the work unit was informed about it. The details would remain on his official file forever.

Ange pointed out various 'must-see' sights from the taxi on the way back to the hotel. 'At least you can say you've seen them,' she said. The Big Goose Pagoda and Little Goose Pagoda were both in the grounds of temples built to house Buddhist scriptures brought back from India in the 8th century. Nearby were ancient-looking dark-red archways. 'Those were put up last year,' Ange said, pointing to the archways.

I was surprised. 'It's hard to know whether anything I see dates from last week or centuries ago,' I said. 'I feel as if I don't have the tools to interpret anything I see.'

When we said goodbye, Ange hugged me. 'I'll pray for you,' she said.

There was one thing I still needed to do before I left Xi'an, and it didn't involved an ancient temple or any other tourist site. Brad from the terracotta warriors tour told me I had to try a snack that I referred to in my notes as a 'mutton pocket'. I never learned its proper Chinese name.

'It's grouse, it's just like a meat and gravy roll at home,' Brad said. We were at an outside stall near the hotel. Brad was wolfing down his food and taking swigs of Coke. When he was finished he burped. 'That's better,' he said. 'I was so hungry I could've eaten the crutch out of a low-flying duck.'

I decided to give it a go. A big aluminium pot sat on a gas ring. Bubbling inside were fatty chunks of meat in a thick brown stew. It smelled great. I gave my order to the teenage boy behind the pot. He stuck a skewer in and pulled out a lump of meat. He placed it on a wooden board with some green chillies and chives, and whacked at it with a cleaver until it was all in tiny pieces. He ladled some of the meat juice from the pot onto the mixture and spooned it all into a piece of steamed bread that had been sliced down the middle.

It was just about the best thing I had ever tasted.

Chapter Four

Topsy

> It is given to very few to be solitary, because people belong together. Many reasons draw people to each other, and the strongest of these is love.
>
> *Monkey* Series 2, 'Keep on Dancing'

The town of Jiuquan has no west gate. Hundreds of years ago the town's priests decreed that if a west gate was built, a flood would destroy the town. This made people uncomfortable. A town needs four gates, they said. So they agreed that the fort of Jiayuguan, about 35 kilometres to the west, was in fact the west gate of Jiuquan.

Floods have never destroyed Jiuquan.

More than 80 years before me, the Trio had moved on from Xi'an and travelled in a straight line – or so it looked on the maps – towards Jiuquan, their new home base in the north of Gansu province, almost halfway across China. Here, after they had settled into the rhythm of regular trips across the Gobi and through some of the most remote areas of China, the Trio became a Quartet. It would be some time before I saw Jiuquan for myself, but the experiences of the next few weeks made me think often about the Trio's lives there.

The path the women took from Xi'an to Jiuquan might have been straight, but it wasn't straightforward. In the winter their cart became alternatively bogged in mud and, when ice broke under them, submerged in water. They travelled along the valley now known as the Hexi corridor, the flat stretch of land between the mountains of Mongolia to the north and Tibet to the south. They left Huozhou in June 1923 and they arrived in Jiuquan in October 1924.

Jiuquan, which was known as Suchow in the Trio's time, was unusual in that most residents were Han Chinese, while the rest of Gansu was predominantly Muslim. Most of Jiuquan had been destroyed in a Muslim uprising in 1862, and when the town was rebuilt the government ordered that no Muslims were to live within the city walls. But the Muslims didn't move away. By the Trio's time, the eastern part of town, just outside the wall, had become the Muslim quarter. Traders from all over Central Asia passed through the eastern marketplace. This was where the Trio heard stories about the Gobi desert, before they set out to cross it themselves. It's where they started learning the Uyghur language (then known as Turki), which was more widely spoken in the areas further northwest. Most of the Trio's new neighbours looked like the people they had left behind in Shanxi, but the Uyghur and Kazak Muslim traders wore beards and heavy sheepskin coats.

The Trio didn't arrive in Jiuquan alone. On the way there they had stopped for six months in the town of Zhangye, where they taught and lived with local Christians who were led by a Chinese medical doctor called Kao. When they moved on to Jiuquan, about thirty members of the Zhangye church came with them to found a Christian community in Jiuquan. The Trio called this group their 'Pioneer Band'.

Topsy

The Trio and their band lived in a Jiuquan inn for a few months, and received a steady stream of local visitors. Many had never seen Westerners before, and they were surprised that the women spoke fluent Mandarin. They spoke about the Trio in front of them, saying 'They are just like ourselves; they have father and mother, brother and sisters the same as we have. There is no difference.'

A merchant then found them a property to rent. The compound had been empty for a while because it was said to be haunted by 'a troublesome spirit who gives a twisted face to everyone who lives in it'. The merchant told them they were probably safe from the spirit because they believed their god would protect them.

The women were housed in a flimsy but attractive pavilion in a garden. Other buildings and courtyards were set up as classrooms and living areas for the Pioneer Band. They planted a vegetable garden on some waste ground, alongside a tent where they held open church services filled with music and stories.

They drew a distinction between these services, which were aimed at bringing in outsiders, and their own preaching and worship services that were just for the Christians. At the private services, Eva and Mildred both preached. This was acceptable to CIM leaders, and to Christians back in England. For years there had been a double standard whereby the only women allowed to preach and teach from the Bible were missionary women. But Eva and Mildred quietly took things a step further by leading communion services, where they distributed the bread and wine, the symbolic blood and body of Christ, to Chinese Christians.

They didn't mention this in letters home, but it got out. The women received at least one angry letter. Their biographer, Platt, devoted four pages of his account to admitting it was shocking and arguing that it was acceptable. 'Their theology and practice were based on what they felt to be permissible by New Testament teaching,' he wrote.

The Jiuquan children turned out to be more interested in the open church services than the adults were, so the Christians started targeting the children. Every evening a boy ran through the town playing a gong, encouraging other children to follow him to the tent. The Trio called him their Pied Piper. The well-behaved children were loaned musical instruments, and the orchestra played along while the other children sang Bible verses set to well-known Chinese tunes. Parents started turning up, although they said they came to see the clever children, not to hear the preaching. When Dr Kao was in town, he would tell Bible stories in serial form, urging the children to come back for the next instalment.

At each service the children were asked to recite a creed about all gods being false except for the one true God. Some of the children parroted the words without thinking, but others took them seriously. They approached the Christians after the service one day and said the time was coming to offer the annual prayers to the household gods. They didn't know what to do. The children were encouraged to go ahead and do the kowtow, while quietly reciting the creed in their hearts.

The children became protective of the Trio. From time to time bands of brigands, sometimes army deserters, would travel through Jiuquan, demanding money and food and terrorising the community. Sometimes they asked about the three foreign women. The children always lied, claiming that there were no foreign women in Jiuquan, or they would lead the men to the wrong side of town.

One day a brigand leader found the Trio in spite of the children. He wanted them to teach him a song. He had heard a snatch of it and was told it was a Christian song. It was called 'Endure Hardness as a Good Soldier'. He wanted to teach it to his men.

In the winter months it wasn't uncommon for beggars to freeze to death overnight in Jiuquan. Stiff bodies would be found on the temple steps and under shop awnings. The Christians held a harvest thanksgiving service at the tent church, and asked the children to help collect food for the beggars' home that had been set up by the city's Mandarin. The Christians also set aside two spare rooms in the compound, where hay was spread on the floor and porridge was served up every morning. Anyone was allowed to sleep there, but men and women had to stay in separate rooms.

One of the beggars was a teenage girl whom the women called Grace. She had been sold into slavery by her desperately poor family and was owned by the governor of the Jiuquan prison, an influential member of the community. He treated his slaves brutally. Grace slept on an earth floor without a blanket, and developed first frostbite and then gangrene in her foot. The Jiuquan Christians rescued her and called Dr Kao across from Zhangye.

The prison governor might have been an important man, but so was Dr Kao. In this case he was angry enough to use his influence. He forced the governor to watch while he amputated Grace's foot, then he handed the man a spade and the gangrenous foot, and ordered him to go outside and bury it.

Grace lived with the Trio for a few months while she recovered, and was then returned to her family. After her mother died she was reduced to begging again for a while, until the Trio returned from a trip to Urumqi, found her at the beggars' home, and organised for a Chinese Christian woman to take her in. She stayed within the local Christian community for the rest of her life. Mildred and Francesca wrote a children's book about her that ended with her marrying a Christian man, as if this was the highest pinnacle of a woman's ambition, although I can't imagine any of them believed this for themselves.

When Grace was forced to live on the streets, she had an occasional begging companion, a deaf-mute girl whose nickname, Gwa Gwa, translated as Little Lonely. The two girls sometimes huddled together for warmth on freezing nights. The deaf girl always followed people who gave her money or food, insisting that she do some kind of work for them in exchange.

The Trio attributed Gwa Gwa's pride to her Mongolian ancestry. Her father was a tribal chieftan from the Mongolian grasslands to the north of Jiuquan. In about 1918 he travelled south to a Buddhist festival at a monastery in the Tibetan foothills, in what is now China's Qinghai province. As an important visitor, he was given his pick of the local girls to sleep with, and the next day she was pregnant.

I laughed when I read about Gwa Gwa's father in Platt's biography of the Trio. It described him as going on his way without thought of the consequences, 'like many another man before him, whether in the West or the East'.

So the baby girl was born, and three weeks later a relative travelled to Jiuquan and sold her to a childless woman, who petted her and dressed her up in a silk cap with an embroidered cat's face on one side and tinkling silver bells hanging down the other side.

After a few years it became clear that the child couldn't hear or speak. The pretty clothes were put away. When Gwa Gwa was six years old and her foster mother gave birth to a boy of her own, the girl's fate was sealed. She was dressed in rags and put out to beg. She was only allowed to come home, where she slept on the floor, if she brought money with her. Her foster mother mainly used the money to buy opium.

The other beggars could shout and implore people to help them, but Gwa Gwa could only tap on doors with her stick. It was easy for people to ignore her. Sometimes she would open a door to a courtyard and let herself in, but this was risky because of the watchdogs. She couldn't hear them barking, and sometimes didn't know they were there until she felt their teeth. Her legs were covered with infected bites. She had deeper sores, too, where her foster mother burned her with the fire poker as punishment for coming home empty-handed.

Topsy

She was thin, dirty and bleeding when she tapped her stick against the Trio's door for the first time. They gave her some food and cleaned up her legs and called her a poor little mite. But she wasn't the first beggar child they had met, and they sent her on her way.

The next day Gwa Gwa's foster mother turned up in her best clothes, demanding to see the foreign devils. She said their dog had wounded her poor little child and she wanted restitution. Before Eva could answer, the cook lost his temper and shouted, 'We have no dogs here, and what is more, the ladies have actually bandaged the legs of your good-for-nothing child with their most expensive ointment. You're a fine one to dress up, and your child with not a rag to cover her. Why does she go begging? Are you a beggar too?'

The woman became nervous and blamed Gwa Gwa for misleading her. 'I'll thrash her for that,' she said, turning to leave.

That was a mistake. Eva was furious. She called after the woman, suggesting that when a well-dressed woman sends her child out to beg, she might come to the attention of the authorities.

The Trio started asking questions about Gwa Gwa. The children who attended their services told them about her family, and how her foster mother beat her. The children offered to help, promising they would give food to Gwa Gwa and keep the dogs away from her.

Gwa Gwa began coming to the Trio's house every day for soup and bread. When they went away to preach and sell Bibles at festivals in Mongolia and Tibet, they made sure the cook looked after her. They let her sweep the yard or carry kindling in exchange for food.

In 1927 the Trio loaded up the mule cart and travelled all the way through northwest China to Russia. From there they would catch a train across Europe to England, where they would visit relatives and speak about China at conventions and conferences. As the cart left Jiuquan, Gwa Gwa ran after them, through the streets and all the way into the open countryside. It was too much for

Mildred. She stopped the cart, walked back down the road to the girl, and explained that she had to go back or she would get lost. All the way back to England Mildred kept picturing Gwa Gwa's desolate little face.

Gwa Gwa visited the Jiuquan Christians every day for the next year. The cook always gave her a hot meal. Sometimes she slept in the straw-strewn room with the other beggars instead of going home. When she stepped into the courtyard one day in late 1928 and saw the Trio's baggage, she made an excited noise and threw her stick in the air. The women were relieved that she was still alive, and gave her a new pair of cotton trousers.

That night, while Gwa Gwa was asleep, her foster mother took her new trousers and exchanged them for opium. It was the final straw for the Trio. They set up negotiations through Chinese friends and the Mandarin, and they bought Gwa Gwa from her foster parents.

She was officially passed to the Trio on Christmas Eve, 1928. That night Little Lonely was given her first bath, and a new set of clothes, and calico socks to pull over her scarred legs. She was told she had a new name, Ah Lien, which meant Love Bond.

Ah Lien might have had a beautiful meaning, but it was a hard name for a lip-reader to recognise. So the Trio called her Topsy, and she remained Topsy for the rest of her long life. The name on her passport was Eileen Guy, an Anglicisation of Ah Lien Kai. Kai was Mildred's Chinese name.

Topsy now seems an unfortunate name, although it probably seemed appropriate to the Trio. It was from the best-selling novel of the 19th century, Harriet Beecher Stowe's *Uncle Tom's Cabin*. When the book was first published, its sympathetic descriptions of black characters had such an impact that the work is credited with bringing an end to slavery in America. Now it's better known as a source of patronising racial stereotypes. Topsy was the simple black slave girl who had been abused but learned to trust again through the love of a saintly white girl called Eva.

Racist implications aside, Topsy was also a child's name. Perhaps the Trio didn't think about Topsy growing to be an adult.

The Trio led disciplined lives, and they were determined that Topsy would too. Life on the streets had taught Topsy to be self-reliant and strong-willed, but it had not helped her develop the qualities of obedience and gentleness that were valued in middle-class households when the Trio were children.

So a battle of the wills began. When Topsy was asked to do something, she was expected to do it straight away, properly and without arguing. This rarely happened. When special food was put out in preparation for guests, Topsy was not to steal sweet things and hide them in her baggy trousers. When she was questioned about the whereabouts of the sweets, she was not to make it worse by lying about it, especially after the sweets fell out the bottom of her trousers in front of everyone.

She would sob loudly for hours when she was punished. If you had been scarred with a hot poker and mauled by dogs in the past, being sent to your room or having your hand smacked or your beloved picture of Princess Elizabeth turned to the wall might seem like much more bearable punishment. Perhaps it's harder, and more confusing, to be hurt by someone you love, and who loves you.

There's no doubt there was a love bond between Topsy and her 'three mamas', as she referred to them after she learned to write and sign. But the women were not sentimental guardians. They didn't dote, at least not in their writings. Letters to friends and family have no glowing reports about her progress. In the whole of *The Gobi Desert*, Topsy is only mentioned once, in passing, as 'a Mongolian child who was with us'.

Mildred and Francesca wrote a children's book called *The Story of Topsy* in which she was presented as anything but a saint. Stories about her sweet-stealing and temper tantrums were interspersed with her adventures with the Trio along the Silk Road. The book contained beautiful photos of young Topsy riding horses and camels ('As for her riding – why, no-one who saw Topsy astride a pony could doubt she was a child of the Mongolian plains, so fearless was she and sure of herself').

To the Trio, Topsy was their daughter, but she was also a parable. She had been redeemed, they wrote, and 'later on she would learn of the Saviour who redeemed her, not with gold or silver, but with His own most precious blood.' All her life Topsy retained an absolute faith that it was Jesus who had saved her.

Chapter Five

Xining

> If there is any plan in the universe, it can only be evolving consciousness. This is the difference between human and animal. People feel love and grief for others.
> *Monkey* Season 2, 'At the Top of the Mountain'

I lay on the top berth on the overnight train from Xi'an to Lanzhou and practiced ordering yak. I had been eating a lot of dumpling soup and steamed bread, mainly because I knew how to order them in Mandarin. Now I was heading down to yak country, and I wanted to eat like a local.

I looked in my phrasebook and underlined all the dishes I wanted to order. I said the names out loud. Nobody else in the compartment could have heard me over the instrumental version of Air Supply's 'All out of Love', which was blasting out next to my left ear.

Sha-guo was a meat-filled hot pot that sounded good. *Suan-nai*, yak-milk yogurt, sounded tasty too. *Sha-guo, sha-guo*, I recited along with the rattling of the train. Then that bloody Celine Dion song started up again.

The only reason I was going to Lanzhou was to change trains; from there I would travel south to Xining, the capital of Qinghai province. I was aware that I was straying off the Trio's path. When they left Xi'an they had travelled first to Jiuquan, and only later had they taken short trips south to Qinghai. I would have liked to follow the Trio exactly, but this would have meant some backtracking, and I only had limited time before I met up with Jack in Jiayuguan.

The province of Qinghai was historically part of the Tibetan world. It officially became a province of the Republic of China in 1928, during the time when the Trio visited the region, but the women continued to refer to it as Tibet. The whole time the Trio lived in the area, Qinghai was, in reality, ruled in part by the thirteenth Dalai Lama (who ruled absolutely in the rest of the Tibetan world) but mostly by Chinese Muslim warlords. Qinghai was the only part of the Tibetan world where the communists had complete control after the People's Republic of China was declared in 1949, so in the late 1950s it was unaffected when the People's Liberation Army moved into the rest of Tibet, crushing the rule of the priests and forcing the fourteenth Dalai Lama into exile in India.

The Trio and members of the Pioneer Band regularly travelled south from Jiuquan and through the foothills to Qinghai to attend Buddhist festivals. They set up tents and handed out scriptures and had long talks about religion with monks, often staying at a monastery on a hill. They called the monastery Kan-lung.

Before I left Australia, I had spent a lot of time online, trying to find information about Kan-lung monastery. I found nothing. The Trio's hand-drawn map placed the monastery in a spot that was empty on modern maps. When I posted questions about Kan-lung on various online China travel forums, people told me I was probably looking for Kumbum, a famous monastery just outside Xining. I knew it wasn't the same place, but in the end I resigned myself to going to Xining and visiting Kumbum anyway, just to see a Tibetan monastery.

Early in the morning the train slowed down on the outskirts of Lanzhou. We chugged past the backs of multi-storey concrete blocks where sewage appeared to be running down the walls. Further away, past more cubes of dirty concrete, smoke billowed out of industrial chimneys.

The Trio liked Lanzhou, and described it as beautifully situated and cosmopolitan. Today the town is famously polluted, even by Chinese standards.

In Xi'an, I had only been able to get a ticket as far as Lanzhou, and I expected to be trapped there for days. The hotel receptionist, who had sent a man to buy my ticket, warned me that a seat on a Xining train could be hard to come by. But when my train pulled into Lanzhou station, I walked straight to the ticket office, had the most fluent Mandarin conversation I had ever had, and within half an hour was waiting for the 8.20 a.m. Xining train, ticket in hand.

This was my first trip by what the guidebook described as 'soft seat' class; it had been the only ticket available and the seats proved to be not especially soft. Women wearing starched, frilly aprons walked up and down the aisle with huge teapots, refilling the passengers' cups. Outside, a soft drizzle fell. Once we got past the suburbs of Lanzhou, the landscape was startlingly green, and the rivers were muddy and swollen. We moved slowly uphill.

In the distance, outside my window, I could see a range of jagged hills. When I looked across at the peaks I thought about something my mother told me in India. She said the Indian hills were the wrong shape; they were too pointy and young. In Australia the landscape was so old that the edges had all been rounded. When my mother was homesick, the shape of the Indian hills bothered her. At the time I didn't understand. The only things I missed about Australia, then, were ice creams and my grandparents. These days I didn't stay away from Australia for long enough to miss anything about it too much.

After four hours on the train, we arrived in Xining. The sky was overcast and I was surprised at how cold the air was. I could see my breath as I climbed the stairs from the underpass up to the square where the taxi drivers were clustered.

At the top of the stairs, a young man was standing under a shop awning, shielding himself from the drizzle. He smiled and asked where I was staying. This man's manner was so gentle – and his English was so good – that I stopped and smiled back at him. I told him I was looking for the Post Hotel. His face lit up and he said 'That's where I'm from, see!' He pulled a notebook out of his anorak pocket and showed me a page where POST HOTEL was written in shaky capital letters. I wondered how many hotel names were written in that notebook.

The man shook my hand and introduced himself. I'll call him Wang. 'OK, I'll come with you,' I said. Wang put his notebook back in his pocket and pulled his anorak hood over his head. He held an umbrella over my head and led me around the side of the square, steering me away from puddles and unexpectedly reversing taxis.

The hotel was only a few doors away from the station, and the location was not quite where my guidebook had described it. The sign out the front said Hongguang Hotel. 'That doesn't say Post Hotel,' I said.

'That's the Chinese name,' Wang said. I didn't want him to be scamming me, but it was patently not the Post Hotel. I didn't argue.

Wang helped me sign in. The room cost 35 yuan a night, far less than anywhere else I had stayed. It was small and smelled musty. The blankets were pilled and stained, but there were plenty of them. There was even a television.

Xining

Wang followed me into the room and asked what I wanted to do in Xining. I explained that I wanted to go to the Kumbum monastery because I was researching some English women who had travelled in Qinghai, and I wanted to see the kind of monasteries they had visited.

Wang drew me a map of Xining, and showed me where to catch the minibus to Kumbum. He called the monastery by its Chinese name, Ta'er Si. 'You like temples, I think,' he said. 'The head monk at Ta'er Si drives a Mercedes. Maybe after Ta'er Si we go to a better temple and see a Living Buddha. I can take you.' I said yes, that would be good. I didn't know how much it might cost me, or if I would even see him again.

We shook hands again and he left me to unpack. I pulled out a woollen cardigan that I had almost decided to leave behind in Melbourne. I hadn't expected this kind of cold in the summer months.

When the rain stopped, I walked outside to find some yak to eat. The Trio hadn't shared my enthusiasm for eating yak meat. The monks at Kan-lung ate it raw, they reported, along with parched corn, butter, yak's milk and tea. The Trio thought even the butter was suspect, as it tended to be flecked with yak hair. They brought their own food on the mule cart from Jiuquan. The yaks that hadn't yet been killed and cooked were fierce looking, Mildred wrote, but were of a 'mild and peaceful disposition'. It was the dogs you had to watch.

I crossed a bridge opposite the railway station and walked uphill towards the town's main shopping strip, Dongguan Dajie. I turned and looked back down at the station. In any other context the building would have looked imposing, but here it was dwarfed by the sheer stony cliffs behind it. The town couldn't sprawl past the station. It was forced to stop, hemmed in by the mountains.

I walked a long way up the main street. Many people wore Muslim headgear. They did not look Tibetan, so I assumed they were Chinese Muslims, known as Hui. There had been a sizeable Hui population in this area since the 17th century, and Mildred had mentioned them in *The Gobi Desert*, describing the white embroidered caps worn by the men. Many men in Xining still wore these caps. The women today covered their hair with black scarves, but they wore ordinary pants and shirts like the Han women. I had imagined Chinese people wearing blue Mao suits, but the women in China dressed much like women in the West, only more neatly, and their hair always seemed to be perfectly groomed.

Beggars were lined up on the footpath outside the mosque. Most of them had severed limbs or deep burns, which I assumed were mainly the results of industrial accidents. They all wore white embroidered caps. Worshippers started emptying out of the mosque. Men chatted to each other while they strapped prayer mats to the backs of motorbikes. Most of them handed coins to the beggars. Alms-giving is a pillar of Islam, so clearly the worshippers were easy marks.

One shop sold pieces of fur. The teenage boy in the shop wore a glossy fur hat. The tiger skin on display might not have been real, but there was no doubt about a smaller piece hanging on the wall: it was ginger-coloured, with a white patch. '*Ze shi mao ma?*' I asked. I was careful to use the right tone for *mao*, which can mean either 'cat' or 'fur', depending on the inflection.

The boy looked at me and paused. Could I handle the truth? He suddenly smiled and said yes, it was cat. I made a shocked face, just to amuse him, and he laughed.

Almost every food stall and restaurant had a signboard painted to show a bright-green meadow and a bright-blue sky. The animals you could expect to find served up there were pictured, gambolling in the field, oblivious to their eventual fate. Other signs showed dishes floating in the sky over the field. Most of the signs featured sheep. I kept walking until I saw a picture of two hairy yaks.

The yak restaurant was dark inside, and there were no other patrons. I couldn't even see any waiting staff. I sat down and coughed loudly.

Soon a Tibetan woman appeared at the kitchen door. Her eyes widened in surprise when she saw me. She look around for something under the cashier's counter, then handed me a limp cardboard menu, entirely in Chinese. I studied it, even though I couldn't understand any of the characters. I realised I would have to use my phrasebook. But when I opened my bag to get out the book, I remembered I had left it on my bed at the hotel. The woman stood behind the counter and stared at me without smiling. Without taking her eyes off me she called out to her friend in the kitchen, who wandered out and joined her in staring. I tried to remember the word for yak, or stew, or even noodles, and nothing came. All my Mandarin had left me. I remembered one word, only because it was a word I often used in India.

'Cha,' I said weakly.

The woman brought me a cup of tea. Her friend laughed.

I was hungrier than ever. I drank the tea and kept walking up Dongguang Dajie. After a few blocks I reached a more prosperous part of town, with boutiques and jewellery stores and bookshops. Then I saw a restaurant sign. It was quite different to those in the rest of town, but it was very familiar. The red-and-white sign depicted an elderly Caucasian man with white hair and a goatee beard. The Colonel wore a bow tie. He looked kindly. 'There's no shame in eating when you're hungry,' he seemed to say. So I went inside for some fried chicken.

The next morning I walked through the town again, following Wang's map to the bus stop. An old man directed me away from the minibuses towards a taxi, which I shared with three young men wearing business suits. Inside, the roof of the taxi was decorated with pictures of Disney characters, mainly from the extended Duck and McDuck family.

The sky was grey, light rain was falling, and the sides of the roads had turned to mud. We travelled uphill, past shining wet trees, and I noticed something white scattered on the ground and over the bushes. I wondered if some kind of fertiliser had been put down. It almost looked like snow. It took another ten minutes of staring out the window before I realised that it *was* snow.

I had low expectations of Kumbum monastery. Of the six major temple complexes of the Yellow Hat sect of Tibetan Buddhism, this was the easiest for tourists to reach. The more I had read about it, the more I got the impression it was a museum rather than a working monastery, a place with hordes of tourists but few monks. It would be about as similar to the Trio's elusive Kan-lung monastery as my KFC was to yak hot pot.

The unseasonable cold and rain probably worked in my favour. After I bought a ticket and ran the gauntlet of souvenir sellers at the entrance, I saw few other visitors. I saw monks in purple robes, and some colourfully dressed Tibetan women who seemed to be attached to the temple. One of them held up a screaming baby and asked me for money. She continued to smile and wave in a friendly way after I shook my head.

There was a scattering of snow on the roofs, and on the flowers planted along the pathways. Each building had a plaque attached to it, explaining the name or purpose of the building in a range of languages. The plaques looked much newer than the walls and doors they were screwed into.

At the first door I walked though, a young monk with rosy cheeks was sitting on a stool and checking tickets. He had a sleek, fat tabby cat asleep in his robe, with just its head sticking out. I smiled and patted the cat's head. I was glad it had escaped the furrier. The monk smiled at me. He was about fourteen, and beautiful.

Through the door was a courtyard with raised balconies around it. A shrine was built around a large image of the Buddha at the far end. Looking down on the courtyard were mangy-looking stuffed animals with glass eyes that stared in different directions. The unevenly stuffed yak looked particularly deranged.

A monk chanted and lit incense sticks at a metal burner that looked hundreds of years old. The shrine itself was a colourful clutter of drapery and candles and ornaments and framed paintings and photos of lamas and offerings of fruit and incense. I was reminded of the window displays in shops in fashionable suburbs at home, the kind of places my boyfriend would drag me away from, calling the contents 'hippy junk'. I recognised the same prayer flags that my student friends hung in their front windows.

A young Chinese woman in tight jeans and an Adidas sweatshirt bowed and prayed in front of the Buddha. Then she got up and pushed some folded money into a clear plastic box in front of the shrine. The box was almost full of money, mostly notes rather than coins.

When I turned to leave I saw a banner that depicted a series of skulls with red eyes and long tongues. I can't say I was scared, exactly, but I remembered how images of the goddess Kali and her necklace of skulls had frightened me as a child in India. I imagined the Trio would have found this kind of imagery fairly confronting. When she described Buddhist temples, Mildred uncharacteristically used the kind of language you would expect from a pantomime Victorian missionary:

> The hours of the temple offices were marked by calls to worship sounded on the great conch shells, and at this signal all the Tibetans would troop towards the temple and up the central flight of steep stone steps into the demon-haunted atmosphere of the Satan-ruled hall.

I wandered from room to room. The murals and paintings on the walls all looked far more Indian than Chinese. One room contained backlit photos of festivals being celebrated at the monastery, and glass cases with the costumes worn in the photos. I was the only person in the room until a thin, wrinkled old monk walked in and approached me. I held out my ticket but he waved it away.

'*Yige ma?*' he asked – 'Are you alone?' He had only three or four teeth.

I nodded. He watched me while I looked at the photos. As I was leaving he spoke to me again, saying something I couldn't understand and holding out his arms to indicate something big. Then he pointed at me, smiling and nodding. I realised he was talking about how big I was. He kept murmuring 'big' while he touched my hips and upper arms. He seemed to be pleased. He was just reaching for my breasts when I stepped back and said 'no' rather less forcefully than I should have. But he backed off, still smiling as I left.

I can't imagine any of my missionary women being felt up, let alone by a monk. They were often described as 'formidable'. Formidability is a quality that I lack entirely.

The final room in the temple complex contained yak-butter sculptures. I had laughed the night before when I read about the sculptures. I imagined the kind of lumpy offerings produced in high-school pottery classes, or the mashed-potato mountain Richard Dreyfus made in *Close Encounters of the Third Kind*. In fact, the religious scenes carved from butter were the most impressive things I saw that day. They were intricate and brilliantly coloured and looked nothing like butter. One scene inside a glass case stretched across the whole wall, with detailed deities and animals and flowers tangled together. They smelled tasty, too, like shortbread. I remembered the Mandarin phrase for 'I'm hungry' and said it under my breath. '*Wo oerle.*' Pronounced right, it sounded like a rumbling stomach. The fried chicken seemed a long time ago. It was time to have another try at eating like a local.

Mr. Lutley. Mr. Dreyer.
Mrs. Lutley. Miss Palmer. Mrs. Dreyer. Miss Rasmussen.

Miss Johnson. Miss Hoskyn. Miss Higgs. Miss French.
Miss A. Hoskyn. Miss Gauntlett.

PARTY IV. WHICH ESCAPED FROM SHAN-SI.

To face page 102.

Eva French and other China Inland Mission workers who fled Shanxi during the Boxer Uprising, 1900 [OMF]

EVA FRENCH, MILDRED CABLE, FRANCESCA FRENCH

PHOTO BY VAUGHAN & FREEMAN
44A DOVER STREET, LONDON, W.1

A postcard given out by the Trio in about 1915. Note that the names are incorrect – Francesca and Eva have been transposed.
[Courtesy of Marion Myers]

The Trio enroute to Central Asia from Victoria Station, London, 1928 [Henry House, OMF]

Eva, Francesca and Mildred, early 1930s [OMF]

The Trio and Topsy on the road, about 1930 [OMF]

Photo by]   Dr. G. Whitfield Guinness.

A KAIFENG HOSPITAL PATIENT.
A hopeless case of consumption. Dr. Kao—now in Kanchowfu, Kansu—is talking with him.

Photo by]   [Miss Cable.

A LOCALLY MADE TENT USED BY THE LADIES.
MISS FRENCH IS SPEAKING.

Photo by]   [Miss M. Cable.
The 'Flying Turki' and the 'Gobi Express' leaving Suchow.

Pictures and articles in the China Inland Mission's magazine, 'China's Millions', kept readers in touch with the work of the Trio and their Chinese colleagues, such as Dr Kao

Back in town, I collected my phrasebook and scouted out the restaurants near the railway station. Most of them were just stalls, with a table and a couple of benches and a list of dishes on a board. I stopped at one and asked 'Do you have *sha-guo*?' in careful Mandarin. The teenage girl at the counter stared blankly and called over an older woman. I repeated myself to her. She shook her head. I wasn't sure if this meant she didn't have *sha-guo* or she didn't understand me.

I walked away, feeling anxious. The only people who understood my Mandarin were ticket sellers. I gave myself one more chance and walked into the next stall. A large poster of Chairman Mao covered the wall. He looked as stylised and kindly as the Colonel. I wondered if he was Chairman Cat or Chairman Fur.

A Tibetan woman smiled at me and waved me towards the one table. Ten minutes later she gave me a cast-iron bowl containing layers of meat and vegetables and noodles in a bubbling, spicy broth. It tasted fantastic. 'Is this yak meat?' I asked. The woman nodded and asked if I liked it. 'Very good,' I said. I worked through all the layers and slurped up the remaining liquid.

When I paid the woman I told her I would be back the next day. She smiled and wiped down the table, while a toddler clung to her leg. I would have liked to have clung to her myself. There was something very comforting about her.

My original mission in Qinghai province had been to visit Kanlung monastery, and I was still disappointed not to have found it. But I cheered up a bit after the hot pot. I'd downgraded my mission to 'visit Kumbum monastery and eat some yak', and I'd managed *that* pretty successfully. Now I was ready to go and buy some of the yak-milk yogurt that was sold in clay pots on the footpath near the mosque.

Crossing the bridge that led back towards the mosque, I walked past a beggar sitting on the ground. Most of the beggars here had some obvious physical disability, but this woman appeared to be merely mad. She was middle-aged and tiny, with Tibetan features. At first I thought she had a baby strapped to her, but it turned out to be a grubby doll. The woman cradled the doll as if it was a child, but its porcelain face was turned away from her. Under the dirt the doll's face was white. The woman moaned and rocked the doll. Everyone ignored her.

I had seen this woman every time I crossed the bridge. I had been reading about Topsy, and whenever I saw her I thought about Topsy's real mother, who must have lived near here, and how she had been forced to give up her child. Maybe the beggar woman had lost a child, and that was what had broken her.

For me, the saddest part of *The Story of Topsy* is not when the little girl is sent out to beg or is attacked by dogs or even when she is burned with the poker. The saddest part is where the Trio travel to the mysterious Kan-lung monastery and watch a ceremonial dance. One of their Chinese friends nudges them and points out a woman who is also watching the dance. 'Gwa Gwa's real mother lives just here,' the Trio's friend says. 'She is one of those women wearing the tall hat, but no one is supposed to know. It is a secret, and no one must tell.' We hear nothing about Topsy's mother again, in this or in any other of the Trio's writings. There is just the one image of her, silently watching the dancers, while being watched by the foreign women who will take her baby to the other side of the world.

I ate my yogurt while standing on the footpath, and returned the clay pot to the smiling Muslim woman who ran the stall. When I got back to the hotel there was a note from Wang under my door. It was written on the back of a bus ticket. It said he would be at the hotel at eight o'clock the next morning and would take me to a monastery.

Chapter Six

Somewhere north of Xining

Buddha uses outrageous coincidences sometimes to awaken piety.

Monkey Series 1, 'Outrageous Coincidences'

'The clang of cymbals, jingle of rattle and tinkle of bell were continuous, while the lilting of the chanting Lamas rose and fell, sometimes in a droning monotone, and sometimes in a high-pitched, excited invocation.' Mildred wrote that, after watching a ceremony at the Kan-lung monastery. I didn't know what I might hear or see at Wang's monastery, but after my experiences at Kumbum I hoped there would be more in the way of jingles and chants, and less in the way of multilingual explanatory plaques.

I got up early, and while I waited for Wang I ate steamed bread with Vegemite from a tube that I would carry from one end of China to the other and back again. When Wang arrived he said we were going on a bus to a temple where tourists don't go. I assumed he must have taken a few there in the past, but I didn't say anything. Wang had already called the monastery, and they had agreed to me having an audience with the Living Buddha who lived there. He was five years old, and had been installed only a few months earlier.

I wasn't sure what I would say to a Living Buddha, but I didn't want to pass up the opportunity. The Trio met a few in their travels, including the head of Kan-lung monastery, who they described as 'a man of exceptional ability and a source of great revenue, being in constant demand to conduct rituals for the benefit of the living and the dead'.

The Trio's friend Dr Kao, who led the Chinese Christians in Zhangye, was friendly with a Living Buddha who sometimes borrowed the Trio's cart. Mildred wrote:

> Buddhists held him to be the reincarnation of a spirit which, having achieved the goal of nirvana, had voluntarily returned to earth to spend a further cycle of lives among men and help them to find their way out of the illusion of sensory things into the realities of annihilated desire.

Mildred also added the aside that 'Living Buddhas, as other men, vary in quality.'

As our bus set off, Wang asked if I had eaten breakfast. Yes, I said, but he either misheard or ignored me. 'So I think we will go to my friend's family in Tu minority village and have some breakfast there.' I had seen a website describing a village just north of Xining that was built to showcase the minority people of the area, particularly the Tu, with their colourful costumes and dances. It sounded like a human zoo.

After about half an hour Wang called out to the bus driver, who pulled over and let us off on a quiet country road. The Tu village, across a grassy field, did not look like a tourist attraction. All I could see was a collection of mud-brick walls sprawled along the base of a hill. When I asked Wang if this was where tourists came to see the dancing, he laughed and said no, this was where the people lived.

The Tu people are descended from Mongolians who settled in the area around the 13th century. They intermarried with Turkic and Tibetan peoples and created their own distinctive culture. Every source I consulted gave me a different figure, but it seemed that around two hundred thousand Tu people lived in Qinghai and Gansu provinces. Wang's friend's family were Tu people.

The sun was surprisingly warm, and for the first time since I arrived in China I could see a blue sky. We walked through the fields along a concrete path that would have been wide enough for a motor-bike but not a car. It was the only way into the village. Inside, the village seemed to be almost deserted. A few ragged children played on the paths between the mud walls. They all stared, and the older children shouted 'Hellooo!' This was the only English word most Chinese people seemed to know.

Inside the village, dusty paths ran between the high walls. The heavy wooden doors in the walls were all closed. There was no indication of what the houses inside might be like. Invisible dogs barked behind the walls as we went past.

When Wang pushed open the door to his friend's parents' compound, the house looked unexpectedly new and clean, with blinding white tiles covering the outside walls. Inside it was spotless, with more white tiling on the floors. A middle-aged woman with a wrestler's build and a sensible short haircut greeted Wang and nodded to me. Then she led us to the living room, which was dominated by a large flat-screen television set. A beach towel was draped across the back of the vinyl couch. Inside a cabinet was a collection of ornaments: a delicate jade Buddha, a porcelain bunny rabbit with big eyes, a glass dolphin jumping over a plastic moon, and a plastic McHappy Meal Hamburgler.

In the yard, a dog strained on its chain and barked without stopping. That dog really wanted to kill me. He had long fur, and a massive head like a bear's. If he had been friendly he would have been very cute, like an enormous stuffed toy. I would have liked to give him a cuddle, if he wasn't threatening to rip my throat out the moment I got close.

I recognised the breed from one of the Trio's books: 'Of all the wild beasts which surround us, the one of which we are most afraid is the domestic dog,' Mildred wrote. 'Among the Tibetan tents he roves at large, a huge, shaggy, dark-brown creature, showing his fearsome teeth.' Her tip for anyone who met such a beast was to keep throwing stones for the dog to chase, and to hold a large stick for the dog to chew on before he got to you, while calling out loudly for help.

> Probably by the time your stock of stones is exhausted and your stick is eaten up, someone will have arrived on the scene. It may be a small naked child about five years old, who will throw her tiny arms around the dog's neck, and he will became quiet in a moment. It is rather humiliating, when you think of that row of silver cups which you won for athletic prowess, to realise that you experienced a sense of relief when your small protectress patronisingly said, 'Don't be afraid, I've got him.'

Wang's Friend's Mother, whose name I never caught, brought us flat bread with bits of green onion in it, and a pot of tea. The tea was very strongly flavoured. Although I generally liked the green tea served up in Chinese restaurants, drinking this was like swigging cheap, warm perfume. I wrinkled up my nose with every mouthful in an attempt to stop the taste going up my nostrils as well as across my taste buds.

Wang's Friend's Mother kept filling up my teacup while she chatted to Wang. I realised I would have to drink very slowly. Unfortunately I wasn't slow enough, and had to use the toilet. To get to the toilet – a walled pit in the corner of the yard – I had to walk within centimetres of where the dog's chain stretched to its fullest extent. I could smell his rancid breath as he bared his teeth at me while I edged past, along the wall.

When I got back from the toilet, my heart still racing, Wang said we had been invited back for dinner in the evening, on our way back from the monastery. 'Thank you, very kind,' I said to Wang's Friend's Mother. She nodded briskly and spoke to Wang. 'She says you must drink more tea before you go,' he said.

After we got away, Wang led me through the village and up a path towards a temple. This wasn't the monastery he had promised me, but simply the local village temple. It sat on a ridge overlooking the village. I was out of breath almost from the start of the walk, and by the end I was panting like an asthmatic Chihuahua. I worried that I was going to faint, and the more worried I got, the harder it was to breathe. I was embarrassed, and I apologised for my lack of fitness. 'It's the altitude, I think.' Wang kindly agreed with me.

From the front of the temple we could see out across the village and fields. Wang said the temple was about three hundred years old but had been renovated recently. The architecture was traditional Qing, the outside walls and roof painted with complicated, bright floral and geometric designs. The temple guard dog was a dirty white colour, and had the same big head as the dog I had just met. It was even more psychotic. Instead of just straining to the length of its chain, it took running leaps at me until the chain snapped tight, throwing the dog backwards and half choking it. The choking didn't stop the dog barking. The barking just changed register a bit.

Inside the temple was the usual collection of banners and incense burners and fruit placed in front of images of the Buddha. In a side room there were larger-than-life-sized clay statues. Wang called them guardians. He said that, in the past, soldiers on the run had come here for protection and had slept among the guardians. One of the sculpted figures carried a lute; it was said to play and sing for the soldier if he was lonely.

I hadn't seen many Buddhist temples, and they were already starting to look the same to me. I thought I should probably have done some kind of 'Introduction to Buddhist Architecture' course before I left Australia that would have helped me interpret all the imagery around me.

Wang and I walked past the crazy dog and back down the hill and through the village to the road, where Wang hailed the next minibus that came past just five minutes later. I wasn't sure if he just knew the timetable well or if this was a busy route. On each bus trip, I paid for both our tickets. Wang had yet to mention money. I was not sure how much it would be appropriate to give him for playing tour guide, or when such a payment should be made. I didn't even know how to bring it up.

Before long, we reached the small town of Huzhu, having passed the tourist version of the Tu village, with its flags waving outside the front gate and three tour buses parked outside. There we changed buses, and travelled on for more than an hour in a bus with inadequate suspension, mostly on rocky, unmade roads, through countryside best classified as Middle of Nowhere. Then the bus took a corner, revealing a stunning vista of snow-covered peaks behind a lake. I gasped when I saw it, and Wang laughed. 'Reservoir, not natural lake,' he said.

We bumped along the side of the reservoir. I was so transfixed with the view that I forgot the numbness of my bottom. Then the bus veered again and we climbed up and down another hill and into a green valley. Wang shouted to the driver, who stopped and let us out.

We were in the tiniest of hamlets. It was just a dusty strip of shopfronts. Wang said he was hungry, but all he could find to buy was a packet of instant noodles, so he ate them raw while we walked uphill, out of the hamlet and towards the monastery. Grassy fields spread out on either side of us. Two old men sat under a tree, sharing a cigarette, with two skinny horses tethered beside them.

When I emailed my parents about the trip to the monastery, my mother emailed back and said 'Were you afraid, being out in an isolated spot with a man you didn't know?'

It hadn't even occurred to me to be worried. 'I'm a lot bigger than him,' I wrote back to my mother. 'Also, Chinese Men Are Not Attracted To Western Women.'

After finishing his crunchy noodles, Wang told me about the Living Buddha, who had recently been chosen from 400 Tibetan families by the Dalai Lama himself – I didn't think to ask how he had done this from exile in India – and had been sent to this monastery because it was quiet and isolated. Wang called the monastery Que Zang. He was friendly with the monk who had been chosen to look after the little boy. I got the impression the monk had to be both scripture teacher and nanny, at least while the boy was still young.

The path widened, and we reached a series of mud-brick walls. I could see carved wooden roofs behind them. Wang opened a door in the wall and ushered me through into a courtyard. There were no multilingual plaques bolted to the doors here. Nothing appeared to have been renovated, or even cleaned, in the recent past. The painted details on the roofs had almost faded away. Someone had left out a mop and leaking bucket, and water was pooling on top of an intricately carved chest.

I stood on the smooth stones of the courtyard while Wang went to look for his friend, the nursemaid monk. I imagined the stones must be very old. At one end of the courtyard a banner with Tibetan script on it hung in front of the Living Buddha's quarters.

After a while Wang reappeared and said we could have an audience in five minutes. 'What gift did you bring him?' he asked.

I hadn't thought about bringing a gift.

'Do you have any coins or sweets from your country?' Wang asked, sounding anxious. I didn't even have any sweets from China. I wished he had asked before we left Xining.

Rummaging through my bag, I found the small photo album with pictures of my family that I showed people during stilted conversations on buses and trains. I could identify all the members of my family in Mandarin. I had a photo of my cat, and I knew how to say 'My cat is a family member too', which always got a laugh.

In the back of the album I had some photocopies of pictures from the Trio's books. I had brought them to show people as I travelled, and to compare the Trio's images with modern-day sights. Some were of Tibetan and Mongolian people in the 1920s. I showed the pictures to Wang, who shrugged as if to say 'Better than nothing'. I pulled the pictures out of the album and held onto them while we waited to be called.

Wang's friend the monk was about thirty. He was tall and broad-shouldered and he smiled a lot. He led us inside and into the Living Buddha's room. The Living Buddha himself was sitting cross-legged on an office chair that had been draped in turmeric-coloured silk. He wore a corduroy windcheater under his purple robe. He had pink cheeks, and he looked serious and, if it's not blasphemous to say so, extremely cute.

Wang and the monk and I sat on a dark-red rug on the floor, at the feet of the Living Buddha. An iron stove with an old teapot on top gave off a warm glow. There was a cosy smell of incense and butter in the air.

The room was filled with an eclectic assortment of toys and pictures and ornaments. It was like the display cabinet in the Tu village, only on a much larger scale. Priceless old images of the Buddha rubbed shoulders with grotty stuffed toys. A plastic electric guitar with a moulded Spiderman figure on the front hung from a hook in the wall below a delicate silk painting of previous Living Buddhas. A framed picture showed a badly Photoshopped montage of old monks hovering in the sky over the monastery. One wall was covered in a faded mural that the monk said was more than two hundred years old.

When I say the monk spoke to me, I mean that he spoke in Mandarin to Wang, who translated to me. When I asked the Living Buddha a question, I spoke to Wang, who spoke in Mandarin to the monk, who spoke in Tibetan to the Living Buddha.

I handed my pictures to the monk, and explained that they were from old books about Tibet that had inspired me to travel here. The monk then handed them to the Living Buddha. He gave them a lot more attention than the average five-year-old would, tracing over the images with his finger and asking the monk questions about them. All the same, I wished I had brought him some sweets. After a few minutes he put the pictures down carefully on the table next to him.

I asked about the Living Buddha's family, and whether he was allowed to see them. The monk said he could see them once a year, but he had to learn to be without them. He had been here a few months, and he didn't cry for his mother anymore. He was not allowed to mix with other children, because he was special.

I tried to think what I would ask a five-year-old at home. I remembered the teenage monk with the cat at Kumbum, so I asked if the Living Buddha had any pets. No, the monk said. We sat quietly. I wondered if I had a Western inability to deal with silence.

After what seemed an age but was probably less than a minute, the Living Buddha nudged the monk and spoke to him quietly. The monk gave him some sheets of paper and a pencil.

'What does he like to draw?' I asked. Wang translated to the monk.

'He likes cars,' the monk said. Sure enough, the Living Buddha soon held up a drawing of a car. I told him it was good, and then I pointed to myself. The Living Buddha giggled and started to draw. Soon he held up a picture of an enormous sphere with a tiny head on top. Pigtails stuck out either side of the head like cow's horns. As impressions of me go, it wasn't bad. To my eternal regret, I didn't ask if I could take the picture home.

'You can take a photograph,' Wang said. I pulled out my camera. The monk helped the Living Buddha adjust his robe and encouraged him to sit up straight. He looked seriously at me.

'Now we can go,' Wang said. We stood up and said goodbye to the Living Buddha, who stayed seated on his office chair and nodded solemnly to us. The monk walked us out of the room.

Outside in the corridor, Wang told me I should give the Living Buddha five yuan to buy a toy. I found a five yuan note and handed it to the monk. I assumed Wang knew what was appropriate. We walked down the corridor, and I stopped at a framed picture of the monastery. It was an aeriel photo, taken in the 1950s. The place was much more extensive then, with buildings spread across the hillside. Wang said most of the monastery complex was destroyed in the 1960s, and there was only one temple left. We were in the monks' quarters rather than a temple now.

'The Cultural Revolution?' I said.

Wang looked around and then he nodded.

I realised how little I knew about this period in Chinese history, a time that still made people speak furtively, forty years later. I knew that Communist Party chairman Mao Zedong had initiated a mass movement of workers and students that had led people to destroy anything connected with religion or other suspect traditions or practices, and that there had been mass jailings and killings in an attempt to stamp out anything connected with capitalism or the West. I knew that it was such a terrible time that it had been officially repudiated by the current government.

'The government didn't like people having religious belief,

because when they meet together the government worries that they plan together,' Wang said.

All my life I've been told that Chinese Christians are persecuted. Terrible stories about tortured pastors were shared in church services and books and mission newsletters. Nobody ever told me that people of other religions suffered the same treatment. In India, Tibetan Buddhist refugees lived in our town and sold shawls and sweaters to tourists. I never thought to ask what they were refugees from, and nobody at church ever mentioned them. There was an assumption that only Christians would keep to their faith in the face of persecution, because, of course, Christianity was the only true faith. In a circular piece of logic, the fact that people would suffer for Christianity was held up as proof of its being true.

But Buddhists and Muslims, like Christians, had held out against the Chinese authorities who hated religion for a whole raft of reasons. The communists were officially atheist, but, as Wang said, they were also opposed to anything that might bring people together and be valued more highly than the state. But people held on to their traditions and their faith when it would have been much easier to abandon them.

Not everyone, of course. In China there were Christians and Muslims and Buddhists who had fallen in line with the Communist Party. Others had colluded with the authorities in ways that might be called either expedience or betrayal. Wang said there were rich head monks at other monasteries who had good relationships with government officials.

I told him that some Chinese Christians joined the Three Self Patriotic Movement or the Catholic Patriotic Association, the only official Christian organisations in China, because it meant they were free to worship, while others believed that no real Christian could join these groups because their first allegiance would have to be to the government, not to Jesus. Wang nodded.

The communists' historic attitude towards Buddhism seemed a bit more complicated than its outright opposition to Christianity and Islam. In recent years Buddhist sites have been cleaned up and put on show for tourists, and I had read that Chairman Mao had often compared himself to cudgel-wielding Monkey, a central character in Chinese Buddhist tradition.

Wang and I walked a short way downhill to the temple. In the grass around the temple were old bricks, the remains of ruined buildings. Inside the temple the light was dim. It looked like the Great Hall at Kumbum, with low benches where the monks sat, and Indian-looking murals on the walls, and there was the same buttery aroma. A whole wall was lined with identical images of the Buddha in glass-fronted cases.

When we went outside again we saw a group of monks talking. While Wang went up and spoke to them, I looked around at the green hills, and behind them to the snow-covered, jagged mountains I had seen reflected in the lake.

When Wang came back, he explained that the monks were planning to conduct a ritual outside the temple, and I was welcome to stay around and watch. He said the monks had come from the Labrang monastery in Gansu, and they had brought their own, more senior Living Buddha with them to lead the ritual. 'The little Living Buddha isn't ready to do these things yet,' he said.

I sat on the paving stones and watched the monks prepare. I was lucky it was a fine day, and that I had brought a jacket I could sit on, because the preparations and ritual took a couple of hours. A small crowd of what looked like local people gathered to watch the monks. The children in particular wore ragged, dirty clothes. The only other obvious outsiders were two expensively dressed Chinese men, taking photos. The children stared at me. The monks ignored everyone.

The monks set up a table and placed bowls of grains and dried beans on it. Then one of them opened a box and brought out a protractor, some cardboard stencils and bottles of coloured sand. They laid the stencils on the ground and poured sand over them to create a multicoloured, circular pattern on the ground.

'That's a mandala, isn't it?' I said to Wang. He nodded.

All the monks bent over to look at the mandala as it was being drawn, and they all appeared to be putting in their two-cents' worth as to how it should be done. Layers of colour were added, making the pattern more and more complicated.

Some of the monks looked as if they were in their early teens, or even younger. Some were horsing around, and had to be told off by the older monks. One of them put on the distinctive yellow curved hat of their sect and began head-butting the temple wall, which amused the other young monks. An older monk shouted at him to take the hat off.

I watched the creation of the mandala from start to finish, for more than an hour. Wang told me it was fine to take photos, but I didn't take many. I didn't want to get in the way.

When the mandala was finished the monks placed some pieces of kindling and wood over it. About ten monks put on gold head-dresses and colourful capes and sat behind a low table. They rang bells and chanted from scriptures laid out before them. The monks sometimes missed their cues or fluffed their lines. As Mildred had noted at Kan-lung monastery eighty years earlier, the pitch of the chants changed from low droning to higher exclamations.

A monk led the old Living Buddha from Labrang to a seat by the pile of wood. The Living Buddha wore a taller, more ornate head-dress than the other monks. He chanted and threw some butter over the wood and set fire to it. Bowls of grains were brought to him, and he threw handfuls of each grain into the fire.

Some of the older people in the crowd bowed or even lay down with their faces to the ground. The children just stared.

Then the remaining monks circled around the fire. Some of them blew long trumpets. They wore the same yellow hats that the boys had been playing with.

The procession was still circling the flames when Wang tapped me on the shoulder and said it was time to go.

By the time we changed buses in Huzhu – one missed bus, a long wait being giggled at while watching a truck being slowly loaded with potatoes, and a fat-jiggling, smoke-filled bus ride later – night had well and truly fallen. I was tired and hungry, and I hoped that dinner in the Tu village would not drag on too late. I thought longingly about my little hotel room back in Xining, about my books and my Scrabble and my MP3 player packed with songs that my boyfriend had carefully chosen for me. I didn't want to spend an evening making polite conversation in a strained mixture of English and Chinese.

We got off the bus outside the village. As we walked up the path, Wang said casually, 'It's too late to catch the last bus to Xining'. He said I would be allowed to stay the night at his friend's parents' house for free. He spoke as if it was a great treat for me to be allowed to stay there in the village.

'They're expecting me at the hotel,' I said. I was too tired to be gracious. I felt like bursting into tears. 'I didn't bring any sleeping things.'

Wang shrugged. He said he would call the hotel. I knew I should be grateful that strangers were about to feed me dinner and give me a bed for the night. But for the first time since I left Australia, I was homesick.

Wang's Friend's Mother greeted us and the dog roared at us. Wang explained why we were late, and dinner was reheated and served to us in front of the television. A Chinese opera was being broadcast. Women in ghostly make-up and gold headpieces sang about problems that I couldn't understand. We ate mounds of rice, a slippery tofu dish and salty mixed vegetables. We were given more perfumed tea.

Wang's Friend's Mother was not happy with the amount I ate. Every time I stopped eating she shouted at me. I told Wang to tell her the food was very good and I was very grateful, but I was full. She listened. Then she said I should stop and drink some tea. She said the tea would help me wash down the food, then I would have room for more.

The married daughters of the family, who had helped cook the food, stayed in the kitchen. One of the daughters had a son who was about a year old. He wore pants with a split crotch, which I gathered was the preferred method of toilet training in China. He was clearly the love of Wang's Friend's Mother's life, and she fussed over him and sent him toddling across the room towards me. I knew it was my job to admire him, so I told Wang to say how cute he was, and I spoke some nonsensical baby talk at him. Wang's Friend's Mother looked at me and said something to Wang.

'She says you have no children,' he said.

'That's right,' I said. I picked up my bag and pulled out my notebook. 'I am going to write in my diary now,' I said to Wang. The opera blared out. The dog barked without stopping. I scrawled for an hour without looking up, while Wang chatted with Wang's Friend's Mother and her husband.

Eventually one of the married daughters took me to another room, where a quilt and pillows were laid out on a raised platform. I thanked her, she left, and I lay down in my clothes. The platform was hard. I needed to pee, but I wasn't going to try to get past that bloody dog in the dark. I thought I was going to lie awake feeling uncomfortable and resentful for hours, but I fell into a heavy sleep almost straight away.

The next morning I was given the food I couldn't finish the night before, fried up like a Chinese version of bubble and squeak. It was quite improved, actually. Wang's Friend's Mother watched and nodded approvingly. I felt ashamed of myself for the previous night's grumpiness. I had been fed and housed and nobody had asked anything of me in return. I couldn't imagine a stray Chinese traveller who turned up in an Australian country town being treated so well.

Wang's Friend's Mother left the room and came back with some plastic shopping bags. 'She wants to show you the Tu crafts that her daughters make,' Wang said. Rainbow-striped bags and wall hangings and embroidered pieces of fabric and what looked like Christmas-tree ornaments were laid out. I admired them politely, and Wang told me I could buy anything I liked at a cheap price. I chose a couple of pieces. The prices seemed high to me, but I didn't think I was in a position to start bargaining. I paid up, and Wang asked if I was ready to go back to Xining.

Yes, I said, picking up my bag.

There was just one more thing, Wang said. I should give the family some money because they had given me food and a bed.

I sighed. 'How much?' I said.

Wang took a step back and smiled and said that was up to me. He pulled the hood of his anorak over his head, and I noticed that rain had started falling outside.

'I don't know how much is right,' I said, without smiling back. 'I really don't know, but *you* know. Please, you have to tell me.' I knew I was overstepping some kind of cultural boundary here, that I was causing Wang to lose face, but I wasn't sure exactly where the boundary lay, and like any fair-dinkum Australian I just wanted Wang to be upfront with me.

He muttered and said maybe 30 yuan, so I gave them 50 yuan, just to show that I was in nobody's debt. I really wanted a shower and a change of clothes. Mud splashed up the back of my trousers as we ran through the field towards the bus.

By the time we reached Xining the rain was pelting down. Wang insisted that I go straight to the hotel while he went to the bus station to buy my bus ticket to Zhangye for the next morning. When he knocked on my door a little later with the ticket, he was drenched. Rain dripped off his anorak and onto the carpet. I paid him for the damp ticket, and he said that now he had to go.

I thanked him for taking me out and looking after me. Then I gave him a 100 yuan note. I wanted him to know I really was grateful. I felt awkward, I didn't know if I had done the right thing.

'Oh no,' he said. I insisted, and shook his hand.

Wang looked at me, and at the 100 yuan, and he paused, as if he was trying to work up the courage to say something shameful.

'I must tell you the truth,' he said. 'This is not the Post Hotel.'

There is a postscript to this story.

When I got back to Australia I searched online to find out more about 'Que Zang', the name Wang gave to the monastery we had visited together. Google turned up nothing under that name, and although I knew the monastery could have many alternative names and spellings, I couldn't find any that fitted.

At the same time, I was still trying to find information about Kan-lung, the monastery on a hillside that the Trio used to visit, the place where Topsy's birth mother lived. Again, I found nothing.

Then I decided to combine a search for Huzhu, the closest town of any size to Que Zang, with the word 'monastery'.

The following paragraph came up on three separate Chinese websites:

Located 30 kilometers east of the Tu Autonomous County of Huzhu, 65 kilometers from Xining, Gun-lung Monastery was established in 1604, the 32nd year during the reign of Emperor Wanli of the Ming Dynasty. The monastery was first run by Gyese (Rgyalsras), the Seventh Living Buddha, and is now run by the 13th Living Buddha.

I seemed to have found the monastery I had visited. But even more exciting was the name give to the monastery. I knew that the Chinese sound that used to be transliterated as a K, as in Dr Kao, was now spelled with a G. It was an easy step from Gun-lung to Kan-lung.

It seemed that I had been led, completely accidentally, right off the maps and outside of the bounds of the tourist guides to the very monastery that the Trio visited in the 1920s. It was one of the key sites in the Trio's books, and one of the places I had most wanted to visit, and I had been there without knowing it. The villagers watching the ancient rituals with me could easily have been Topsy's relatives.

'The world often seems unfair to people who believe in fate, yet the fact is the universe works, and against all odds,' the narrator says in *Monkey*. 'Sometimes, to make it all work, the Buddha has to resort to outrageous coincidences.'

Chapter Seven

Zhangye

> Time moves, not like a river from here to there – we do that. Time moves in waves, it ebbs and flows. There is a time for everything.
>
> *Monkey* Series 2, 'The Dogs of Death'

The Trio had a hard time getting to the town of Zhangye. They were on the final leg of their cross-China trek from Xi'an to their new base in Jiuquan, and the rough mountain tracks took their cart over rocks, up and down sand hills and through fields of mud. When one mud pit proved too much for the contrivance, the axle broke and the cart became stuck. Evening fell and the women expected to be stranded overnight.

Enter our hero, Dr Kao. This was the Trio's first meeting with the doctor who would become their firm friend, and I wouldn't have blamed any of them if their spinster hearts were set slightly aflutter.

At the moment when our courage reached its low ebb, for the short daylight was rapidly waning and there seemed no prospect of extricating the cart, two galloping horsemen appeared on the horizon, and in a few moments Dr Kao swung himself from the saddle, and advanced to meet us with cordial and cheering words.

The doctor sent his companion back to Zhangye to fetch help, and had stern words with the carter. He told the women that this carter had just finished his third jail term for destroying travellers' property. Dr Kao knew what everyone was up to. He was a take-charge kind of guy.

Not surprisingly for a natural leader, Dr Kao found it hard to get along with foreign men. Even the best of them would have radiated a sense of superiority and treated him as an underling. But as leader of the Zhangye church, Dr Kao believed the community needed the kind of Bible teaching that only trained missionaries could provide. So in 1923 he had asked the community to pray for two experienced women. Soon the Trio arrived.

About 150 people attended the first Sunday church service after the women reached Zhangye. Dr Kao told the crowd that God had been gracious enough to send them three women when they had asked for two. He hoped the women would settle in Zhangye. The women believed God had called them to Jiuquan, further northwest, but they agreed to stay for six months, teaching and training teachers.

A missionary called J.O. Fraser travelled through Gansu during this time, compiling a field report about missionary activity in the region. He wrote:

> I don't think we have in the whole of the CIM a more capable teacher of any subject than Miss Cable ... The thoroughness with which she teaches the Scriptures to Dr Kao's young men is almost appalling! She makes them go through the whole Bible – no

skipping – Minor Prophets, Revelation, everything ... Miss Cable asks you what book you are reading and if you aren't reading anything wants to know why you aren't.

Zhangye is a small town by Chinese standards, but it has two claims to fame. The first is its Sleeping Buddha, which is 35 metres long. The second is that the world's most famous traveller, Marco Polo, lived there late in the 13th century. Some say he was the governor of the town for a while. I liked the idea of the massive Buddha, and I thought Zhangye was a significant enough place in the Trio's travels for me to see it for myself. I didn't know that, like the Trio, I would have a hard time getting there.

Before Wang went to buy my ticket, he warned me that the bus trip to Zhangye might take an unusual route because some roads had been closed. He asked if I was sure I wanted to go to Zhangye by bus rather than going back to Lanzhou and then on to Zhangye by train.

I looked at the map and told him it was far more straightforward to take the bus due north over the hills to Zhangye. I didn't understand his concern. Surely he knew I was used to local buses and bad roads by now.

My ticket was for the best seat on the bus, the single seat at the front, near the driver. This meant I wouldn't have second-hand smoke blown in my face, and I would have an unimpeded view out the front window. Of course, if we had an accident it would probably be the worst seat on the bus. I would be flung straight through the front window. I remembered how an old boyfriend had habitually referred to the front passenger seat of my car as the 'death seat'.

The view from the death seat was astounding right from the start of the trip. We headed towards jagged, barren mountains covered in loose rocks, and we wound our way up and up. The road was narrow. The only signs of life were occasional shaggy goats that skipped along nonexistent paths and somehow managed not to fall down sheer drops. The sides of the road were splashed with snow.

I idly wondered how high we had climbed. Xining was about 2300 metres above sea level, and we had been driving steadily uphill for a couple of hours. My guidebook said altitude sickness could kick in at 2700 metres, and warned about the resulting headaches, nausea and confusion, but I didn't think I was likely to be affected. I had spent my childhood in India living at about 2300 metres, and we always laughed at visitors who became breathless when they first encountered our thin mountain air.

The bus dropped into a valley where the sunlight sparkled over clear streams forded by old stone bridges. Herds of goats and huge, long-haired yaks drank at the waterside. I really needed to pee.

'When toilet?' I asked the driver. He stared ahead as if he hadn't heard me, but five minutes later he pulled up at a group of shops by a stream, and indicated that I should go outside. Almost every man on the bus got out and unzipped straight away by the stream, in full view of nearby villagers. The Chinese are more comfortable with communal toilet-going than most people, I thought. A woman from the bus led me behind a concrete wall to where a couple of holes had been dug, and we squatted together. She watched me the whole time, nodding and smiling.

We got back on the bus. Outside, an old woman walked past holding a rope that was fastened around the neck of a yak calf, as if she was taking it for a walk. We drove on, past more streams and yaks and mud-brick villages surrounded by poplar trees. I thought I had never seen anything so picturesque in my life. That was my last coherent thought for about five hours.

We veered up into the mountains again, and the snow by the road got heavier. After a while, muddy snow was all I could see around us in every direction. The sky was overcast. The road was a single unmade lane, and the bus seemed to be straining to get through the mud. We rattled slowly through the mountains for a long time. I ate steamed bread with Vegemite from a paper bag, and listened to Johnny Cash's *Live at Folsom Prison* on my MP3 player.

There were no warning signs to what came next. In what felt like an instant, we were suddenly parked next to a strip of shops and stalls in a mountain hamlet. Johnny wasn't singing anymore. I looked out the window and saw that one of the bus tyres was being changed. I had not gone to sleep. Time had just skipped, like a record.

I felt nauseated, like I do when I'm recovering from a migraine. Passengers got back on the bus, and the instrumental version of Chicago's 'You're the Inspiration' started up from the front speakers as we continued on through the snow. I took deep breaths and told myself the altitude must have made me black out, but I would be all right from then on. I rehearsed how I would ask a taxi driver in Zhangye to take me to the Liangmao Hotel.

I wasn't all right. Time kept skipping. I dreamt without really sleeping. In my first dream I had arrived in Zhangye and was taking a taxi to the hotel. Then I was back on the bus, feeling lucid again, looking down at my hands and out the front window and across at the driver. Then my head ached and my brain misfired like an old car engine and I dreamed I was in Zhangye again. I'm not sure that I could have explained what was wrong, even if anyone around me had been able to understand English. I felt as if the electronic pathways in my brain were leading to the wrong places. I imagined my brain was a mess of coloured wires that sparked and smoked as they shorted.

I had a dream in which I knocked on the door of my friend Louisa's house. In waking life Louisa looks after intellectually disabled adults. In my dream she opened the door and said 'I have a surprise for you.' She led me into a dark room and switched on a lamp and I saw an old Chinese woman with long hair asleep in a bed. It was Topsy. Louisa shook her shoulder gently. 'Wake up Topsy, she's here,' she said. Topsy sat up and smiled at me and we embraced. We were both so happy that we cried.

'I thought you were dead,' I said.

'I wanted people to think that,' she said. 'I was tired. But I've been here waiting for you.'

Then I was back on the bus.

The lucid periods were getting longer by the time we descended into Gansu province. We had left the snow behind, and were on a two-lane, asphalt road with flat green fields on each side. Muddy ridges ran between the fields.

A couple of hours later, in the early evening, we pulled into Zhangye. I had been on the bus for ten hours. It had been at least an hour since I had felt any serious confusion, and I hoped the descent from the hills had fixed whatever had been wrong with my brain. A taxi took me straight from the bus stand to the Liangmao Hotel. I had never been so relieved to arrive anywhere. My clothes were creased and grubby, and if I looked anywhere near as tired and unsteady as I felt, I must have looked a bit frightening. The receptionist looked at me and shook her head before I had a chance to say anything. I showed her where the guidebook listed the hotel, but she waved me away. That was when I burst into tears.

The receptionist ignored me and stared at her computer screen. I might still be standing there now, but another woman who was mopping the floor called over a boy who looked about five years old and put his hand in mine.

The little boy led me a couple of blocks down the road to a grand hotel with marble columns and uniformed doormen, then he let my hand go, saluted and ran back down the street. I blew my nose on the only thing I could find, the paper bag my steamed bread had been wrapped in.

The front-desk manager at the grand hotel turned out to be the kindest woman in the whole of China. I told her I had been refused a bed in the Liangmao Hotel and I could not afford to stay at her hotel. I tried not to blub again. The woman put me in a taxi to the Zhangye Hotel, which she said was both moderately priced and accepted foreigners. She gave me a map of Zhangye and recommended some cheap restaurants. Then she gave me her home phone number. If I had any problems with the Zhangye Hotel, she said, I could come and stay with her and her mother.

The receptionist at the Zhangye hotel was immaculately made up, and had long red fingernails that she tapped on the counter while I filled in all the usual forms in triplicate. She looked deeply unimpressed with me. I was just grateful that I was allowed to stay.

Upstairs in my room I splashed cold water on my face, then I went back outside in the dusk to buy some nuts and bananas for dinner; I thought I'd heard they were good for the brain.

I sat on the end of my bed and ate a banana. On CCTV9 I watched the same travelogue about a southern Chinese village and its textile production that I had seen three times before in the past week. The layout of the hotel room was identical to every other hotel room in China, with two single beds and a desk, and I could smell stale cigarette smoke. I did not feel good. I felt as if I was very hung over.

I showered and lay down and had a little cry. I couldn't tell if my brain was back to normal, or if something had broken irreversibly. I didn't think about how being permanently confused might affect the rest of my travels. I thought further ahead, about whether I would ever be able to work again, and whether my boyfriend would still love me if I couldn't think or speak properly. I saw myself sitting on my couch at home, staring blankly ahead. Then I slept like the dead.

The next morning a woman came to my door to give me a breakfast voucher. I hadn't eaten a proper Chinese breakfast yet, and wasn't sure what it would consist of. It turned out that Chinese breakfast buffets are heavy on the raw peanuts, cold pickled vegetables, steamed-bread rolls and boiled eggs. Warm soymilk was served up in glasses. I saw what looked like a thin, steaming porridge, but I couldn't face it. It looked a bit too much like Indian boarding-school food.

The tables in the hotel restaurant were large enough to seat about ten, so I had no choice but to perch at the side of a table on my own. All the other guests were men in suits. I would have liked to drop a couple of rolls and boiled eggs in my bag to eat at lunchtime, but every time I looked around one of the besuited men was staring at me.

The eggs and vegetables, not to mention the ten-hour sleep, made me feel much better. I was no longer on the verge of tears, and I felt I could remember all the Chinese I had ever been taught. I breezed over to the reception desk and asked fluently where I could find the Sleeping Buddha. The receptionist with the long nails looked somewhat surprised. No doubt she remembered the limp, non-Chinese-speaking mess I had been the day before.

It turned out that the famous Buddha was right behind the hotel. When the Trio lived in Zhangye in 1923, the complex of buildings that housed the Buddha was still a working temple, and had a fairly chaotic atmosphere. Today it's a museum with the Sleeping Buddha as its centrepiece, and everyone speaks in the hushed tones that people save for museums and churches.

The Buddha had a friendly face. His eyes were half open. Considering the open eyes, he should probably have been called the Resting Buddha. I looked at the image for a long time, trying to decide how best to convey its size; it was like two train carriages with another two train carriages on top.

Zhangye

Mildred wrote that Zhangye's Buddha was so big that pigeons nested in its nostrils. It's probably kept cleaner than it once was, and I couldn't imagine the pigeons getting the opportunity to nest anywhere on it these days. The attendant in the Buddha's building had a tough look about her, and I imagined her shaking her broom at any sacrilegious birds.

Mildred had written that the Buddha was expected to get up from his sleep one day, join forces with other enormous Buddhas in the northwest, and 'set the whole world to rights'.

I left the Buddha and looked at the other buildings in the temple complex, most of which contained collections of paintings, scrolls and relics. I wandered from building to building for want of anything else to do with the rest of my day. Then I saw an ink painting that made me stop and look more closely.

The painting was on a scroll that stretched across a whole wall, and it showed a group of men having a party. Food and drink was laid out in front of them. Some of them were richly dressed. Others played musical instruments. A little boy and a pet monkey cavorted in front of them. The men looked happy. Three women sat in the far right-hand corner of the picture. They were watching the men. They had weary looks on their faces. One woman rested her chin on her hand. You could see her sighing. She would be cleaning up monkey vomit and dispensing hangover medications the next morning.

I was still smiling when I left and walked out into the streets of Zhangye. The three women, sitting aside from the men, made me think again about the Trio, and especially of Eva. Platt wrote that once, when the Trio heard that a friend in England was getting divorced, Eva sympathised with the wife, saying 'Well, just fancy what it must be like having to live with *one* man all your life.'

Eva, Francesca and Mildred all remained single all their lives, and Mildred is the only one who appears to have had any kind of romantic involvement.

While she was studying medicine in London, before she went to China, Mildred was engaged to a man from her church. They planned to work in China together. For some reason – perhaps he was scared by the news of the Boxer Uprising – Mildred's fiancee decided he no longer wanted to be a missionary, and he sent her a letter. It was either him or China.

Mildred doesn't seem to have hesitated in choosing China. But she was deeply hurt. She wrote about it in Victorian terms, and in the third person.

> Unless she take a devious course, and deny her vocation, she must pursue her pathway alone. In one hour the brightest things of life burnt themselves to ashes, and joy removed itself so far from her that it took years to court it back.

Shy, genteel Francesca would probably have fitted into Edwardian middle-class wife-and-motherhood if circumstances had been different. Eva would have hated it.

Nearly everyone I talked to about the Trio wanted to know about their sex lives. 'Were they virgins?' people kept asking me. 'Were they lesbians?' I usually answered 'probably' to the first question and 'probably not' to the second, and I sometimes followed up with a warning about imposing 21st-century values onto Victorian women. I think they functioned well as an unconventional family unit, albeit one that didn't involve men or sex. They liked their independence, and they were busy and fulfilled in their work.

In Marina Warner's introduction to the 1984 Virago edition of *The Gobi Desert*, she suggested, as if she rather liked the idea, that the Trio were lesbians, but then rather reluctantly rejected the idea. I think that was probably wise.

I walked through the streets of Zhangye, where, as usual, everyone stared at me and a few people shouted 'hellooo'. Marco Polo described Zhangye as 'the town of more gods than men', but I didn't see any temples. Perhaps more shoe shops than men, but maybe times had changed. I even tried out a useful new Mandarin phrase: '*Kan-kan*', which translates as 'I'm just having a look,' and, if said to shoe-shop girls in a confident tone, let me browse in peace.

It was nearly midday when I got back to the hotel; I needed to either book in for another night or leave. I sat down to watch the CCTV9 news. The lead story was about the pianist Richard Clayderman, who was going to give a live concert in Beijing. I ate some nuts and my last banana, and threw my clothes in my pack. I didn't need to spend another day in Zhangye.

I signed out with a minute to spare, and asked the receptionist to write 'Jiayuguan' in Chinese characters for me, to help me recognise my bus. She obliged, and gave me an unexpected smile when I thanked her and said goodbye. I took a taxi to the bus station and found a Jiayuguan bus almost straight away. Soon we were driving away in the direction of the Gobi desert.

Chapter Eight

Jiayuguan

> Regret little. Regret belongs with the past. The future is a dream never realised, the past is a phantom – ghosts and dreams. Now is the only reality, and you will need all of yourself to live it.
>
> *Monkey* Series 2, 'The Fountain of Youth'

Every man on the bus to Jiayuguan smoked. I didn't note which easy-listening classic in instrumental form was playing. I was too busy staring out the window at the view Mildred had described: 'On the Tibetan side the snow-covered Richtofen Range came closer and closer, while the Mongolian hills gradually diminished in size until they became mere sand-dunes, and then drifted off into the flat expanse of the Gobi Desert.'

Travelling along this stretch of road from Zhangye to Jiuquan, the final stretch of the Trio's epic trip toward their new lives, had taken the women and their band several weeks. They stopped at villages along the way, staying at inns and farmhouses. One isolated spot that they called Camel Town consisted of some Buddhist ruins and a lean-to where an elderly couple lived.

The landscape got flatter and browner. I looked carefully for what could be ruins. I saw abandoned mud-brick walls on the plain on either side of the road, but it was impossible to tell how old they were.

When we passed through villages I noticed the same style of signage that I had seen outside Xining food stalls. But instead of sheep and plates of noodles floating over green fields, I saw kitchen sinks, motorbike parts and screwdrivers floating in the painted clouds.

Four hours after we left Zhangye, the bus stopped for five minutes in Jiuquan. This was one of the most important stops on my itinerary, the town where the Trio had settled and adopted Topsy. They were based here for thirteen years, and it's where I hoped to find some evidence of their lives – I imagined meeting a wrinkled old lady who had known them, or finding a church like the one in Huozhou where the pastor remembered their names. But I didn't get out of the bus. I planned to base myself in Jiayuguan, 35 kilometres further west, and make day trips back to Jiuquan. From the window, the bus-station lot looked like every other bus-station lot I'd ever seen.

Half an hour later I was in Jiayuguan town. The military fort of Jiayuguan Pass, which marks the western end of China proper, was built in 1372. For nearly six hundred years there was no town of Jiayuguan as such. There was just the fort, and a small township that had grown up around the fort to service it.

The Gobi Desert begins with the Trio living in the fort, preparing for their first trip into the Gobi. According to Mildred, three types of people lived in the fort. The oldest residents were the innkeepers, the shop owners and the blacksmiths, who doubled as veterinarians. They were proud of never having travelled outside of Jiayuguan.

Living further inside the fort were the army officers and their families. They hated the place, with its howling winds and swirling sands. The wives gossiped, play mah-jong and smoked opium as a distraction. The only other residents were travellers who were just passing through. They were mostly traders and exiles.

Nobody lived at the fort now, except for a couple of caretakers and security guards. It was a tourist attraction five kilometres west of the new town of Jiayuguan. The town itself was full of expensive-looking shops, and I didn't see any beggars there. It's supposed to be more well-off than average because people have to be lured there with high wages to compensate for living in the wilds of northern Gansu.

I found a room at the Xiongguan Hotel, which the guidebook described as spotless, though it wasn't. Like every room in every hotel in China, my room smelled as if someone had just smoked a packet of cigarettes in there. In the hotel's favour, each room was supplied with a huge vacuum flask of boiling water that was renewed every few hours.

An undercover market with a cooked-food section was just a short walk up Xinhua Zhinglu. Past the stalls of camouflage-print sneakers and polyester t-shirts, a husband-and-wife team were cooking the same mutton pockets I had enjoyed in Xi'an. I ate two of them. The couple seemed like the happiest people in the world. I had no idea what they were saying, but they kept laughing and teasing each other and (presumably) making jokes about me.

It had been a long day. I walked back to the hotel and watched television. The lead news story on CCTV9 was about an outbreak of bird flu in Qinghai, the province I had left two days earlier. The only poultry I could remember eating in Qinghai was at KFC, and if the urban legends were true, that may not even have been chicken, so I figured I was probably safe.

I caught a taxi to Jiayuguan fort early the next morning, and walked up the steep road to the main gate.

The Trio always approached Jiayuguan from Jiuquan. It's a journey that now takes 25 minutes by minibus, but it took more than six hours by mule cart.

> At a distance of about two miles a high gate-tower of many stories came in sight, flanked on either side by a clay wall, which on the south stretched for seven miles to the foot of the Tibetan mountains. On this side lay green meadows richly watered by springs, and for this reason the name Kaiyukwan has been given, meaning 'The Barrier of the Pleasant Valley' ... Under the shadow of the walls a stream is crossed by a wooden bridge, and from here the path mounts steeply to the door of the southern quarter, where all the inns are situated.

Jiayuguan Pass looked exactly as an ancient Chinese fortress should, with crenellated walls and archways and high, elegantly curved gates. Inside it was quiet and empty, with reconstructed houses and just a few souvenir shops. It couldn't have been more different from the bustling community that the Trio described. Between buildings there were patches of grass and small trees, and growing under the trees were purple irises. Mildred wrote that purple irises grew beside the road between Jiuquan and Jiayuguan.

I took out my copies of the Trio's pictures and found the same internal gateways they had photographed. The paving stones underneath the arches were the same shape that they were in the old photos, with grooves worn away where hundreds of wheels had rolled across them.

At the far end of the fort I climbed the stairs to the top of the walls. You could see what a perfect place this was to build a fortress. The ruins of the western end of the Great Wall trailed off toward the snow-capped Tibetan Qilian Shan range on my left. The black Hei Shan mountains of Inner Mongolia were on my right.

Straight ahead of me was the Gobi desert. This was where it started.

I had expected to see roads and shops and all kinds of development, but the view to the northwest was almost exactly what the Trio would have seen when they set out on their first journey into the desert. It was flat and stony and featureless. Near the wall of the fort were about a dozen camels and their drivers.

I climbed back down the stairs and walked to the northwestern gate, which Mildred called the Travellers Gate or the Gate of Sighs. The gate is almost a tunnel, under a long archway, and it's the final exit from the fort. The walls were once covered in writing, final poems and words of mourning from exiles, criminals and disgraced officials who were about to be spat out of the mouth of China and into the unknown. The walls are clean and blank now.

I carried my copy of *The Gobi Desert* with me, and stopped under the gate to read.

> Just outside the gate was a high stony mound which blocked the view. It had been thrown up to act as a barrier against the elemental and inimical spirits of the Gobi, for the simple-minded men of the garrison would never credit the goblins with sense enough to find their way round the mound and into the fortress.

The mound was still there. I walked over it and stood on the rocky ground of the Gobi. A young man wearing camouflage pants and a baseball cap ran over to me and motioned towards the camels. 'You ride,' he said.

I shook my head. The truth is I was scared of the camels. The back of a camel seemed a long way from the ground. The Trio had always favoured mule-cart travel over camel caravans, apparently for much the same reason.

> The camel litter is spoken of in caravan circles as a luxurious way of crossing the desert, and we were often urged to take advantage of its ease. It was doubtless recorded to our credit that we were unwilling to spend extra money on our own comfort, but the fact was that nothing would have induced us to expose ourselves to the torture of being shut up in a small wooden box for long hours of heat and cold, unable to relax a muscle until such time as it would please the *bash* to order the beasts to kneel. Moreover, anyone possessing a gift of imagination could visualise the position of that box if the camel that carried it went mad and ran amuck. Such things have happened before and may happen again.

The Trio owned a mule cart they called 'The Flying Turki' (not to be confused with a turkey, Mildred reminded readers), but for their first trip into the desert they bought a new cart that they called their Kou Wai ('outside the mouth') cart or the Gobi Express ('a name that would at any rate give us the illusion that we were moving quickly'). The wheels were eight feet across, which gave them good clearance over gullies and streams, and the cart had a hood stuffed with grass matting to protect the travellers from the sun. The cart and the mules' saddlebags were packed carefully with provisions, copies of pamphlets and scriptures in six different languages, and a foot-pumped harmonium keyboard to accompany their hymn-singing. The lead mule, Molly, had come all the way from Shanxi with the Trio, and they openly loved her. Mildred wrote about Molly more affectionately than she did about Topsy. 'Our beautiful Molly,' they called her.

These carts crossed and recrossed the Gobi desert for the next thirteen years. Between 1923 and 1936 the Trio travelled all the way between Jiuquan and Urumqi – more than 1600 kilometres of the old Silk Road – five times, in addition to many other, shorter trips. On most of their journeys they were accompanied by Chinese evangelists Elder and Mrs Liu, as well as various cart drivers and Brother Chen, who had come from Shanxi with them. After 1928 Topsy always travelled with them. Members of the party took turns in riding, walking and sitting on the cart.

It's sometimes hard to tell from the Trio's writings who was with them on each trip. Sometimes they intentionally protected the identities of their Chinese colleagues. After they returned to England for good, and wrote many of their books, they had no way of knowing what repercussions their Christian friends in Gansu might be facing, from whichever local official or warlord was in charge, for having been close to foreigners

I had originally been inspired to travel all the way from Melbourne to Jiayuguan because of Mildred's description of how she threw a stone against the fortress wall before leaving on her first trip into the desert. The soldiers told her it was good luck if the stone rebounded, and she noted the cheeping noise the rock made as it hit the wall, like a twittering bird. I imagined that throwing my own rock would be the high point of my trip. But now that I was here, looking at the back wall of the fort, I held back. I wasn't ready.

I decided I would come back to the fort another day, after I had visited Jiuquan and seen the Trio's old compound and talked to people who had known them. Like Mildred, I would toss my fateful stone at the wall just before I headed into the Gobi desert, to mark the start of what I thought of as my real journey.

I turned back and walked through the fort again, and followed the signs pointing to the Great Wall Museum. The museum building was new, with high ceilings and dim lighting and air-conditioning. It contained artifacts and maps and pictures of the fort. In one room I saw a stone carving of two birds in a circle, with the fort behind them. This was written next to it:

> At both sides of the main entrance if you strike on stone with another you will hear the faint 'jug jug'. A legend says during the year of Zhende in the Ming Dynasty, a lot of swallows nested their home inside the city of JiaYu Pass. One day, the two swallows flied out for hunting food. A sun fall, they were merrily fling to the inside Pass. As soon as the female one flew into the city gate, suddenly there was a blustering gale, the male swallow lost his way. When he found the Pass gate, it was tightly closed. The male swallow bumped his head to the city gate in an impulse. The female swallow waited and waited, but the male swallow never came back, she was heart stricken and made the 'jug, jug' at times. And people say that is the undying soul of the female swallow.

It was easy to see how the story could have changed over the centuries. The soldiers in the 1920s might not have known the legend about the birds, but the tradition of the stones had continued. Later that day, at an Internet cafe near the Jiayuguan post office, I found variations of the story online. One said that generals would bring their families to throw rocks against the wall as a prayer before they rode away on a campaign.

The next morning, the weather looked fine, so I left the hotel wearing sandals, a t-shirt and thin cotton trousers. I threw my umbrella in my bag, just in case. The bus station was just a couple of blocks away, but before I got there the rain had started falling heavily.

'One to Jiuquan,' I said to the woman behind the ticket desk. She shook her head and pointed to a desk on the other side of the room. I walked across. 'One to Jiuquan,' I said to the man at the desk. He indicated I should give him my bag. I made a confused face and said. 'I don't understand. I want to go to Jiuquan,' I tried again, in my best Mandarin.

'Yes, Jiuquan,' he said. Then he asked for my bag again.

I went back to the ticket desk. 'One to Jiuquan,' I said. The woman sighed and pointed to the other desk. I pulled out my guide-book and showed her the Chinese characters for Jiuquan.

'Oh, Jiuquan!' she said. She laughed and called out to the man at the other desk. He started laughing too. I couldn't tell the difference between their pronunciation and mine, but they made it clear that when I said 'Jiuquan' it sounded exactly like 'left-luggage desk'. I shrugged and took my ticket.

By the time the minibus reached Jiuquan, less than half an hour later, the temperature had dropped and the rain was bucketing down. I really wished I had worn socks and sneakers.

I sat down in the bus station and pulled a map and some photos out of my bag. The map was very basic and about ten years out of date. A street called Canghou Jie had been highlighted on the map with a yellow marker. The photos were taken in 1992, and showed a middle-aged Chinese couple sitting in a tumbledown courtyard with what looked like piles of old building materials in the background.

The photos had been taken by an English linguistics professor called Patricia East who lived in Munich. Back in Australia, when I was planning my trip, I had exchanged emails with Patricia. She told me that in the early 1990s, when she was living and working in China, she had fallen in love with Xinjiang province. Searching for a way to write about the area through the eyes of a Westerner, Patricia had discovered the Trio's books. She followed their journeys through Gansu and Xinjiang. Then she went back to England and met Topsy, who was in her seventies, and William Platt, the Trio's friend and biographer; he had since become a Reverend Doctor but was 99 years old and becoming vague in his memories, and he died soon afterwards.

I said 'damn' out loud when I started reading Patricia's first email. Not only had someone already written the book I wanted to write, but a brilliant Englishwoman who spoke Mandarin and Uyghur had written the book I wanted to write.

Actually, Patricia was the best thing that could have happened to me. She went on to say that she had written about her experiences but she had not published the account. She gave me the impression she had moved on to other interests. She sent me files of all her writing. She said that if I ever came to Germany, she would show me photos of Xinjiang and letters from Topsy.

A few months later I had dinner with Patricia in her flat in Munich. She wore a black wool dress and a heavy gold necklace that looked Tibetan. Her sculptures and rugs had the same look. 'It was all classy Tibetan, not cheap hippy junk,' I wrote to my boyfriend the next day. The flat was lined with packed bookshelves.

We ate pasta and drank Italian wine and talked for hours. When I told Patricia I was on my way to look at archives in England she wished me luck. She said she had found no private diaries and few personal letters. All she had to work from were the Trio's published writings, Platt's biography, and a few papers from their final years in England, as well as the memories of some of their colleagues who had probably since died. Patricia said these old friends had laughed out loud when she asked them if the Trio were lesbians.

Patricia gave me articles and photographs she thought I would find interesting, and she gave me copies of her letters from Topsy. They had written to each other up until Topsy's death in 1998.

The photographs I was looking at in the Jiuquan bus station were of the compound in Jiuquan where the Trio had lived. In 1992,

Patricia had talked to people on the streets here, asking if they knew where the foreign Christians used to live. A man had taken her to Canghou Jie, which she translated as Behind Granary Street. Some of the old buildings were still there, and Patricia spoke to a woman who said this was once a Christian community. She took pictures of the woman and her husband sitting in their courtyard, smiling. Now I hoped the map and pictures would lead me to the same place.

I put my umbrella up and walked outside. Muddy water streamed over my feet. I stopped every second person and asked them how to get to Canghou Jie. They all pointed me in the same direction, and I walked down the street until I saw a sign that said 'Canghou Jie' in Chinese and English.

I walked from one end of Canghou Jie to the other and back again, and I saw nothing that resembled Patricia's photos or description. Most buildings in the street had at least two storeys, and they were all built from concrete and tiles. They did not look startlingly new, but they could easily have been built in the thirteen years since Patricia had been here. Some buildings had small shopfronts on the ground floor. The shops sold a random assortment of goods. One had lightbulbs, mousetraps and beans on display. The sky was so overcast that the shops were lit up with fluorescent tube lights.

I looked around for an older person to talk to, but the shops seemed to be staffed entirely by teenagers. I spoke to the girl who sat behind the basket of beans, and showed her one of the photographs. 'Is this Canghou Jie?' I asked, pointing at the photograph. She looked confused and gestured towards the street. 'Canghou Jie,' she said. I showed her the photograph again and she shook her head. She said she didn't know.

Not knowing quite what to do next, I walked back to the main road and up to the drum tower, a solid building that used to be the town's east gate, and stood underneath it to escape from the rain. On an adjacent corner I saw a brightly lit fast-food restaurant called Dicos. It looked as if it would be warm and dry, which it was.

It was also quite surreal. I splashed across the street. A woman in a yellow t-shirt greeted me at the door and held it open. 'How do you do?' she said. 'Um ... hello,' I said. I had not heard any English spoken for days. The woman turned towards a crowd of small children who stood in the corner of the restaurant. They all looked about eight years old. I made a surprised face at the woman. 'Yes, lots of children,' she said, again in English. The children all looked Han Chinese. In the Trio's day Jiuquan had few Muslim residents, and that didn't appear to have changed.

Teddy bears, balloons and plastic flowers hung from the ceiling. I ordered a chicken burger and lemonade, and took my tray to a table where I could see the children. Young couples who I assumed were parents sat and watched the children. I couldn't help but think of the band of children that the Trio befriended here in Jiuquan, and the parents who would gather to watch them.

The woman who had spoken to me had two helpers, teenage girls who also wore yellow t-shirts. The t-shirts had 'You & Me English School' printed on them. A television set in the corner of the room showed cartoon characters singing in English, and the children sang along. What they lacked in tunefulness they made up for in enthusiasm.

The children sang 'You Are My Sunshine', and they clapped along to a chant that went 'How are you? I am fine!' The teachers held up cards with animals on them, and the children shouted out the names in English.

After a few songs the children were told to take a break, and a group of them came straight up to my table. The pushiest little girl had a crazy collection of hairclips and bobbles and fluorescent-coloured scrunchies in her hair. She asked me questions in English, and I tried to answer in both English and Mandarin.

What is your name?

What country are you from?
What is your favourite colour?
What is your favourite animal?
What is your favourite flower?

They were all good questions. I should have thought to ask them of the Living Buddha. I showed the children the photo of my cat. Parents started pushing the shy children forward and prodding them in the back. 'Talk to her!' they said. So each shy child in turn would giggle and ask:

What is your name?
What country are you from?
What is your favourite colour?
What is your favourite animal?
What is your favourite flower?

The teacher pushed her way through the crowd of children and said hello to me. She said it was good for the children to talk to a native English-speaker.

It occurred to me that the teacher might be able to help me. I told her that I was looking for information about some English women who used to live in Jiuquan, and wondered if on another day I could pay her or one of her assistants to do some translating for me. I said I would like to talk to some Jiuquan Christians. I imagined us walking back up Canghou Jie and talking to old people and getting invited to visit a church where people would smile and clasp my hands like the Christians in Huozhou. Then the teacher behaved exactly as if she had not heard me. 'Yes, now come and speak to the other children,' she said. She pulled me towards another group of children, who asked me the same questions.

The teacher called all the children together. While they were gathering around the television set she shook my hand and thanked me. 'Now, goodbye,' she said firmly, and she walked away. It was clear that although she could not say 'no' outright, she did not want to get involved.

I sat back down. I didn't know where to find another English speaker in Jiuquan. I suddenly felt foolish for having imagined that I could travel to China alone, with just a few Mandarin phrases, and expect to uncover any kind of information about people and events of eighty years ago. Whatever I had expected to find in Jiuquan, it wasn't there.

There was one more site I wanted to see in Jiuquan. The town's name means Spring of Wine, and there are at least two explanations for this, both relating to a small lake outside the eastern gate. One story tells how a battalion of soldiers was camped near the spring after a successful battle. The general was sent some wine by the emperor as a thank-you gift, and he poured it into the spring so that all his soldiers could have a share.

The other explanation is simply that the spring's water tastes good. When the Trio first moved to Jiuquan, then known as Suchow, Mildred wrote:

> We were taken to a lovely lake outside the town with pavilions standing on its brink and a temple surrounded by trees on a small island in the centre. 'The water of this spring,' they said, 'is so pure and fresh that it tastes like wine, and Suchow regards it as a very sacred trust, for everyone who drinks this water is strengthened and refreshed by it.'

The weather was so bad, and I was so disheartened by the day so far, that I decided not to waste my time walking around in the rain trying to find a lake that was marked only by an arrow on an out-of-date map. For all I knew it had been filled in with concrete. I left the light and warmth of Dicos and went outside into the pouring rain and began walking back towards the bus station. My feet had passed cold and gone straight to numb.

Water streamed down the footpath. As I trudged along, thinking about the hot shower I would have when I got back to the hotel, I must have stepped on the edge of a metal sewer cover, and suddenly it flipped open and one of my legs went all the way down into something wet and slimy. I clawed my way to my feet, grazing my hands. My umbrella blew away down the street.

I limped over to the nearest shop. One trouser leg was particularly wet, but I was damp and muddy all over. I started shaking. I wasn't sure what to do next. A young woman opened the shop door and called me in. It was a musical instrument shop. The woman pointed to the leather stool at the piano. I pointed to my wet leg and said 'I'm smelly' in Mandarin, but she insisted I sit down. She brought me a towel and let me pat myself down; she brought me a cup of green tea and then she went outside.

Two young men sat in the shop, playing unplugged electric guitars. They took turns playing soft-rock riffs and praising each other's playing. One of them played the opening of the Guns N' Roses song 'Sweet Child of Mine'. The men played softly enough that I could hear a piano lesson in the back room.

The woman came back with my umbrella. All the spokes were broken. I thanked her, and she laughed and held up her hand as if to say 'it's nothing'. After tea and a few deep breaths, I thanked her again and headed back out into the rain. My umbrella was now almost useless, but I held it above my head anyway. The limp spokes hung pathetically around my head, as I limped up to the bus station.

For a change I was glad of the cigarette smoke in the bus. It masked the smell of my leg. Everyone was a bit damp, and the windows were steamed up. The man sitting next to me put his bag of potatoes between us, and it dug into my hip for the whole trip.

When I got back to the hotel I stripped off, balled up my filthy clothes in a plastic bag, and jumped straight under the shower. I turned on the hot tap. It gurgled and produced a short-lived, cold trickle.

'Shit', I said out loud. 'Buggery sod.'

I checked the water in my vacuum flask. It was almost boiling. I emptied it into the sink and scrubbed myself down. After I'd put on some clean, warm clothes, I walked downstairs and bought a new umbrella at the shop in the hotel foyer. Then I went back to the Internet cafe and wrote an email to my boyfriend. The subject line was My Horrible Morning. I told him that I had fallen down a drain and skinned my knee and that I didn't know where to start in uncovering information about the Trio in Jiuquan and this job was harder than I thought it would be. I didn't know if I would have anything to write in my book. But I told him I wasn't going to be a cry-baby. After all, I had found the Trio's church in Huozhou, I had met a Living Buddha, and I had even carried out a few Mandarin conversations. I was excited about the imminent arrival of my brother, and the thought of our finally heading into the Gobi desert. 'Things can only get better from here on,' I wrote. I was almost right.

It was early in the afternoon and I had time on my hands. So I'm not going to apologise for the fact that, like most solo travellers without a fixed schedule, I organised my day around searching out food. I figured that the late-morning Dicos burger must have been my breakfast, in which case it was perfectly reasonable for me to go to the market and buy another of those mutton pockets for lunch. At the market the jolly couple welcomed me like a long-lost child. I sat on their bench and scoffed down the meat and bread, and it tasted just as good as it had the previous day.

I would have laughed if anyone had told me that was the last mutton pocket I would eat in China. But when I got back to the hotel my stomach felt unsettled. I thought I had indigestion, so I lay on the bed and watched television.

CCTV9 was showing a report about an anti-Chingrish campaign run by the *China Daily* newspaper in preparation for the Olympic games in Beijing. People were encouraged to use correct English in signs and brochures so as not to confuse foreign visitors, or make them laugh.

Some examples of Chingrish were shown at the launch of the campaign. One sign said 'Deformed Man Toilet'. Another, in a supermarket aisle, said 'Sex Thing'. In my first few days in China I had taken photos every time I saw this kind of thing ('Look! It says "Exing Wisher" on the fire extinguisher!'), but I soon discovered how pervasive it was, and then I stopped noticing. I figured the wobbly English I encountered was way better than my Mandarin.

I had been watching television for about ten minutes when I realised I was not simply bloated from overeating. I went to the bathroom and bent over the sink and reacquainted myself, at alarming velocity, with my mutton pocket.

Over the next two days ... suffice to say I was thoroughly emptied, over and over, every way possible. The trip between the bed and the bathroom would exhaust me so much that I had to have a sleep each time I returned to the bed. I made it to the downstairs shop a couple of times, and stocked up on its most appealing soft drink, a sugary, very slightly soapy concoction called Future Lemon, which I diluted with water and sipped between naps and trips to the bathroom. Every time I went back up the stairs with my Future Lemon, I told the receptionist that I was sick. I needed somebody to know. She just nodded.

I felt too awful to read. Instead I played Scrabble, so badly that the Easy setting beat me every time. I discovered that CCTV9 was especially boring in large doses. I watched many hours of press conferences about textile import and export regulations, from which

I gathered that the Chinese were unhappy about restrictions that European countries were placing on Chinese exports. At one press conference, an Italian journalist asked a question and one of the Chinese politicians responded by talking about Marco Polo. He said Marco Polo was an Italian who was a great friend of China, and that he would be surprised and saddened by the unfair way that modern-day Italy was restricting modern-day China's right to sell as many t-shirts as it wanted.

After two days of television, sleep and Future Lemon, I started to feel marginally better. I put some clean clothes on and went downstairs to the foyer, where I sat on a plastic chair and read *The Gobi Desert*, looking up every now and then. Soon a tall man with a beard and a battered stockman's hat walked into the foyer. He carried a backpack. I squealed, jumped up and hugged him, and led him to the reception desk.

'*Ze shi wode didi*!' I said to the receptionist. 'This is my little brother!'

Chapter Nine

Into the Gobi

> No-one can know himself. Therefore people will live behind many masks and call themselves by many names, when all that matters is the effect we have on others. Thus even a monster may want to be kind, friendly and gentle.
>
> *Monkey* Series 2, 'Such a Nice Monster'

My brother, Jack, had been enthusiastic about my trip to China right from the start. He had spent hours online, looking at maps and chat rooms and other travellers' photo albums, emailing me links every time he found new information.

One night his wife, Alex, had looked over his shoulder at the Chinese train timetable on the computer screen and asked if he would like to go with me. He, in turn, politely asked me if I would mind. We had spent years as travelling companions in India, and I couldn't think of a better person to cross the desert with.

Two days before meeting me in Jiayuguan, Jack had flown into Guangzhou from Melbourne, then made his way northwest overland. He planned to travel as far as Urumqi with me, then fly southeast to Kashgar.

The first thing Jack did when we got up to my room was plug his digital camera into my iBook so he could show me all the photos he had taken in the past two days. Most of them were pictures of Chingrish signage and packaging. 'No Smoking the bed please' was on a plaque in his first hotel room. In the hotel bathroom, he had photographed a packet that said For Man Only. The instructions said it was for washing the genitals, after which the man should use a pasteurised towel. 'Please use at ease,' the packet said.

I told Jack I was switching my Scrabble game to two-person mode now that I had real-life competition. Then I told him about my disappointing trip to Jiuquan and how I had to go back and find the Spring of Wine lake. I talked until my mouth was dry. It felt like ages since I had spoken anything but the most stilted English. Now I couldn't stop.

I thought Jack might want to rest or eat after spending the night on a train, but he was on some kind of travel rush and claimed he didn't need any sleep. 'Come on, let's go find your Spring of Wine,' he said.

So we took the bus to Jiuquan. When we got there the air was dry and hot; as I walked my brother down the main street to show him where I fell into the sewer, it was hard to imagine rivers of rain gushing along the street just a few days earlier. We walked down Canghou Jie again, just to confirm that there was nothing in the street but new buildings. Jack made me stand in the middle of the street while he took a photo, shouting instructions at me from the side of the road.

'Look sad!' he said. 'You're disappointed!'

The Spring of Wine was a long walk down a main road on the

eastern side of the drum tower, but it was not difficult to find. We paid 30 yuan at a ticket booth to enter the park around the Spring of Wine, which turned out to be a small and not terribly clean lake. A concrete sculpture of soldiers and horses had been built around the point where the water bubbled up. We walked on a concrete bridge that zigzagged across the water.

Boats were available for hire. They looked like repurposed exercise bikes. The seats were so high that we couldn't imagine how you could pedal one and not overturn. None of the boats were in use when we were there, so we didn't get the chance to find out by watching other people. There were only a few other tourists at the spring, sitting on benches and watching the water. A small Ferris wheel was unattended.

'Well, there's your spring,' Jack said. 'Can we see the fort now?'

We caught a taxi from outside the park and asked to go to Jiayuguan Fort. The driver seemed to understand, but he shouted something that I couldn't follow.

'Is he annoyed?' Jack asked.

'I don't think so,' I said. I explained how, for a while, I had thought everyone in China was angry, but the language just sounds emphatic and emotional to an English speaker. In Chinese the meaning of a word is conveyed through its tone. By way of illustration, I demonstrated how, with the tones in the right places, 'Ma ma ma' can mean 'Is mother a horse?'

Jack said I was showing off. He didn't think this was a phrase he was likely to be using.

When we reached the fort I showed Jack around and we climbed the walls to look out over the new town in one direction and the empty Gobi in the other. I pointed out what looked like a nuclear reactor in the distance, back in the direction of the town.

I was hot and sweaty from climbing the stone stairs. Mildred had described the fort as noisy and busy, but it seemed strangely quiet now, up on a hill away from the traffic. The few other visitors looked a long way away, in the courtyards beneath us. We looked up as a plane zoomed above us, breaking the silence. I had noticed a lot of fast, low-flying aircraft since I had been in Jiayuguan. 'I think that was a MiG,' Jack said. 'Is there some kind of military base near here?'

It was a good question. I had read warnings, in guidebooks and online, that much of western Inner Mongolia, the region just north of Jiayuguan, was off-limits to travellers. Nuclear testing and dumping had been reported there. In journalist-speak, there was a 'heavy military presence'. Near Jiuquan was China's first space centre, from where the country's second manned space flight was about to be launched. I didn't have a local guide and I was relying on public transport, so I had no way to follow the Trio's trips north into western Inner Mongolia. Their descriptions were mainly of sandstorms and wide empty spaces and the same kinds of Buddhist festivals that they attended in Tibet, which sounded enough like other places I had visited, or would soon be seeing, that I didn't worry too much about missing out.

When Jack and I reached the far side of Jiayuguan fort and walked over the spirit mound, I told him I had got up the courage to ride a camel. I had seen photos of glossy, fluffy Bactrian camels in the Trio's books. In one impossibly cute picture, Topsy had her arms around a baby camel. 'I probably need to do this,' I said. So we glanced in the general direction of the camel touts, and they were all over us within seconds.

We negotiated a price and chose a camel. They all looked patchier than the camels in the Trio's pictures. I wondered if camels moult in the summer. The camels all had rods through their noses, attached to ropes held by the driver. On either side of my camel's rod, holding it in place, was the plastic lid from a Coke bottle. 'Take a picture of the Coke lids,' I said to Jack. 'It's an allegory about Coca-communism, it's a metaphor for socialism with Chinese characteristics!'

Jack looked confused. 'Socialism with Chinese characteristics,' I said again. I tried to explain that this was what the government called its system of mixing one-party totalitarian government with free-market economics and '...well, having Coke posters everywhere'.

Jack shrugged and took a photo, and then half a dozen touts helped me onto the camel's back and it slowly stood up. Then it farted. Jack backed up a few paces and held up his camera. I felt a bit light-headed. I remembered Mildred's comments about bolting camels.

'Jack,' I called. He came closer and lowered the camera. 'I don't think I want to go for a ride.'

He sighed. 'But you want photos?'

'Yes, take photos of me, make it look like I'm riding.' The camel made a loud humphing noise and I put on my best fake smile.

The last thing I had to do before I left the fort was to finally throw a rock against the back wall. Like the Trio and so many before me, I had to see if I would have a safe journey. The fort must have been renovated recently; there was no dented patch by the Travellers Gate to show where people had thown stones at the wall over the centuries. So I chose a piece of wall at random and picked up a rock, and threw it. When it bounced back, I heard a definite peep that did, in fact, sound like a baby chick. Jack was still photographing camels a few hundred metres away, but I turned and waved at him and gave him the thumbs up.

I was ready to cross the Gobi desert.

We left early the next morning. The road from Jiayuguan into the desert runs close to the fort, so I was following the Trio's route closely. Our destination was Dunhuang, a town the Trio had visited many times and where they had been trapped for months during a siege.

Our bus was large and bright pink, with over-active air-conditioning. I felt a chill on my skin as soon as we stepped onto it. This was the first bus trip I'd taken where the No Smoking sign was actually obeyed.

I stared out the window at the desert. I had imagined it would be fine golden sand and rolling dunes. When I thought of the Gobi desert I pictured the scenery from *Lawrence of Arabia*. If I had read the Trio's books more closely I would have been alerted by Mildred's constant use of the words 'stony' and 'desolate'.

The Gobi, I discovered, is mainly flat. It's more grey than golden, and more rocky than sandy. There are subtle changes in the shape and colour of the landscape along the way, which the Trio learned to recognise and appreciate. But in my first few hours of watching the desert, I felt as if I was moving along the bottom of an enormous, unattractive quarry.

On each of the Trio's regular journeys across the desert, their party had left Jiayuguan in the evening and travelled through the night to avoid the heat. The first time they started into the desert, Mildred walked alongside the cart for a few miles until the stones hurt her feet. She noted the absolute silence of the desert, where 'there was not even a blade of grass to rustle, a leaf to move, a bird to stir in its nest, nor an insect on the wing to fly past'.

On that first trip into the Gobi, Mildred had a moment of doubt:

> Although the journeys which lay behind had often seemed long, slow and tedious, yet they always led to a kindly shelter for the night, towards a goal which lay within measurable distance, and gave certain promise of a return to a welcoming home. In China the wayside inn had had its unfailing atmosphere of cordiality and pleasant intercourse, but this place had none of these amenities. The life of China's main roads was one of stirring activity, with

something happening every moment to interest or amuse. What faced me here might be the burden of boundless monotony. Should I ever distinguish one stage from the other? Might I not even die, not, as some had done, of thirst or fatigue, but of boredom? In the end, should I make good my quest, or would the desert prove too much for me?

The Trio's first stop, after about ten hours of travelling, was always a small oasis they called the Village of the Muslim Tomb. The caretaker who had first showed Mildred the tomb, with its domed roof, told her it housed a Muslim pilgrim who had travelled from lands to the west. Legend had it that he would awaken one day. His body was placed in a vault covered only by a cloth, because the caretaker didn't want the revived pilgrim to hit his head on a coffin or stone slab when the angel called his name and he sat upright.

About an hour into the desert we saw a few scrappy trees and some buildings. The bus stopped at the side of the road to pick up a passenger. Across the road a heavy gate was held shut by a padlocked chain. There was Arabic writing on the gate. Behind it was a green domed roof. Perhaps this was the same place.

I poked Jack. He was humming along to the instrumental version of Foreigner's 'I Want to Know what Love Is'.

'Do you think that's it?' I said. 'Can I say I saw the tomb?'

'It can't hurt to make stuff up,' Jack said.

'By which you mean I can't make stuff up,' I said. I pouted. The bus drove on, back into the desert.

My theory had always been that a lot of travel books were written by English public-school-educated, chambray-shirt-wearing men with money and resources behind them. If one of those writers had been researching the Trio, he would have found their books in specialty bookshops in London where he was on a first-name basis with the charmingly eccentric owners. In Jiayuguan, he would have hired a four-wheel drive, a driver and a translator. They would have travelled out to the Muslim Tomb village together, discovered the tomb and spoken to the caretaker. The caretaker would have told the translator fascinating stories and taken everyone home for lunch. When questioned about the Trio, he would have remembered his grandfather talking about three grey-haired Englishwomen. The writer would have taken beautiful photos with his expensive camera.

I really hated my toffee-nosed rival. He would have gone to the prohibited parts of Inner Mongolia, too, bribing officials from a bottomless purse.

'But I'm just a woman from the bottom of the world who's watching stuff from the bus and speaking a few words of Chinese that nobody can understand,' I said.

'Oh, boo hoo,' Jack said. 'You're seeing things the way most travellers see them.'

To cheer me up, Jack said he would buy me dinner when we reached Dunhuang. I still hadn't eaten anything since I was first sick, three days earlier.

Dunhuang was a lot further away than either of us realised. The ticket-seller in Jiayuguan had told us the bus trip would take about six hours. But we kept coming across roadworking crews, and the bus had to veer off and crawl along dusty unmade stretches of gravel. There was an unending emptiness to the wider view. Occasionally we drove past the remains of mud-brick walls. They could have been the ruins of a 7th century Buddhist city, or the week-old construction of road workers.

The next building we came across was a mammoth petrol station. It was the only sign of life we could see in any direction. The bus stopped to refuel and Jack got out to look around. I told him to buy me some Future Lemon. I looked out the window and saw him taking photos of the petrol pumps and the shade cloths and the unusual pyramid-shaped roof.

My brother is an engineer, and he is very practical. He likes things that are useful, and when he travels he doesn't always pay attention to the sights that are supposed to interest tourists.

'Remember Mysore Palace?' I said when he got back on the bus. When Jack and I were small children in India, our father took us to the palace of the rulers of the princely state of Mysore. The palace was full of intricate mosaic-work and soaring carved ceilings, and paintings and armour and weapons. The artworks and artifacts were kept behind coloured rope barricades.

When we got home, our mother asked what we thought of the palace. 'It was amazing,' Jack said. 'I've never seen such thick nylon rope before.'

After another hour we reached a small town where the ticket collector herded all the bus passengers onto a dirty minibus that already contained a few smokers. We sat down across the aisle from a smiling old couple and headed back into the desert.

The minibus was not air-conditioned. Most people kept their windows closed. I opened mine, but closed it again after dust blew into my eyes. The view outside did not change.

I tried to imagine moving along this route at the speed of a mule cart. I was already starting to understand Mildred's fears about being bored to death. From time to time, on the bus, Jack and I would see things on the horizon and ask each other 'Is that water?' or 'Are those trees?' and we would start to make things out very gradually as we got closer. Sometimes something was actually there, but sometimes it would disappear. The Trio must have gone through the same frustrations, only about twenty times more slowly. If I thought the bus was hot, the covered cart must have been nightmarishly stuffy during the day.

It was hard to believe that this skinny stretch of asphalt through this boredom-inducing landscape was once the most important road in the world.

'We're actually on the Silk Road,' I said to Jack. 'This is where East and West met; it's how people exchanged ideas and goods; it's the reason why people changed religions and put different spices in their food and added new notes to their musical scales and started wearing different kinds of cloth.' I was excited about travelling on such a historically significant route. Major civilisations had fought and traded and merged around this part of the road – Buddhist India, Confucian China, Western Christendom, Orthodox Russia and Islam had all been here. 'It's like the navel of the earth,' I said.

'Actually, I'm pretty sure I've heard Africa described that way,' Jack said.

Marco Polo came down this road in the 12th century. He was one of the many travellers through this region who wrote about the spirits that haunt the desert, calling people off the road so that they lose their way. He wrote that the Gobi was full of evil spirits who lured travellers into danger. Monkey and his companions had frequent run-ins with them. Soldiers and traders warned the Trio about them.

Mildred wrote that the voices could be clearly heard, and on an early trip she had asked the carter to stop and follow them. 'Never listen to those voices,' the carter said. 'It is not a man's cry, and those who follow it may never come back to the caravan.'

The Trio got used to hearing and seeing things that were not there. Mildred wrote:

> Mirage is the desert traveller's constant companion and his perpetual torment. As soon as the sun is high on the horizon, the sand begins to glitter like water and appears to move like wavelets, while the clumps of camel-thorn look like tall bushes or stunted trees, and seem to be set by the edge of a lake.

We stopped at another petrol station. An old man got onto the bus and sat in the seat in front of us. He smelled of sweat, and his suit coat was old and greasy. He was swigging from a bottle of Tsing Tao beer. Jack and I were both perspiring and dusty by now. We both watched the old man for a while. I looked at Jack. We said 'Mmmm ... beer.'

We had been on the bus for about six hours when we pulled into an oasis town with wide, tree-lined streets and a large, ugly sculpture at the central roundabout. Almost every town in China has one of these. Although I can close my eyes and picture the streets around it, I must admit that I have no recollection of the statue itself. The notes I wrote that night say, rather unhelpfully, 'large, ugly sculpture'.

We pulled into the bus station and I asked the old couple if this was Dunhuang. They nodded, but showed no signs of leaving the bus themselves, so Jack and I said goodbye, strapped on our packs and climbed out into the sunshine. The ticket collector was on the roof of the bus, tightening the ropes around the bags. He became quite agitated when he saw us with our packs on.

'Anxi!' he shouted.

'This isn't Dunhuang?'

'No, it's Anxi!' he said. He shouted something I couldn't understand, but it was almost certainly along the lines of 'Get back on the bus, idiots!'

We got back on the bus. The old couple laughed. I wasn't sure if this was some kind of face saving, or if they were just genuinely amused that we had nearly got stranded.

'So Anxi didn't disappear under the sand,' I commented to Jack.

'Was it supposed to?'

In the 1920s Mildred Cable gave the town about twenty years before the desert covered it. Strong winds blew nearly every day of the year, and sands had drifted to the top of the city walls. She and

Eva and Francesca climbed the walls on their first visit, led by naked children who had been swimming in a nearby irrigation channel.

As usual, they were spending their time just talking to people, mainly women and children. Their missionary activities were always very low-key. In towns like Anxi, where there were few or no Christians, they didn't set up meetings or preach in the town square. They described how when they walked past a half-open door and saw a woman sewing they would compliment her on her stitching. She might then ask them about their own clothes, and where they had been made. She might call a female relative in from another room, and they would all get chatting. The Chinese women often asked about the missionaries' pince-nez glasses, which would be passed around and admired. When the missionaries were asked why they travelled, they talked about their beliefs. Sometimes the Chinese women were uninterested, but sometimes they asked to hear more.

Mildred wrote that the town of Anxi was more important than it appeared. It was the geographic centre of Asia, and was at the junction of two major trade routes. From the walls the Trio looked out at roads leading northeast to Mongolia, northwest to Urumqi, southwest to the Himalayas and southeast to Xi'an and central China.

Successive armies had based themselves at the garrison here. Late in 1931, Mildred, Eva and Francesca were forcibly transported to Anxi under armed guard. Their captors were part of a Muslim army that followed a charismatic, handsome and very young warlord known variously as General Ma, Ma Chung Ying, the Baby General or Thunderbolt.

General Ma was a Hui, a Chinese Muslim. He and his men were well known in Gansu in the late 1920s for their protests against government taxes. They called themselves an army and claimed to be liberating Muslims from government rule, but the Trio referred to them as brigands and accused them of killing and looting indiscriminately. There was always trouble when General Ma's men passed through Jiuquan. The Trio believed General Ma's only aim was to cause trouble and gain more power for himself.

In 1930 the general's army travelled northwest and joined up with angry Uyghur Muslims in the town of Hami. The whole area was in uproar following the death of the khan, the hereditary Uyghur ruler descended from Genghis Khan. Uyghurs made up the majority of the population in the region, and for generations the presence of the khan had given them a sense of autonomy, although the khans had always paid a tribute – including an annual load of Hami's famous melons – to the Chinese emperor in Beijing.

Beijing would probably have been happy for this situation to continue, but the regional governor, a man called Chin, had other ideas. Mildred said Chin was scared of the Muslims. She described him as having 'none of the qualities essential to good rule or wise administration', and he seems to have proved her right in this case. In 1930, when the khan died, Chin jailed the khan's heir and brought in Han Chinese magistrates and officials.

Rebellion was already in the air. Then one of the Han officials raped a Uyghur girl, and the whole region went crazy. General Ma arrived, declaring himself a fellow Muslim who would fight against the oppressors. Hui and Uyghur Muslims had quite different cultures, but the general was welcomed, at least initially. In the course of fighting to liberate Xinjiang, General Ma's army liberated many ordinary people from their money, their food, their sons and their lives. It didn't spare either Hui or Uyghur Muslims. Today there are Uyghur people who still remember, and hate, General Ma.

In October 1931 the 21-year-old general had retreated to Anxi with shotgun wounds to both his legs. His men had occupied the nearby town of Dunhuang, where Jack and I were headed, and the Trio's party had been trapped there for most of the year. Nobody was allowed to leave or enter the town, and food became scarce. Typhus broke out, and Mildred tended to the sick and wounded.

Word got back to the general that one of the foreign women had medicines from the West, and Mildred was summoned to Anxi to dress his wounds. She had no choice. Eva and Francesca insisted on coming with her. Topsy stayed with the Chinese Christians in Dunhuang, who gathered around the Trio's cart and sang 'Guide Me Oh Thou Great Jehovah' before the women left.

The Trio's readers would have been familiar with the words of the hymn, and would have recognised how relevant it was to their difficult journey through the desert.

> Guide me, O thou great Jehovah, pilgrim through this barren land.
> I am weak, but thou art mighty; hold me with thy powerful hand.
> Bread of heaven, bread of heaven, feed me till I want no more.
> Open now the crystal fountain, whence the healing stream doth flow; let the fire and cloudy pillar lead me all my journey through.
> Strong deliverer, strong deliverer, be thou still my strength and shield.

When they reached Anxi the women were kept under guard by 'impudent youths handling loaded muskets'. They noticed one of their mules, looted from their stable in Jiuquan months earlier, being watered at a nearby well. I got the impression that they were as annoyed as they were frightened by the whole situation.

The next morning they were brought before the general, who had requisitioned the best house in Anxi as his quarters. The women were surprised, and unimpressed, by his effeminate and flippant manner. 'He was amiable to us but this was small comfort, for he is notorious for covering savage actions with smooth words.'

While Mildred dressed the general's wounds, he carried out interviews with peasants who had come to beg favours. Sometimes they pleaded for the life of a family member who had displeased the general. The answer was invariably no. The general was afraid of pain, and he asked Mildred if the disinfectant she was preparing for his wounds would hurt. She thought this was ironic, considering that 'before our first interview with him was over, he was giving orders which must have plunged good, honest, hard-working men and women into an abyss of grief.'

The general enjoyed talking to the women, who wondered if they were the only people left in his life who did not flatter him constantly. They were relieved when his wounds healed, and they asked permission to return to Dunhuang.

The women were surprised when permission was granted. The general reminded them that they were still under his control, and gave them a gift. It was a collection of unopened tins of French food, including cheese and pate. The food had been dropped off near Anxi in preparation for explorers on the French Citroen expedition through Xinjiang. General Ma's men had opened a few tins, discovered pork products (and, almost as disgusting to them, cheese), and had not bothered to open any more.

The last time Mildred met with the general she looked him in the eye, gave him a copy of the New Testament in Mandarin, and told him to have a care for his soul. He saluted her, and she left. The women travelled back to Dunhuang without guards, stopping at familiar inns and farmhouses along the way.

When our bus finally reached Dunhuang it had been ten hours since we left Jiuquan. It was a relief to see some greenery and houses, and to smell the faint whiff of sewage in the air that signalled civilisation. It was about six in the evening, and I was ready to eat.

Chapter Ten

Dunhuang

When what is indestructible meets what is irresistible, the female all too often wins.
Monkey Series 1, 'Monkey Swallows the Universe'

There must have been a glut of hotel rooms in Dunhuang. Jack and I followed our map to what the guidebook described as the best-value rooms in town. We went to the reception desk and asked for a room. The sign over the desk said twin rooms were 160 yuan. This seemed like a good price.

'You look first?' the receptionist said. She looked worried. We walked upstairs to see the room, which had cool, tiled floors. We put our bags down proprietarily. 'Very good,' I said.

'OK, we can discount to 70 yuan!' the woman said desperately.

'Oh … very good,' I said. We went downstairs and paid. When we came back up another woman was moving our bags to the next room, which was bigger and had a better view. She smiled and left us alone.

We looked at each other.

'Aren't we hard-arses, we just got a discount and upgrade by …'

'…smiling and looking a bit bewildered and saying "very good"!'

'Do you think if we keep not bargaining they might do our laundry for free?'

We showered and put on clothes that didn't smell of ten hours on a bus through the desert, and we walked out onto one of Dunhuang's main streets, Mingshan Lu. Jack had his heart set on eating the local specialty, donkey meat, but I told him I was sick and steered him into John's Information Cafe, one of a string of backpacker-oriented joints along the Silk Road. The menu was exactly what we imagined it would be, and was remarkably similar to the menus of beachside restaurants for backpackers in India. Banana pancakes, fried rice and French fries were all on offer. We sat in the courtyard and raised our glasses to each other. My rice took a while to arrive, and the beer went straight to my head.

'Why do you want to eat donkey?' I said. 'You always eat the thing that's most likely to make you sick. Remember how sick you got when you ate fish in Delhi? Do you know how far Delhi is from the sea?'

Signs on the walls advertised various tours and services. One message began with the words 'Dear Gusts'. I started to think Chingrish was pretty funny after all.

Not surprisingly, we slept well that night. And in the morning, Jack and I went to Mildred Cable's favourite place in the world.

Dunhuang

On the southeastern edge of Dunhuang, the roads and greenery ended abruptly, and rolling golden sand dunes began. On the far side of the first set of dunes was a temple built next to a crescent-shaped lake.

The first time the Trio visited Dunhuang they climbed the sand dunes in search of the temple.

> We wandered to and fro, looking for some trace of the lake. At every step we sank up to the ankles in the loose, fine sand, but one step more, and there, down at the foot of the hill, as we hoisted ourselves over the last ridge, we saw the lake below us, entrancing, crescent-shaped, sapphire-blue ... like turquoise lying in a fold of opalescent velvet, so deep that its water were said to be unfathomable.

It was Eva, the child of the family, who suggested they should sit and slide down the dunes towards the lake. The three of them took off, bringing the sand rushing down around them. What happened next gave them a surprise: 'as we slid, a loud noise came from the very depths of the hill on which we were, and simultaneously a strong vibration shook the dune as though the strings of some gigantic musical instrument were twanged beneath us.'

When they arrived at the temple the priest said he had heard the thunder of the hills as they approached. Later, they read descriptions of the singing sands of the Gobi in Marco Polo's *Travels*. He said they sounded like 'all kinds of musical instruments'. There are about thirty sand dunes around the world where this phenomena has been reported. Scientists still can't be sure what exactly causes it, but it seems to only happen after a rainstorm, and to sand that has travelled a long way.

Mildred, Eva and Francesca became friendly with the priests at the temple, and over the years they often stayed there when they needed to recuperate and reflect. They lived at the temple guesthouse for some of the time they were trapped in Dunhuang by General Ma's army, and the priests let them hold Christian meetings in the temple grounds. The Trio responded by trying to abide by Buddhist customs while they lived there.

This wasn't always easy. Food became scarce in Dunhuang during the siege, and when they lived at the temple the Trio started to eye the wild pheasants that wandered around the nearby dunes. Those birds looked like easy pickings. They were going to mention this to the head priest, but one day, when they were discussing a farmer who was cruel to his animals, the priest said: 'It is hard to fathom the wickedness of the human heart. You would scarcely believe it, Teachers, but there are people in these farms who would actually kill and eat a wild bird.'

'After that, we did not even allow ourselves to think of roast pheasant,' Mildred wrote.

Jack and I caught a minibus out to the dunes. I told Jack I was going to slide down the singing sands.

I knew the dunes had become a popular spot for Chinese tourists, but I was surprised at just how busy they were. Around the ticket gate, souvenir sellers thrust stuffed toy camels and bottles of water at us. They all seemed desperate to sell us water. They had probably seen plenty of tourists with heat exhaustion.

A high wall was built along the edge of the sands, and we had to pass through a gate and buy a ticket for 80 yuan to get through to the dunes and temple. On the other side of the wall there were more drink stalls, and a herd of honking, harrumphing camels. The camels all had colourful saddles with painted numbers hanging off them. A sign on the wall in English and Chinese told people to take note of their camel's number and make sure not to change camels at any time.

The dunes looked exactly like my *Lawrence of Arabia* fantasies, except that they were crawling with Chinese tourists who were climbing up or sliding down or calling to each other from across the dune-tops. Camel trains were being led around the base of the dunes.

Straight ahead of us, between two dunes, was a concrete-lined pool of water. 'That's not a temple and a crescent lake,' I said to Jack. 'That's new stuff. I'm sure we have to climb over the dunes to reach the temple.'

'Near the top, where the slope was almost perpendicular, exhaustion overcame us and every few steps we sank to the ground,' Mildred wrote. Jack and I started climbing. It was hard to gauge perspective in the sands, and the incline looked gentle at first. But after a while I looked up and saw how tiny the people at the top of the dune appeared to be, and I realised how far there was to go. I was hot and red-faced and could feel my heart beating too fast. Jack strode on ahead, stopping from time to time to shout encouragingly at me.

Near the top I stopped again and looked out across the dunes, and saw the temple and lake below me. They looked almost exactly as they did in the Trio's photographs, only the lake was less than half the size it used to be. It was more like a pond than a lake. It was a dirty green colour.

'Is that it?' Jack said. We looked across and saw that the path we had left to climb the dune led directly between the dunes to the temple. We could have walked straight there without exhausting ourselves. Jack laughed and said the climb was good exercise for me.

We sat on the top of the dune for a long time. As the wind whistled around us, I opened my bag and pulled out a photocopy of a letter from Topsy to Patricia East. The letter was dated February 27, 1993. 'June 1930,' Topsy had written, apropos of nothing. 'Afternoon I went walk three Mamas and Topsy long walk up sand mountain. Pretty crescent warm sand nice drink water. Camel on sand.' Next to this passage Topsy had drawn a picture of the crescent-shaped lake.

Topsy had held onto the image of Mildred's favourite place for decades after Mildred's death. Sitting there, looking down at the temple and lake, I felt as if I should honour both their memories in some way, but I could not think of any appropriate ritual. If I had been a Catholic I might have prayed for their souls. Instead, I put the letter away and turned to Jack.

'I'm going to slide down the dunes just like the Trio did,' I said. I gave Jack my bag, and I sat down at the top of the incline and pushed myself along with my hands. I moved just a few centimetres and sank into the sand. Jack raised his eyebrows.

'I think you probably have to sit on something to slide,' he said. 'Look at those people over there, they're sliding on some kind of toboggan.'

I stood up and brushed the sand off my dress. 'Let's run,' I said. We spread our arms out and hurtled down the dunes in the direction of the temple, towards the camel trains and drink stands.

The temple didn't appear to be in use anymore. There were no priests. All the rooms were either empty or locked, except for a couple of drink stands, some public toilets (I gave them seven out of ten for cleanliness) and a hall where photos of the temple and lake were displayed. The rooms were cool and quiet. Unlike the riotously coloured Tibetan temples, this place had been renovated with plain wood and grey stone and fresh white plaster.

I was sad to see the crescent lake looking like a stagnant puddle. In the final chapter of *The Gobi Desert* Mildred sat by the lake and meditated on the spiritual lessons she had learned in the desert. She questioned why the lake had thrived for so long in spite of the sandstorms that had obliterated whole villages in the area. She drew a spiritual moral from the answer.

> By some mystery of orientation the lake was so placed that every breath which stirred the encircling sand-mounds blew upward and lifted the drift away from the water. I picked up a handful of sand and threw it downward, but the breeze caught it and blew

it back in my face. This, then, was the secret of this exquisite lake's permanence – its exposure to the upward-wafting winds of God, and its deep unfailing source of supply ... every time the sand threatens, the winds of God are there to protect it, and no harm touches it. That is why its peace, its purity and its serenity can never be destroyed. Surely the parable is clear – it is the pure in heart who see God.

We sat on a low wall and looked at the lake, and I read Mildred's parable out loud to Jack. This kind of illustration was familiar to both of us from a lifetime of listening to sermons and Sunday School talks. I could create my own metaphor about God's nature from almost any material you gave me, and slot it into any sermon ('You know, boys and girls, we're all a little bit like that teapot/camel/little boy who wouldn't eat his peas'). It wouldn't make God real.

I didn't say this to Jack. I knew Jack was taking a break from attending church, but I didn't know exactly where he and God were at.

'Mildred's parable's fallen apart a bit, hasn't it,' I said. 'The lake looks kind of crappy.' I wondered if the concrete reservoir we had seen earlier was draining water away from the lake, or if it was there to feed the lake and prevent it from disappearing entirely.

Or maybe Mildred just upset the balance of the place when she took some sand back to England with her.

> Sometimes in my London home I take up a handful of Crescent Lake sand and try to make it sing, but I listen in vain for the echo of the thunder-roll of its voice. Between the leaves of a book I have pressed a small branch of sand-jujube flowers, and whenever I catch its subtle but fading fragrance, I ... long for a place that seems so near and is yet so far away.

We caught a minibus back into Dunhuang. In the centre of town was the usual oversized concrete sculpture, but this one was more attractive and interesting than most. It was a curvy woman standing on one leg and playing a lute behind her head. 'Very rock and roll,' Jack said.

We walked past an Internet cafe, and stopped to email my boyfriend and Jack's wife. Inside, the air-conditioning was turned up high and the soft drinks were almost frozen. They had sold out of Future Lemon, so I tried the icy Future Cola. Jack looked at the bottles and pointed out that all the Future drinks were made by a company called Wahaha.

'Wa ha ha! Wa ha ha!' he said in a horror-movie voice, shaking the bottle at me. In fact, for the rest of the trip he did this every time either of us bought a drink produced by the good people at Wahaha.

Like every other Internet cafe in China, this one was filled with young men playing online games. It was a change from Internet cafes I had visited in India the year before, which were filled with young men downloading pornography. Posters on the wall showed Japanese animated characters with big swords and angular haircuts. I recognized some of them from video games my boyfriend played at home.

I did a search for 'Dunhuang' and 'church'. I didn't expect to find directions straight to the local underground church, but I thought I might find some reference to Christians in the area. I didn't.

What I found was a story about links between religious sites in Dunhuang and in the south of England. The English *Telegraph* newspaper reported that a team of researchers was investigating a distinctive symbol that showed three hares in a circle, joined at the ears. It had been found carved in medieval parish churches in Devon, and was also painted on the walls of 6th-century Buddhist caves outside Dunhuang.

The journalist quoted an archaeologist who said the image must have travelled along the Silk Road from China to the West, and that it must have had a special significance. They were still not sure what the significance was.

The Trio used to wait months, and sometimes years, for the delivery of books and periodicals about the history of the regions they travelled through. I knew I was lucky to live in a time when I could do my research on the road and on the spot.

When we got back to the hotel I unwrapped a new roll of toilet paper. Printed on the wrapper was a map, some Chinese text, and the motif of the three hares, joined at the ears.

That evening we ate at a cheap, simple restaurant with no menu. A signboard outside was all in Chinese except for one item. It said YELLOW NOODLES WITH DONKEY FLESH. That piece of English meant this restaurant had at least one eye on the tourist market, but it looked local enough for Jack.

The woman taking our order did not understand us, and Jack had to take her out into the street and point at the signboard. I ordered pretty much at random and got some noodles with chilli and thinly sliced green things. It reminded me of the kind of meals the Trio ate every day when they were on the road. Their noodles were made on the spot from flour that they ground in Jiuquan, the oil was from the same flask as the oil used for greasing their cart wheels, and the powdered chilli came in twists of paper bought at stalls in oasis towns. The green things were generally some kind of desert herbs that the carter picked up along the road.

Jack's noodles were cold, and they came with a bland vegetable sauce and a side plate of tough, strong-tasting slices of meat. He ate it all, although he wasn't very impressed with the flavour. 'This tastes like ass,' he said, adopting an American accent. He stuck his fork in a piece of donkey meat and held it out for me to try. 'Bite my ass,' he said, determined to repeat his joke until it got a laugh. I took a mouthful. It tasted like boarding-school beef.

That night I heard Jack make at least three trips to the toilet. 'I'm fine, I'm fine,' he said every time he got back into bed.

The next morning there were a couple of crumpled three-hares-brand toilet-paper wrappers on the bathroom floor, but Jack insisted he was well enough to take a day trip to the Mogao caves.

The Mogao caves are the main reason people visit Dunhuang. Unlike the tourists, many of them Japanese, who fly in from the eastern cities to the tiny airport near the caves, we caught a minibus from outside John's Information Cafe. All the other passengers were Chinese men. They wore ties and appeared to know each other. We speculated that they were there on a work trip.

On the outskirts of Dunhuang I saw a man driving a tractor with a tray on the back. On the tray was the skeleton of a freshly killed animal. Bright-red flesh was still stuck to it. At the end of the bones, hanging off the back of the tray, were hooves.

We drove through the desert and past the airport. A young woman with a megaphone sat at the front of the bus and told us about the history of the caves. The Mogao caves are a series of Buddhist temples that were carved into a 1700-metre stretch of sandstone cliff between the 4th and 14th centuries. The caves were decorated with wall paintings and sculptures. Thriving monastic communities were set up here, with artists and calligraphers working alongside the monks and nuns. Rich traders donated new caves, and in return their portraits were included among the wall paintings. Two images of the Buddha, each about 30 metres high, were built into the cliff.

In the 14th century Islam became the dominant religion in the region, and the caves fell out of use. The stairs that linked the caves crumbled away. Pictures of the Buddha had their faces scratched out because Islam forbids the making of images of living creatures. The caves were forgotten for hundreds of years.

At the very end of the 19th century, about the same time that 22-year-old Eva French first reached China, a Taoist Buddhist monk called Wang Yuanlu found the site. He realised its importance, and started to fix it up. He planted trees, cleared sand out of the caves, diverted streams to water the riverbed that ran along the base of the cliff, and built a guesthouse for other monks. He travelled around the region on begging tours, returning with funds for more renovations. In the course of exploring one cave, he discovered a cache of thousands of perfectly preserved scrolls and silk paintings. Unsure what to do with his discovery, he had a door made and locked up the cave.

In 1908 the Hungarian-born explorer Aurel Stein arrived. Stein had heard about the locked cave. He sought out Wang, who was happy to show him around but did not mention the hidden manuscripts. It took a lot of sweet-talking by Stein and his Chinese secretary, Chiang, and the offer of what seemed like a lot of money before Wang agreed to show them the scrolls and let them take some away. Wang decided to trust Stein after learning that they had both chosen the same patron saint – pilgrim Xuan Zang, the priest who brought Buddhist scriptures back from India in the 7th century, and whose journey inspired *Journey to the West* and the legends of Monkey.

In the end, Stein and other European explorers carted off about twenty thousand scrolls containing priceless religious and historic texts in a range of Central Asian languages. Most of them went to European museums and private collectors. Some of them were destroyed in World War II when Allied bombs fell on Berlin.

Wang was paid about 220 British pounds for the scrolls. All the money was used for restoration at the caves. It's not clear whether Wang ever regretted the deals he made.

When the Trio first visited the caves in the late 1920s, Wang was still in charge. The women liked him, and considered him a friend. He invited them to stay in the guesthouse, and they explored the caves in peace. In the evenings they discussed their beliefs. Wang read all the literature the Trio gave him, and he particularly liked John Bunyan's *Pilgrim's Progress*.

Buddhists generally seemed to be very open to the Christian message. This was difficult for the Trio sometimes. A Buddhist would nod and agree with everything they had to say, and would be interested to read more about the life of Jesus. But this was perfectly compatible with remaining a Buddhist. Getting someone to understand the need (as the Trio saw it) to actually renounce Buddhism and embrace Christianity was not so easy.

Today there are some Christians, or at least loosely Christian people who refer to themselves as 'people of faith', who think that some kind of blending of the two faiths adds to them both. In *The Jesus Sutras*, Martin Palmer says the scriptures of the early Chinese church 'united the wisdom and moderation of Taoism and the humanism and compassion of Christianity – the Path of the Buddha and the Way of Jesus'.

But this isn't the way evangelicals think, and it's not the way I was brought up. Even though I had no belief of my own left, something about this all-inclusive faith set my teeth on edge. I didn't like the way modern Westerners treated the faiths of the world as some kind of pick-and-choose, all-you-can-eat buffet. I don't think it would have appealed to the Trio.

The Trio seemed to have made very few converts along the Silk Road, but by this stage they claimed that was not their main aim. They realised how difficult it was to convert Muslims, in particular. They said they were 'planting seeds' by talking to people and giving them books and scriptures to read. They believed that some of the seeds would take root later. They called their methods 'gossiping the gospel'.

Mildred found two images in the Mogao caves that she loved. One was a cherub with folded wings, and the other was a woman with an infant on her lap, a kind of Virgin and Child. She thought these images were signs that there had been a Nestorian Christian influence on the early Buddhist community. She might have been right. Nestorian (or what Martin Palmer calls 'Taoist Christian') scriptures were among the scrolls found in the Library Cave.

The last time the Trio visited the caves, in 1931, they were told that Wang had died. A few days later they received the news that General Ma's army had besieged the Dunhuang oasis, and they hurried back to town to see if their Christian friends were safe.

When we reached the caves we walked past souvenir stands and into a quiet, green garden area. There were no trees here when Wang first arrived. I could see bleached white stupas along the cliff tops in the distances, and I knew one of them must have been Wang's grave.

At the ticket gate Jack and I were rushed through so we could join an English-speaking tour that had already started. We weren't allowed to wander around the caves without a guide. We ran along the tree-lined base of the cliff until we reached the group. The crumbling sandstone cliffs that I had seen in the Trio's pictures had been reinforced with concrete to prevent them from deteriorating further, to protect the wall paintings from sunlight, and to hold up the new walkways that linked the caves.

A young Chinese woman with a perky ponytail was leading the English-speaking group past the Library Cave. It was attached to a much larger cave, where the walls were covered in thousands of identical painted Buddhas. The guide told the story of Abbot Wang and Aurel Stein. I expected she would paint Stein as the villain. I knew the loss of the scrolls had caused a lot of anger in China.

I don't know what the guides tell Chinese tourists, but our guide said Wang's sale to Stein was 'a good thing'. Those are the words she used. She said it gave Wang the money he needed to restore the caves.

The other members of our group nodded in agreement. There were six Americans and a French couple. They were all in their forties or fifties, and they fitted the kind of stereotypes I wouldn't dream of making up. The Americans were overweight, and badly dressed in stretchy knit fabrics. They were very friendly. When we said we were from Australia, one of the women said 'My brother's friend Jim lives in Sydney,' as if we might know him. 'We've been meaning to get down there and see y'all,' she said. I don't think I had ever heard a real-life person say 'y'all' before.

The French couple were lean and tanned and dressed in cool linens. The woman wore a tribal necklace with lumps of amber strung together. They ignored the rest of the group. The only evidence that they were aware of the group's presence was when one of them held up a finger and gave an angry 'shoosh' when anyone talked at the same time as the guide.

We were only allowed to see a few caves. The style of the wall paintings changed from cave to cave. Some looked Indian, while others were like Russian icons.

The guide talked us through some of the stories told in pictures on the wall. One series was about an early incarnation of the Buddha who let a starving tiger eat him in order to save the tiger's life. The pictures of the tiger chomping on the Buddha were pretty gory.

We saw the motif of the three hares, and in another cave the guide pointed out a woman playing the lute behind her head. She said the sculpture in the centre of Dunhuang was based on this image, and had become the symbol of the town.

We followed the guide to the bottom of the cliff and into the cave that housed one of the 30-metre Buddhas. Jack looked a bit grim. I asked if he was all right. He looked at the Buddha's enormous toe. His gritted his teeth and said, softly, 'Toilet'.

'Run,' I said. 'Run like the wind.'

We met up later at the exhibition centre. Most of the displays were copies of scrolls and paintings that had been taken to museums in Europe. Enlarged copies of old photos showed European explorers digging at the caves in the 1910s. I recognised Abbot Wang from a photo I'd seen in a biography of Aurel Stein. He looked wiry and cheerful.

The commentary next to the photos and exhibits was in perfect English. It described who the explorers were, when they visited and what they took away. The tone was politically neutral, although the word 'theft' was used in descriptions of the later American expeditions. I wondered if this was at all influenced by the fact that funding for the exhibition came from Europe. Further up the Silk Road we found explanatory plaques on less famous Buddhist sites that raged in ragged English against thieving Europeans.

Jack and I walked through the gardens and back to the bus. None of the other passengers had returned yet. We climbed up a ridge behind the car park and looked out at the cliffs. They were pockmarked with cave entrances. All around us the desert was rocky and empty. I could see why Mildred was so impressed with the oasis that Wang had created here.

On the way back to town the bus pulled up outside a concrete barn in the countryside. All the men got out and went inside. The woman with the megaphone urged us to go in too. 'It's a mineral exhibition, and you can see it for free,' she said. She sounded very excited.

A sign on the front door said 'Mineral Exhibition'. Just inside, there was a small room where a few polished rocks and crystals sat on shelves. They were dusty and unlabelled. The next door took us into a cavernous hall filled with counters laden with sunglasses and jade jewellery. Each square metre of counter had its own salesgirl. It was most expensive jade I had seen anywhere in China.

'Who'd have thought there'd be a shop in here?' Jack said in mock wonder. The men from our bus tried on sunglasses and posed for each other.

We went back to the bus and waited. From the window we saw an old man walking down the road, muttering to himself. He wore a dirty suit and carried a large piece of raw meat in his hand. When he saw us he smiled and waved the meat at us and shouted something cheerfully.

Jack pulled out his camera.

'I don't know,' I said. 'I think he's saying that this is what's left of the last person who thought he was quaint local colour and tried to take his photo.'

That night we found the central food market, a busy square with tables set up along the street next to a series of stalls where sizzling woks and pans belched clouds of tasty-smelling smoke. Jack stopped at a stall selling mutton pockets. I felt my stomach heave, and I pulled him away.

Fish tanks sat on some of the stalls. The tanks were crowded with writhing fish. Next to the tables were charcoal burners and tins of powdered spices. Occasionally a fish would make a break for freedom and leap out of its tank onto the path, where it would flop about until it was picked up and thrown back into the tank.

Jack's wife, Alex, had emailed him that day, reminding him not to eat fish. She had looked in her atlas and worked out that we were about as far from the coast as you could be anywhere in the world.

The Trio and Topsy, London, 1937 [Hay Wrightson]

Topsy Riding Molly.

Eileen Guy, known to her friends as Topsy, in 1994. She holds a photo of herself with the Trio. [Patricia East]

Topsy in her English garden.

Photos of the young Topsy from Mildred and Francesca's book for children, 'The Story of Topsy'.

The author poses for an ill-conceived publicity shot

Monkey (Sun Wukong) with the demon queen's iron fan, surveying the Flaming Hills outside Turpan

Melon seller, Hami: Cartloads of Hami melons were once sent to the Chinese emperor as a tribute from the Uyghur rulers of Xinjiang

[all pics Jackson James]

Jiayuguan Fort, Xinjiang [Jackson James]

The author atop a sand dune outside Dunhuang, overlooking the temple and crescent lake [Jackson James]

'Remember Delhi,' she wrote. But we decided these must be freshwater fish, perhaps some kind of farmed trout or carp, and if they were alive just minutes before we ate them we were probably safe.

At a stall chosen pretty much at random, we asked a man wearing an apron to cook us a fish. We sat down and watched as he stuck his hand in the tank and pulled out a fish. He hit it on the head with the blunt end of his knife, then flipped the knife around and sliced the fish down the middle. He pulled out the guts and threw them in a bucket, scraped off the scales, and spread the fish on a metal grill that had a long handle. He rubbed spices from each of his tins onto the fish – my guess was chilli, cumin and coriander – and put the grill on the burner. The fish's journey from swimming to grilling had taken little more than a minute. Jack and I applauded, the chef bowed, and the chef's wife giggled. The fish was spicy, and went well with ice-cold beer.

Another stall had a sign that showed a big fat man wearing a Muslim cap and standing with his hands spread in front of the Taj Mahal. The writing on the sign was in an Arabic script. The man did not look Chinese.

The stall was covered in mounds of kebabs, big lumps of meat threaded onto metal skewers. Behind the kebabs was the man whose picture hung above us. He called us over and greeted us as if we were old friends. 'You American?' he said in English. It was the first thing many Uyghur people said to us.

'*Bu shi, Aodaliya*,' I said. The man shook his head. 'No Chinese,' he said. 'I am Uyghur, Kashgari man.'

'We're from Australia,' I said.

'Australia!' he said. 'You like meat!'

We had no choice but to order a plate of kebabs, which were as good as any of the many grilled kebabs we ate along the Silk Road over the next couple of weeks. Jack took a photo of the Kashgari man standing in front of his sign, in the same welcoming pose as his doppelganger. The French couple from the Mogao caves walked past. I waved, but they stared right through us. Jack and I giggled, and I realised how happy I was to have him with me. After weeks alone, I was travelling, just as the Trio had before me, with a trusted companion.

When we left Dunhuang we decided we weren't up to another bumpy ten-hour bus trip through the desert. Instead we took a short minibus ride to the small town of Liuyuan, where we met the Shanghai to Urumqi train. Our destination was the town of Hami, the next stop on the train line, about four hours away. The sky and the desert were both grey, and the view from the train window was flat and featureless in every direction.

On one of their later visits to Dunhuang, after they were caught in the siege of the city, the Trio departed rather more dramatically than we did. When they returned from tending General Ma in Anxi they started plotting how to sneak out of the besieged town. One day in April 1932 they packed the carts and left their rooms strewn with possessions, so it looked as if they had only left for the day. They left mugs on the table and quilts on the kang. The party avoided the main roads and headed straight into the desert. Mildred wrote:

> There seemed but one chance in a hundred that we could get past the border guards, but events proved that the move was accurately timed by One wiser than ourselves, and when we reached the clear cut line where oasis joins desert the Guard was mysteriously absent, we walked past into unsentinelled Gobi, and in due time reached the Turkestan border at Baboon Pass.

This was the short version of the journey that the Trio sent family and friends at home to assure them they were safe. They left out the nights of sleeping under the stars, the struggle to cook in a pit so that the flames of their fire did not attract attention, the threat of quicksand in unfamiliar desert tracts, the poisoned wells and the corpses of soldiers and horses that they stumbled across.

Before they reached the border they were stopped by horsemen, who galloped up behind the cart. The men said they were soldiers of General Ma, and that he had forbidden anyone to travel to Turkestan without a special permit. They demanded to see the permit. The women did not have one, but they counted on the fact that the men were illiterate.

Mildred asked Eva, who was sitting in the cart, to give her their passport. The Central Government passport was a document that all missionaries had to carry. It was impressive looking, with a scarlet seal, but it had nothing to do with General Ma.

The two men fingered the passport, testing the thickness of the paper and the strength of the seal. They decided that such an important document could only have been issued by General Ma, and they saluted the women, letting them pass on.

It took another four days to reach the military post known as Baboon Pass at the border of Turkestan, the province now known as Xinjiang Uyghur Autonomous Region. They didn't know what they might find there, or who would have control of the pass.

Chapter Eleven

Hami

> What is truth, when we lie to ourselves about so much, and know so little? What is the universe made of? How big is it? Is it eternal? Which politics are best for society? Even Pigsy understands that certainty is only another delusion.
> *Monkey* Series 1, 'Truth and the Grey Gloves Devil'

After days of monotonous travel across the Gobi gravel, a change of scenery was usually welcome to the Trio. But they were never too keen to reach the border post at Baboon Pass. It was a forbidding place. Black and grey rocks towered over a ravine where a stream used to run. In 1932, when the Trio arrived there on the run from Dunhuang, it was just a trickle of stagnant water.

The three women had bad memories of Baboon Pass. In 1929 they had been detained there for days before they received permission to pass through. When they questioned the officer in charge about the wait, he sighed. 'I know Westerners well,' he said. 'They are always in a hurry.' The inns were filled with soldiers, so the party had to camp on waste ground, in the middle of flies and rubbish.

When they did get a room, it was the most wretched place they had ever stayed in. There were no doors, and men walked in and out of the Trio's room. When they asked for a bowl of water, the innkeeper shook his head. 'Always washing,' he said. 'These foreign women are extraordinarily clean.'

About a thousand soldiers had been stationed at Baboon Pass in 1929. Some were civilians who had been seized and forced into the army when they tried to cross the border. Their uniforms were the same colour as the granite in the ravine, and the soldiers posted to look out for Muslim rebel soldiers were camouflaged against the rocks.

In the light of all this, it's not surprising that when the women made their escape from Dunhuang, they were relieved to find Baboon Pass deserted. They gave a prayer of thanks and stopped for some brackish water before moving on into Xinjiang, past the granite hills, towards an oasis where they had been cared for in the past. They felt more and more safe. They believed God had been guiding them, and would continue to protect them.

The women travelled through small oasis towns all the way to Turpan. Since they left Dunhuang they had pushed themselves and their mules to the limit. They had eaten nothing but hastily cooked noodles. At an oasis outside Turpan they decided they had to stop.

Mildred recounted in detail the hot bread, lump sugar and new-laid eggs that they ate. Muslim visitors brought them fruit. The local magistrate's wife, a Russian woman, invited the Trio to her house for lunch. She opened a bottle of champagne, but, perhaps in deference to the sensibilities of the missionaries, called it a 'special fruit drink'.

> The puritanical member of our party [presumably Mildred] did not recognise it, never having tasted champagne in her life, and

was only made aware of a lapse from grace by the mischievous look in her comrade's eye; but the smart one of the three [Eva, without a doubt] emptied her glass and accepted more before the label on the bottle came in sight and told its tale.

It was pretty much a given among evangelical Christians of the era (not to mention the Muslims the Trio stayed with) that you did not drink alcohol, and the women were obviously happy to go along with the rules. But they could joke about a 'lapse of grace', and they agreed that being gracious to their hostess was more important than making a show of their righteousness.

When I was very young, and certainly when my parents and grandparents were young, there was a lot of talk among Christians about certain things being 'worldly'. These were things that were not explicitly condemned in the Bible, but Christians shunned them anyway. A marker of having been born again was that you gave up these things. Dancing, smoking, drinking, going to the cinema, listening to 'secular' music, having long hair or short hair (depending on your gender), wearing flared trousers or tapered trousers (depending on the era); these were all at some stage considered worldly. If something was described as worldly it might be fashionable, or unusual, or not quite respectable, or just plain fun.

I always resented these attitudes, even though they were starting to break down while I was growing up. My parents followed the rules themselves, but they made a point of saying they could distinguish between essential Biblical rules and nonessential cultural ones. After I turned eighteen I, in turn, made a point of drinking alcohol, smoking cigarettes and dancing at nightclubs, in the sure knowledge that while my parents might not like it, they couldn't tell me I was going against God's law.

One of reasons I liked the Trio was that they held these cultural strictures lightly. They didn't waste their energy rebelling against them – Francesca, for example, stopped playing cards and going to the theatre when she was converted. But they saw the difference between respectable middle-class Christian culture and the core of their faith, and the core of their faith was the only thing they wanted to impart in China. Behaving respectably by the standards of the people around them was important, but only because they didn't want to offend people or give them a bad impression of Christ's followers.

So Eva enjoyed her champagne, and they all started to breathe easy after weeks of fear. But an escape story wouldn't be complete without a dramatic incident just when everyone thinks the horror is over.

The group travelled overnight into the desert. Early the next day they stopped at an oasis inn and prepared their beds. Mildred went to check that the mules were properly stabled. Later, when Eva walked through the stable yard, she found Mildred lying on her face in the stable muck, unconscious and bleeding profusely from a gash in her forehead. A donkey had kicked her in the head.

There was a rush to help her. One of their carters (whom they always referred to as 'Sir Thomas Cook' because he made all their travel arrangements) ran to interrogate the donkey's owner, who brushed him off, 'merely seeming to view an infidel's head as the legitimate kicking ground for a donkey privileged to belong to one of the faithful'.

Eva and Francesca were horrified. They sat by Mildred's side in the dirty, noisy, fly-ridden inn, trying to get some water down her throat, waiting for her to die. She wasn't young, and they were hundreds of miles away from medical help. The sisters watched for days as their dearest friend drifted in and out of consciousness.

Eva must have been especially frustrated. She had always relied on Mildred to deal with these things. Eva had hated the nursing component of her missionary training in England so much that she had fainted in the hospital one day, and had been excused from completing the unit. Now she had no choice but to help with the nursing.

Finally, Eva and Francesca took the risk of moving Mildred. The whole party relocated to a camp site on the edge of the oasis. They had to sleep in tents, but there was shade and quiet and running water. Muslim friends helped care for Mildred.

After ten days of tears and prayers, Mildred began to recover. There were more tears, and more prayers, and the party finally moved on towards Turpan.

The Shanghai–Urumqi train line passes south of Baboon Pass, so Jack and I had no way of knowing when we had crossed the border from Gansu province into Xinjiang. The desert view didn't change at the border, but the politics did. To pass the time I started telling Jack what I had learned about Xinjiang.

Xinjiang has a history of partial autonomy from Beijing. Until 1932 the hereditary khans, who Mildred called 'the kings of the Gobi', were based in Hami and acted as symbolic leaders for the Muslim Uyghur people of Xinjiang. Uyghurs used to make up the clear majority of Xinjiang's population, but by 2000 the population was about 45% Uyghur and 41% Han. There have been quite deliberate, successful government campaigns to change the ethnic make-up of the region. After all, if Xinjiang is mainly Han there can be no reason for Uyghurs to keep demanding independence from China.

At home I had enjoyed a website called 'The Shanghai Diaries', run by an American journalist called Dan Washburn. He told stories about his travels around China, and I liked the way he mentioned toilet facilities when he described places. I sent him some fan mail and told him about my own travel plans. He put me in touch with his former Chinese teacher, Liu Yi, whose family were Christians from a small village in Shanxi. It was Yi, in turn, who had put me in touch with his friend Paul, who worked at Linfen University, and who had taken me out to Huozhou and helped me find the church the Trio built.

Dan described the relationship between Xinjiang and the Chinese government better than I could. This is how he began his story about travelling in Xinjiang.

> China might as well add 'restive' to its already long and disingenuous name for the Xinjiang Uyghur Autonomous Region. Read a newspaper or magazine story about this vast and mysterious northwestern non-province, and 'restive' will undoubtedly show up somewhere. This makes me chuckle. My dictionary defines autonomous like this: 'not controlled by others; independent' and restive like this: 'difficult to control'.
>
> China-watchers disagree about whether there is still a viable Uyghur separatist movement. The last real signs in Xinjiang came in 1997, when a crowd clashed with military police in Ghulja and three buses were blown up in Urumqi.
>
> Things have been quiet ever since. That hasn't stopped the Chinese government from jailing a lot of Uyghurs in the aftermath of September 11, 2001, under the guise of cracking down on Muslim terrorists. How many people were arrested, how many remain in jail and how many were executed depends on who you listen to. Amnesty International puts the number of people detained since 2001 in the tens of thousands, and there are only eight million or so Uyghurs in Xinjiang.
>
> Uyghur Muslims don't have an easy time in Xinjiang. It's hard to get ahead without being a member of the Communist Party, and for that you have to be an atheist. Nobody under eighteen is allowed to

attend a mosque or receive religious instruction. It's similar to the situation for Buddhists in Tibet, only Xinjiang is not as well known in the West. It has no charismatic equivalent of Richard Gere or the Dalai Lama to champion its cause.

What Xinjiang does have, if I may be so flippant, is some very attractive men. I told Jack that perhaps they needed to produce a sexy fundraising calendar. I pointed out a group of Uyghur men who sat together on the train, across the aisle from us. They looked Eurasian; some of them looked almost Middle Eastern. They were in their late twenties or early thirties, and they looked, well, kind of cool. One of the men had rock'n'roll sideburns. Another wore natty pyjamas covered in dragons. The men passed around something that looked and smelled like a joint.

One of the men strummed a guitar. It was a little out of tune. Sometimes he sang along softly, and at other times the other men joined in. The songs had a melancholy, minor-key, Middle Eastern sound.

Everything about this group, the friendly interaction between them and the casual way they lounged around and sang in public, made them different from the Han Chinese we had met along the way. I told myself that I shouldn't start making assumptions about whole races from the behaviour of a few men. Mildred described Uyghur people as being more emotional and impetuous than the more reserved Chinese, but I was uncomfortable with this kind of generalisation.

The men were laughing and having some kind of friendly argument. The man in the pyjamas picked up the guitar and held it out the window, teasing the guitar player. Then, quite deliberately, he threw the guitar out into the Gobi desert.

'Did you see that?' I said to Jack. 'Did he really just throw a guitar out the window?'

The men sat down and kept laughing and chatting. Soon the guitar player came over and spoke to us. 'Are you American?' he asked.

When Jack said we were Australian the man smiled and said 'You ride good horses in Australia.' He told us he had seen an Australian film that featured impressive animals and riding. His name was Akmed. Like many Uyghur men, he spoke reasonably fluent English.

I had to ask him why the guitar was thrown out the window. He laughed, and waved his hand dismissively. 'Oh, just angry,' he said. I was not sure if his friend was angry, or they were angry at the guitar for being out of tune, or if the explanation was more complicated. It turned out they had been on the train for nearly two days, so perhaps they were all suffering from cabin fever. They couldn't afford to travel by sleeper class, so they had been sitting up since they left Shanghai.

The men were on their way home to Xinjiang after two years in Shanghai. They had been working as musicians and dancers, performing a floor show at a Uyghur restaurant. Akmed said his wife was a dancer. He pointed to a group of women who were sitting together further down the carriage. A young woman waved at us. She had big eyes, and black hair that reached to her waist.

The men were excited about going home. Family members were going to meet them in Urumqi. They were only a few hours away from home, and some of the men were opening plastic packaging and getting out new shirts that they must have bought especially for the homecoming. They took turns going to the bathroom and coming back stripped to the waist, with damp, combed hair.

I wished I was travelling with a female friend, someone I could nudge and exchange looks with.

Akmed asked us if we spoke any Uyghur. We admitted we hadn't yet studied our Central Asian phrasebook, which contained a few Uyghur words, so Akmed gave us a crash course, teaching us a couple of greetings and useful words, including 'brother' and 'sister' so that we could explain our relationship. He made us repeat the phrases back to him a few times, and he wrote them phonetically in capital letters in my notebook.

When the desert gave way to the greenery of the Hami oasis, Jack and I strapped on our packs and said goodbye and thank you in Uyghur.

'Don't just see Urumqi and Kashgar,' Akmed said. 'Big cities are the same everywhere. To see Xinjiang you must see small towns.'

The first couple of times the Trio visited Hami, in the mid to late 1920s, Khan Maksud Shah ruled the region from his carved wooden throne in the Hami palace. He had to pay tribute to the Chinese government, just as his ancestors served the emperor. But he was by all accounts a wise and diplomatic ruler who helped unify and stabilise Xinjiang's Muslims. His chief minister and advisor was a canny man called Yolbas, who was known as the Tiger Prince.

In the 1920s Hami was full of parks and streams, flowers and fruit, and markets crammed with goods and people from all over Central Asia. It was (and still is) particularly famous for its sweet melons. The Trio set up a stall and sold Christian books in the market. Francesca was the chief bookseller, and she claimed to have found the psychological trick to getting books into people's hands. She said you couldn't display the books too carefully, or seem too keen to sell them. Being desperate to sell meant that you wanted to get rid of something. You had to behave as if you didn't care.

While she sat with her casually strewn books, Francesca chatted to Muslim stallholders, who were keen to talk about religion. In conversation with Muslims, the women were often told that Jesus was indeed a great prophet and that the Bible contained many truths. The women were generally accepted because they did not eat pork, they helped the sick and they were seen to live moral lives.

Whenever they visited Hami, the Trio stayed in an inn run by a Muslim family called Ma. The household was run by the elderly Mrs

Ma, who thoroughly approved of the Trio. 'The combination of our grey hairs, celibate state and pilgrim life make a great appeal to her moral ideals,' Mildred wrote.

On one visit, they found Mrs Ma sick in bed but refusing to see a male doctor. Mildred did her best with the drugs she had. The old woman made a complete recovery, and she and her household became even more attached to the Trio. Her eleven-year-old grandson took Mildred aside and confided that his mother and aunts were 'devoid of sense'. He thanked Mildred for saving his grandmother's life, saying that without her control the household would have gone to pieces.

The Trio firmly believed that by befriending women they were gaining access to whole Muslim and Buddhist families in ways that would have been impossible for male missionaries. They thought that women had the real spiritual influence in the household. I had to accept that the Trio had a lot of knowledge about the cultures they lived in. But I wondered if they put too much emphasis on this idea.

The Trio didn't try to convert people to middle-class English morality, but that doesn't mean that their backgrounds didn't influence the way the three women thought. Through the 19th century, British Christianity had become more and more feminised. Angels, which had previously been thought of as masculine or androgynous, became female. It became accepted wisdom that the woman was the spiritual centre of the household. Stories abounded of men who were saved from alcoholism or gambling or other vices by a Good Woman.

This kind of thinking was pretty much dead by the time I was growing up evangelical, but the Trio obviously brought these assumptions with them to China. Whether they were right – whether women had as much influence as they thought, either in England or in China – is harder to tell. When whole families are converted in Bible stories – and these are set in a part of the world not too far removed from the deserts of Central Asia – it is always the man of the house who makes the decision.

The men were certainly in charge in the Hami khan's household. After the Trio shared a meal with the women of his harem, Mildred described the wives as gorgeously dressed in brilliant silks, and utterly ignorant of anything outside the palace walls.

In the harem the Trio were fed fruit and piles of fragrant pilau. Mildred often wrote in detail about food, perhaps because their diet was so monotonous, and she rhapsodised about the sweets and sultanas and nuts.

The Hami women tried to make conversation, asking the Trio about their travels. One woman said, 'You must some time have travelled through women's land where there are no men at all but only women, and also through the country where people are round and have a hole through their bodies like copper cash so that they can be strung together.' This idea became (only slightly) less bizarre to me after I saw old Chinese coins in a museum in Dunhuang. Sure enough, the coins had holes through the middle of them.

The wives also shared palace gossip, including the news that the khan was very weak and would probably not live for much longer.

Mildred was not impressed with the way the women lived, even though she was keen to meet them. 'They were slaves whose invisible cages were none the less fearsome because the prisoners were fed with luxurious food and wore delicate silken robes,' she wrote.

All the same, there was an allure to royal life. In June 1930 the Tiger Prince Yolbas turned up at the Ma inn and invited the Trio and Topsy to holiday in the khan's summer palace. They jumped at the chance. An escort travelled the 30 miles out to the palace with them. The khan put out a proclamation that they were his honoured guests, and it was posted along the road to the palace. It turned out to be the last document to which he affixed his royal seal.

The palace was set on an estate full of flowers and fruit trees. Servants were there to cook their food and do their bidding. The gardens were a series of enclosures connected by low doors in high walls, and Mildred wrote that they felt like Alice in Wonderland. They explored and picked fruit. In the evenings, dancing girls performed for them. The missionaries then sang hymns, or what the servants and dancing girls called 'pilgrim songs'.

The Trio even did something that sounds suspiciously like skinny-dipping:

> The whole of this earthly paradise was watered by one rushing torrent tumbling down from the snow hills behind the pink granite rocks, and each afternoon three stealthy missionaries leapt into its invigorating waters, and all the bathless days were forgotten in the joys of its riotous cascades.

Eight days after the Trio arrived at the palace, they were woken by a messenger who galloped into the grounds. 'The khan is dead,' he called. All the men left immediately for Hami, to join the mourning ceremonies. The women weren't sure what to do.

It would be weeks before the Chinese government officially dismantled the khanate and imprisoned the khan's son Nazir in Urumqi. But people could see what was coming, and anyone with a lawless bent took advantage of the intervening time when it was not clear who had the authority. Within days of the khan's death, bandits turned up at the summer palace and set up camp alongside the Trio.

'Our cook had the real villager's attitude towards bandits, and, as he could not run away from them, he prepared to treat them like the most honoured guests,' Mildred wrote. The women invited the bandits to join in prayers in the morning, and Eva preached about the parable of the prodigal son. The bandits had disappeared the next day (sermons have that affect on me, too) and the Trio took the chance to hitch up the mules and head back towards Jiuquan. On the way home Eva came down with cholera. As they did later with Mildred's donkey-kick injury, they found a quiet camping spot to nurse her.

> When next we saw Camul [Hami], the heir to the Khan's throne was a prisoner, his town residence was demolished, and the Summer Palace had been burnt to the ground ... The ladies of the court no longer wore emerald silk but dressed in the blue cotton of the ordinary peasant women, and were thankful to hide themselves among the common people and to forget they had ever been princesses.

The instrumental version of Kool and the Gang's 'Cherish' was playing in the lobby at the Hami Trade Hotel when we arrived.

Our room was exactly the same as all the other rooms we had stayed in, only the surfaces were shinier, and the price reflected that. In the bathroom, boxes printed with the hotel's name contained individual soaps, toothbrushes and shower caps. I belatedly realised that stealing a toothbrush from every hotel I stayed in would have helped me keep track of all the hotel names.

Jack and I walked out into the streets in the evening. It was eight o'clock according to the clocks in the hotel lobby, and our watches, but it felt like mid-afternoon. Xinjiang officially runs on Beijing time, in spite of being two time zones behind Beijing geographically.

In every Chinese town I had visited, signs and notices had been in Chinese script, and sometimes in English. In Hami, everything was in both Chinese and Uyghur, which was written using an Arabic script. We saw hardly any English. The exception was the signage at the Dicos fried-chicken restaurant.

Weeks earlier, when I visited Patricia East in Munich, she told me that the Uyghur language was not related to Arabic but was in fact closer to Turkish. For a few years, Xinjiang schools had taught Uyghur children to read and write using the roman alphabet, but the authorities had enforced a change back to the Arabic script. Perhaps the government didn't like the fact that learning the roman alphabet gave Uyghur people an advantage in learning English.

Uyghur is a notoriously difficult language to learn. The Trio struggled to speak it, and never became fluent.

> A few colloquialisms gain us the credit of being better speakers than we are, and where we are ungrammatical in our use of the many thousand declensions (which needless to say we mostly are, especially in the difficult Double Compound Presumptive and Hearsay Perfect!) the bystanders readily put us right.

The Trio's nearest missionary neighbour, George Hunter of Urumqi, spent nearly fifty years learning the language, compiling a Uyghur grammar and dictionary and translating the Bible into Uyghur. He didn't go out much, nor did he gain many converts.

Apart from the Uyghur signs, central Hami looked much like any other Chinese town, with the requisite ugly central sculpture and dirty concrete shops and buildings and small market areas and hundreds of busy people on bicycles. In one of the market arcades I saw bright-coloured batik and velvet dresses with sparkly trims. The Uyghur women typically wore looser, more modest skirts and sleeves than the Han women, but the clothes were colourful and distinctive. I thought about the glamorous women of the Hami harem. They wore headscarves, but not the hijab that covers all the hair and neck.

I didn't see the hijab, let alone the all-enveloping burka, anywhere in China.

An elderly Uyghur man with a long beard approached Jack and clasped both his hands. Jack greeted him with one of Akmed's phrases, 'Yakhshimu siz'. The man responded, then he gestured to Jack's beard. 'Musulman?' he asked. 'Kristiyan,' Jack said. The man nodded and walked on. This happened a few times over the next couple of weeks. Jack's beard, and perhaps my loose Indian clothes and headscarf, seemed to suggest to people that we were Muslims.

As we kept walking we saw people setting up outdoor eating areas on the wide footpaths in front of shops and restaurants. Alongside the chairs and tables were huge charcoal-burning stoves on wheels. They were the grand-daddies of the little stoves the Dunhuang stallholders used for cooking fish. A whole row of cooks could stand behind one of these monsters. They had intricate metalwork roofs with arches and crescent designs. They looked like steaming steel mosques on wheels.

Piles of kebabs were built up on tables next to the cookers. Some restaurants had what looked like old oil drums set up next to the tables. We walked over and looked inside a drum. The young cook laughed and encouraged us to take a peek. Coals glowed at the bottom. The inside was lined with clay, and discs of bread were stuck to the walls. It was just like a north Indian tandoor oven.

Once the cooking started, all the restaurateurs started shouting at us to come and eat at their place. Sometimes they yelled in English, sometimes in Uyghur. Others just made hissing and whooping noises to attract our attention.

We ordered food at the biggest charcoal cooker, where seven young men cooked kebabs at the same time, hamming it up for Jack's camera without missing a turn. The kebabs were, of course, delicious. None of the Muslim stalls sold alcohol, so on the way back to the hotel we stopped in at a Han-run grocery store and bought a bottle of beer to drink while we played Scrabble in our hotel room. The beer brand was one we hadn't seen before, and the label had a picture of cucumbers on it. I thought the beer tasted a little bit like cucumber. Which, surprisingly, isn't a bad thing. I thrashed Jack by using all my letters to put SHIRTING on a triple word.

The next morning we set out down Zhongshan Road, heading for the Muslim quarter and the tombs of the Uyghur khans. I carried an out-of-date map from an out-of-print book. As usual, I had a bottle of water and *The Gobi Desert* in my bag.

We followed the road south. We expected to find what the Trio and more recent Silk Road travellers found – a maze of adobe mud houses, markets and a general air of lively chaos. Instead, we walked into a shimmering clean block that looked like a modern Islamic city. We could have been in Riyadh. Only there were almost no people here.

On either side of the wide streets were rows of identical buildings joined together and painted in pastel colours. They had vaguely Arabic architectural touches like arched windows. The upstairs windows weren't curtained, and we could see that the rooms were empty. The ground floors were mostly shops, but most of these were empty too. There were no grocery stores. One store sold sequin-covered wedding dresses. Another sold what looked like ornamental varnished tree stumps. There were no customers in the shops.

It looked very much as if the old Muslim quarter had been razed and a new one erected. The people who used to live here had either rejected it or couldn't afford to live in it. There was nobody there to ask what had happened. There was no bustle. When Jack stood in the middle of the road to take a photo, there was no traffic to run him down.

A white sculpture in a bone-dry fountain sat in the middle of the new block. The sky was vivid blue, the air was hot and still, and the fountain threw off a glare. The sculpture depicted a ring of stylised Uyghur figures who were probably supposed to be dancing, but they looked as if they were goose-stepping. A toddler and a toothless old woman in a headscarf sat by the sculpture. A lone cyclist rode down the middle of the street.

I still don't know when and why Hami's Muslim quarter was transformed. But the more I read, and the more I queried people, the more I realised this kind of thing was not unusual. Historic neighbourhoods were being knocked down all over China. Authorities said they were improving hygiene and living standards for residents, but people displaced from their houses could not always afford to live in the new buildings.

A few weeks later, an English expat in Shanghai told me he had started to dread returning to his favourite historic sites around the country. Too many of them had disappeared in just the few years he had been in China. 'It's all about officials getting kickbacks from building contractors,' he said.

Jack and I kept walking south. The new neighbourhood ended abruptly and life started again, almost immediately. We walked along an unmade path, past vegetable stalls and mud-brick houses and men who were chatting and smoking. We asked directions to the tombs, and were sent across a main road to more backstreets. We walked past a meat stall where a bloody hoof hung on a string out the front.

Eventually we found the ticket gate for the tombs of the khans. The Uyghur woman at the booth seemed to be having a nap behind her window. It was that kind of day. We tapped on the window and she started and slid the window open. She gave us a glossy ticket with Chinese and Uyghur text on it. The only English phrase, printed across pictures of the tombs, stated: 'The Race Greatness Creates Human Civilization Treasure'.

We thanked the woman in Uyghur, which made her smile in surprise. She left the booth and called the gardener over and spoke to him, gesturing at us. Even when it became clear that we couldn't say much else in Uyghur, she patted our shoulders in a friendly way.

Historic sites in China tend to have very formal, sculpted gardens around them. But the garden around the tombs had not been so severely tended, and it contained shady trees and long grass and twisting vines of hardy flowers. There were no other visitors there.

The most striking building on the grounds was the main tomb. It was a cube, covered in painted tiles, with a domed green roof. Inside, the tombs were plain white, roughly coffin-shaped and huddled close together, filling the whole floor space. Most of the tombs were draped with bright-coloured rugs. We had seen the rugs being sold at stalls in Hami the previous evening. Small signs were placed on some of the tombs, with the name of the dead khan in English, Uyghur and Chinese. Maksud Shah was among them.

The caretaker, a wrinkled man wearing a panama hat, appeared at the door and gestured for us to follow him. He took us to a newer building next to the mosque and unlocked the door. A collection of robes worn by the khans hung against the wall. At the end of the room was the wooden throne of Maksud Shah.

I recognised the throne straight away. There was a photo of it in *The Gobi Desert*. I pulled out the book and showed the picture to the caretaker. He didn't seem surprised. He just said 'ah' and pointed me towards a framed magazine article hanging on the wall.

The heading on the article was 'Mildred Cable Tour in Hami'. The rest of the text was in Mandarin. Next to the text were reproductions of photos from *The Gobi Desert*, including the picture of the throne. The magazine appeared to be some kind of Xinjiang tourism publication.

We walked outside and around to the mosque. The inside walls were painted with calligraphy and floral designs. A forest of slim, dark-red wooden pillars held up the roof. Shafts of sunlight shone in, and a family of swallows flew through, weaving between the pillars.

The mosque was only used occasionally for special ceremonies, and was empty most of the year. But it still felt like a living, breathing space rather than a museum.

I looked up at the wooden ceiling, and told Jack that some places felt empty even when they were full of people. The Forbidden City in Beijing and Hagia Sofia in Istanbul were two of the deadest places I had ever visited, in spite of the crowds.

'But this place is still alive,' I said.

'There was lots of really cool scaffolding inside Hagia Sofia,' Jack said, after a pause. I sighed.

Outside I looked up at the green minaret of the mosque, topped with a crescent. Behind it, a block or so away and mirroring the shape of the minaret, was an industrial crane. The red communist flag, with its hammer and sickle, fluttered from the top.

While we were sitting on a bench under a tree, the caretaker approached us with the gardener and another young man, and indicated that they wanted to look at *The Gobi Desert*. The three men sat on the bench next to us and looked at the photos, reading the captions out loud phonetically and commenting to each other.

When they reached the picture of General Ma, the men shook their heads sadly. The caretaker held the book away at arm's length, as if he didn't want to be too close to the general. When they turned the page and saw a picture of Yolbas, the khan's chief minister, the men smiled. 'Ah, Yolbas, Yolbas,' they said, as if they had unexpectedly met an old and treasured friend.

Neither man spoke any English. We communicated that we were Australian, brother and sister, and no, we weren't Muslim. The caretaker pointed to Jack's beard, which was fast becoming the main focus of every conversation we had. Jack asked how to say 'beard' in

Uyghur, and he was very pleased with the answer: *saqal*. 'I'm so cool with my *saqal*,' he said.

When we left the grounds the three men and the ticket seller stood by the gates and waved us off on our hot walk back to the hotel. When we got back we packed our bags. We were about to catch a train across the desert to Daheyan, the nearest station to the oasis of Turpan, and then a bus on to Turpan. I knew Turpan was the hottest place in China, and that it was famous for its large and poisonous insects. Extreme heat and spiders being among my least favourite things in the world, I was a little nervous.

Chapter Twelve

Turpan

> Yet even silence cannot make a wise man out of a fool, wherever he travels.
>
> *Monkey* Series 1, 'Monkey meets the Demon Digger'

Easter 1930. On the evening before Good Friday, the strongest wind since the turn of the century swept across the Gobi. The Trio and their party were staying at an isolated inn in the desert between Hami and Turpan. They heard a strange howl, then a shower of small stones fell around them. The walls of the inn shuddered and the full force of the wind hit them.

Nobody could sleep that night. At about midnight, Mildred became convinced that the mules were in danger. She called the carters, who unwillingly struggled across the courtyard to the stables with her. They led the mules out into the courtyard, and within moments the beams and rafters of the stable collapsed.

Three rooms were blown down, and all the people and animals at the inn ended up huddling in one room. Window openings became unblocked, and layers of sand and dried stable manure were blown over all their belongings. The women were just relieved that everyone survived. Over the next few days they met travellers who recounted stories of horses and sacks of grain being lifted from the ground and blown away into the desert.

Our trip from Hami to Turpan was a tad less thrilling. Our train journey from Hami to Daheyan was a single leg of the epic Shanghai to Urumqi line, and all around us, bleary-eyed passengers wearing creased clothes had been in the same seats for two days. None of them looked out of the window. They already knew what rocky, flat desert looked like.

Late in the morning Jack and I got off the train in Daheyan, about 50 kilometres from Turpan, and caught a bus that travelled over a grey gravel plain for about an hour. The sky was wide and almost the same grey as the desert. The view was identical in every direction. We bumped along on the rocks, along the side of what looked like an asphalt road that had crumbled apart or been washed away in a flood. Pebbles pinged against the underside of the bus.

Jack was watching the driver, who wore mirrored sunglasses and drove with only one hand, or sometimes with his knees. The driver pulled a pile of business cards out of his shirt pocket and looked through them until he found the one he wanted. Then he made a call on his mobile phone. The rattle of the bus made it difficult to hear what he was saying.

'He's talking about us,' Jack said.

When we reached the outskirts of Turpan the bus pulled over at the side of the road to pick up a Uyghur man. The man hadn't signalled to the driver. He was tall and plump and wore polished shoes and a gold chain. He nodded to the driver, than sat down next to us.

'Where are you from?' he said, in English.

Jack told him. 'Good to meet you,' he said, shaking Jack's hand. 'I am Mamet. Where are you staying?'

Jack said we were going to the Jiaotong Hotel. Mamet tut-tutted and shook his head. 'Very noisy,' he said. 'If you like, I'll take you to a better place, very clean, very quiet, very good price for you.'

'We want to be in the centre of town, near the market,' I said.

'This is very centre of town, near to everything,' Mamet said. 'Come and look, if you don't like I'll drive you to the Jiaotong.' He shouted something to the bus driver.

Five minutes later the bus pulled over in front of a gleaming white new building. It didn't feel like the centre of town. Mamet hustled us off the bus. Nobody else got out.

The rooms at Mamet's hotel were clean and the price was reasonable. 'Where's the market?' I asked. Mamet pointed out the window to an empty block of land across the street. 'Special market sets up there at night,' he said. I showed him my map of Turpan and asked him to show me where we were. It turned out we were very close to the edge of the map, and a long way from anything else.

We told Mamet that his hotel was very nice but we wanted to stay in the town centre. He remained as friendly as ever and insisted on driving us to the Jiaotong. We got into the car and Mamet turned on the tape player. A familiar tune started playing. It was Kylie Minogue's 'I Just Can't Get You out of My Head'. The lyrics weren't sung in English, but the line that went 'la la lah, la la la-la lah' was easy enough to translate.

'Listen Jack, it's our Kylie in Chinese!' I said.

'No, no, not Chinese,' Mamet said proudly. 'This is a Uyghur song.'

Mamet was very keen for us to book a spot on his minibus tour of the sights of Turpan. 'You will go on my tour tomorrow,' he said. When we said we wanted to spend the next day looking around but might do a tour the day after that, he said 'OK, but you do my tour.'

The Jiaotong was more expensive than Mamet's hotel, and it had a stuffy smell, but it was directly opposite the market, on a busy street. Outside the hotel were stalls on wheels, covered in piles of melons and elaborately twisted bread.

Mamet spoke to the receptionist. He told us he had negotiated a cheaper price for us. Then he shook Jack's hand and said 'You will come on my tour tomorrow. There, we have shaken on it, so we've made a deal that can't be broken.'

Our room smelled of smoke, but the air-conditioning worked well. 'Hottest place in China,' I said to Jack, not for the first time, or the last.

Mildred Cable claimed temperatures had reached more than 50 degrees centigrade when the Trio passed through the Turpan basin. As well as being the hottest place in China, it is also the second-lowest place on earth, after the Dead Sea, at 155 metres below sea level.

Before the arrival of air-conditioning it took a lot of ingenuity to live comfortably in Turpan. For the Uyghur people in the villages surrounding Turpan, it still does. Mildred described their thick mudbrick walls, deep verandas and cool underground rooms. She said the streets were kept shaded by trellises covered in grape vines that stretched from one side of the road to the other.

Grapes are still big business in Turpan, mainly because the climate is ideal for drying them; if Hami is famous for its melons, Turpan is best known for its raisins. It's also well known for its insects. I read out to Jack the list of creepy things we might encounter, according to *The Gobi Desert*. They included:

* [a] jumping spider with long legs and a hairy body as large as a pigeon's egg [that] leaps on its prey and makes a crunching noise with its jaws;

* another [spider that] burrows holes in the ground, and its bite is as painful as that of a scorpion;
* cockroaches ... over two inches in length, with long feelers and red eyes which make them a repulsive sight; and
* large and virulent scorpions which creep under sleeping-mats, drop on to the unconscious sleeper from the beams or hide themselves in his shoes.

I had also heard more-recent reports of insect sightings. Patricia East had told me about fat ticks she had brushed off her skin in the desert west of Turpan. Her Uyghur guide said people who were bitten by them would suffer fever and madness. He had mimed it for her, with his head lolling, his tongue hanging out and his eyes rolling back.

Jack and I sat quietly for a moment. We decided we needed a drink. We both checked our shoes carefully before we left.

We really needed that drink by the end of the walk. The air was bone dry as well as hot. We ended up at the Turpan branch of John's Information Cafe, down a sidestreet that seemed to function as a de facto driveway for the large Turpan Hotel complex. It was one of the few streets we saw in Turpan where vine-covered trellises still shaded the road. An old Uyghur man drove a donkey cart down the street.

The cafe was in a courtyard with a thatched roof hung with plastic grape vines. As we drank cold beer and ate 'Kashgar Pizza' – hard circles of bread strewn with sesame seeds, and piled with spicy vegetables – young Uyghur men at the next table played cards and drank Cokes. When we had finished eating one of the men approached us. 'May I sit?' he asked. He waited until we said yes before pulling up a chair.

The man introduced himself as Akbar, and he asked if we were interested in doing a minibus tour. He said it would cost 50 yuan, which was the same price as Mamet's tour.

We told him we would think about it. 'OK, thanks for listen,' he said, getting up and returning to his table. His whole style couldn't have been more different from Mamet's pushy patter.

Which is why it is so embarrassing to admit what happened when we returned to our hotel in the evening, after visiting the market. Mamet was in the lobby, talking to some Chinese tourists. He charged over. 'You come on my tour *tomorrow*,' he said, taking Jack's hand. Jack and I looked at each other. Neither of us is very good at saying no to people, and after our long day, it just seemed easier to give in. 'OK,' Jack said. 'We'll do your tour tomorrow.'

Like other markets throughout China, Turpan market had piles of fruit and vegetables and rounds of bread and freshly slaughtered hanging meats; it also had mounds of sultanas and what looked like figs, and fabric stalls selling bolts of a distinctive silk with a tie-dyed design. The women behind the stalls wore long, loose dresses made from the silk, and gauzy headscarves. Flesh-coloured stockings were sold at shops and stands and, from what I could see of their ankles, most of the Uyghur women wore them, in spite of the heat.

I wasn't the only person looking at the Uyghur womens' legs. Jack said the women were beautiful, with their thick eyebrows and amber-coloured eyes and rosy cheeks. 'Mmm, pretty ladies,' he said, mimicking Pigsy from *Monkey*, who indiscriminately chased anything in a skirt. Pigsy even licked his lips when the priest Tripitaka disguised himself as a woman.

We walked around the cooked-food section of the market, which was dominated by kebab stands. The charcoal burners were like the ones we had seen in Hami, but many of them also had an enormous wok that was full of rice mixed up with meat and grated carrot and spices. 'Pilau, pilau,' the stallholders called, gesturing to the rice.

One of the stalls had a crowd around it, so Jack and I climbed some stairs a few metres away to see what was being sold. It appeared to be some kind of natural-medicine stand. Leaves, roots, nuts and powders were laid out in boxes in front of a man who was obviously spruiking the wondrous properties of his wares.

Next to some leaves was a pile of dried-out lizards. Jack pointed them out. 'What do you think the lizards are for?' he said.

'Lizard on a stick,' I said.

I explained. There was a scene in the director's cut of *Conan the Barbarian* where Arnold Schwarzenegger, as the eponymous Conan, went to a marketplace not unlike this one, where the only food for sale was barbecued lizard on a stick. 'Lizard on a stick,' the seller repeated, and finally Arnie was seen walking away, taking bites out of his lizard on a stick.

Most of the men gathered around the stall wore the distinctive Muslim skullcap, known as a doppa, which seemed to be specific to Turpan. The caps were embroidered in shades of grey, and the patterns reminded me more than anything of the intricate dot-work of Australian Aboriginal paintings.

Back at the hotel, I re-read the Turpan chapter of *The Gobi Desert*. Mildred's description of the Turpan market showed that little had changed in the past eighty-odd years. She mentioned rolls of tie-dyed fabric, and embroidered skullcaps, and piles of dried fruit and freshly baked bread.

> The favourite dish of the Turki, however, is pilau, which is made in a large cauldron from the fattest of the mutton, cut small and cooked with rice, chopped carrots and seedless raisins. There is always a seller of pilau in the market.

'Listen Jack,' I said. He was watching CCTV9. Local and foreign experts were talking about the economic benefits China would gain from hosting the Beijing Olympics. I threw my tube of Vegemite at him and read aloud some of Mildred's comments:

> The Turfan herbalist displays a remarkable selection of Central Asian drugs, including gentian, nux vomica, fennel, cardamom, liquorice root, saffron, ginger, rhubarb, cinnamon, camphor, digitalis, oak-apples, capsicum, aniseed, coriander seed, pomegranate bark, asafoetida, dried poppy-heads, seeds of the castor-oil plant, valerian, juniper, sesame, pine-kernels, stramonium, hyoscyamus, strophanthus and camel-thorn sugar. These and many other drugs are laid out in open wooden boxes.

'She doesn't mention lizards,' Jack said.
'No, but she devotes a couple of pages to melons.'
I put the book down and opened the window. There was some kind of ruckus outside. On the street, next to one of the melon carts, a fight was in progress. A man and a woman were shouting at each other. The woman was bigger than the man, and she wore lots of make-up. She was hitting the man with her handbag. He was slapping at her like a girl. A crowd was gathering around them, shouting and egging them on. I shut the window again, mainly to take the strain off the air-conditioning.

Jack changed the channel to a local station that was screening what appeared to be a soap opera about a Uyghur family. A young man left the family home and his aged parents. A montage showed him getting ahead in the big city. In the next scene he returned home, wearing a shiny new suit and having grown a bushy moustache. He clasped the hands of his aged parents, but they did not embrace him because they were in awe of his newfound sophistication. His siblings looked at him suspiciously.

The young man took a package out of his bag. The camera zoomed in on the package, which was emblazoned with the words

'Aram Nutritional Powder'. He mixed the powder into two glasses of water and gave them to his parents. They drank down the mixture, and looked at their son with pride. One of the siblings smiled and the tension was broken. The aged mother hugged her son, and everyone cheered.

We had arranged to meet Mamet outside the hotel at 8.30 the next morning. At about eight we stepped out the front door, planning to buy some breakfast in the market, but Mamet was waiting and he pushed us straight into his bus. He shook his head as if disappointed that we were late. A Chinese man was sitting in front of us. The rest of the bus was empty.

Mamet asked us for our money quietly, gesturing with his head towards the Chinese man and holding a finger to his lips, indicating that we shouldn't tell the man what a good deal we had been given. Considering all the other tour operators charged the same bog-standard price of 50 yuan, I suspect the Chinese man got exactly the same deal that we did.

We sat on the stationary bus for about an hour. From time to time Mamet wandered back to the doorway for a chat. Another fist fight broke out on the footpath. Mamet said they were fighting about melons.

Two young Israeli guys got on the bus. Mamet consulted with the bus driver, before telling us the rest of the group had slept in and the bus would take us to our first stop, then come back for the stragglers. With that, the bus started up and drove through the shady backstreets to the Emin mosque.

The mudbrick mosque was built in 1777. It was simple and geometric, all sharp lines and corners, with no colours or decoration. It was the antithesis of the complicated, curly, multicoloured Tibetan temples. The mosque was overshadowed by its rounded minaret. Pictures of the minaret appear on all the tourist literature for the Turpan oasis.

The mosque and minaret looked exactly as they did in the Trio's photos, apart from the satellite dish on the roof. They were still surrounded by fields of grape vines. I pulled out *The Gobi Desert* to show Jack the old photos, and the Israeli men asked me about the book. I said it was by some early travellers to the region.

One of the men said he was reading *From Heaven Lake*, Vikram Seth's account of his overland trip from Xinjiang to India.

'Oh, we both loved that,' I said. Jack and I often exchanged books about India, just as we often bought each other banana chips and curried peanuts, or lapsed into Indian English when teasing each other.

The man raised his eyebrows. 'Really,' he said. 'I think it's quite immature and shallow. You can tell it's his first book.'

That sort of ended the conversation. I thought about the joyful passage near the end of the book where Seth has almost reached India and seems to be hurtling through the countryside, running down the hills towards his home. That evening, Jack told me he had also thought about that passage; we discovered we had both welled up with tears when Seth described how unexpectedly moved he was by the Indian sights – 'water buffalo; trucks copiously ornamented with religious symbols and hopelessly overloaded with wordly goods; bands of red chillies spread out to dry on the ground and on the rooftops' – that were so familiar to us, too.

When the bus turned up to collect us from the mosque, every seat was full. Mamet had obviously overbooked. The Israeli men muttered to each other, but Jack and I confronted Mamet, who had just got out of a following car. 'Look here, we've all paid for this tour and there aren't enough seats for us,' I said. 'What are you going to do about it?'

I could hear myself using an officious memsahib tone. I sounded like the missionary women in India when they haggled with rickshaw-wallahs or scolded lazy domestics. I hated myself for using that voice. But it did the job. Mamet sighed and shook his head, 'OK, you go in the car, still pay the same price.'

A Japanese couple were sitting in the back of the car. I squeezed in next to them, and Jack sat next to the driver. The couple had probably paid a lot of money to have an air-conditioned car to themselves, but they were more gracious than I would have been about having to make room for two large and sweaty strangers.

The driver's name was Omar. It didn't take long for Omar and Jack to work out which English, Uyghur and Chinese words they could both understand. It wasn't a long list, but they cheerfully communicated as much as they could. Omar drove us through brown, dusty countryside that looked like central Australia.

On the plains we saw mudbrick buildings where every second brick was missing. We asked Omar what they were for, and he conveyed that they were for drying grapes. The hot wind blew straight through the lattice of bricks, but the grapes were kept out of direct sunlight.

Omar took us to two ruined Buddhist cities, Jiaohe and Goachang. They were both founded around the 7th century and had been deserted since about the 14th century. They had been so worn down by treasure-hunters and tourists that they were little more than widespread sandy mounds in the desert. We wandered about, keeping a wary eye out for jumping spiders. We could just make out walls and archways.

Albert von Le Coq was one of the first explorers here. In 1906 he found a wall painting at Gaochang that he took home to Berlin, and he identified the figures in the painting as members of the Manichaean sect. Manichaeanism combined Christian, Buddhist and Zoroastrian beliefs, with a central tenet that the universe and each person in it had a dual nature, with light and darkness always fighting for control. Others have since interpreted the scene as more straightforwardly Christian, with a priest serving communion bread and wine to Uyghur and Chinese believers. The truth might be somewhere in between.

To most Uyghurs in Xinjiang today, the words Uyghur and Muslim are almost interchangeable. But the Uyghurs had a Christian phase from around the 8th to the 12th centuries that seems to have mixed Nestorianism, Manichaeanism and a few other 'isms' for good measure. At least one historian thinks the presence of these Turkic Christians in China might have fed the persistent belief in Europe that there was an undiscovered Asian Christian empire in the far east, ruled by the mythical Prester John.

'Prester who?' Jack said when I started talking about this. I couldn't blame him for never having heard of Prester John. You don't hear a lot about him in history classes, mainly because he never existed. From about the 12th century, European writers placed him variously in Mongolia, Ethiopia and India, describing him as the king of a vast Christian empire that survived among the Muslims and heathen of the rest of the Orient, or Africa, or India (all much the same thing to Europeans of the Middle Ages).

Jack and I walked through Gaochang. When Aurel Stein explored Gaochang in 1914 he identified temples, monasteries and tombs, but there's little to see of these now. In the 1920s the Trio saw farmers knocking down buildings with pickaxes and scraping frescoes off the walls to use on their fields, as the pigments were supposed to make good fertiliser. Mildred described how they camped overnight at Gaochang. They watched local women sifting through the ruins to find useable items like pots but ignoring the more ornamental relics.

We walked as far as we could in the heat, determined to get our entry fee's worth. The sky was huge and cloudless. We sat in the shade under an archway and drank some water, which was warm by now. Other people who had obviously rested in the same spot had left their empty Coke bottles on the ground. They were the only relics we saw.

It didn't matter how much water we drank. Our mouths felt dry all the time. Not for the first time, I thought about the Trio's long trips through the desert, when they had to carry all their water and hope that none of the wells along the way had dried up. Dying of thirst would have been a real possibility. I hadn't really grasped what an extraordinarily harsh place the desert must have been for travellers in the days before telephones and cars and air-conditioning. If you didn't plan ahead properly, you were stuffed. If nobody in your party knew the roads well enough and a sandstorm covered the path, you could wander in circles until you died.

The next stop was the Bezeklik caves. It was like a small version of the Mogao caves outside Dunhuang. Caves had been carved into the side of a gorge in the barren hills outside Turpan. Buddhist murals had been painted onto clay plastered on the cave walls, but most of the caves were empty now, because explorers had sawed the frescoes off the walls and taken them back to Europe. Rectangular slabs of mural were missing from all the caves. The place looked vandalised.

In each cave, plaques in Chinese and English described the pictures that had once been there, and stated which explorer had taken them. Words like 'looted', 'theft' and 'stolen' were used. Most of the signs mentioned Albert von Le Coq, with a few dishonourable mentions to Aurel Stein.

To get to the caves, Omar had driven us through a range of shimmering red mountains known as the Flaming Hills. Mildred wrote about them: 'The denuded sandstone and bare conglomerate is furrowed with narrow gullies. In hot weather the rays of the sun, striking on their barrenness, makes the whole hillside quiver as though it were licked by rising flames.'

I had seen an unrealistic version of these hills bursting into flames in an episode of *Monkey*. Monkey and his fellow pilgrims reached a range of literal hills of fire that they could not pass. A demon queen had set the hills aflame, and the only way to put them out was with the queen's magic fan. The queen would not give up her fan, for complicated reasons to do with her bitterness over her estranged husband, a water-buffalo spirit who had left her for a demanding bimbo called Jade Face. It was up to Monkey, Pigsy and Sandy to reunite the couple. This involved, among many other plot twists, Monkey turning himself into a magic strawberry, and Pigsy trying to seduce Jade Face but forgetting to hide his pig ears.

This turned out to be one of the best-known stories in Asia. It is one of the longest stories in *Journey to the West*. There have been many film, television and cartoon versions of the story, where the queen is known as Princess Iron Fan and her husband is the Ox King. Some versions of the story have Monkey burning his bottom in his attempt to cross the hills, which explains why monkeys have red bottoms.

The popularity of the story goes some way towards explaining the excitement of the Japanese couple when we reached the Bezeklik caves. At the edge of the car park, away from the ticket office and the stairs down to the caves, was a modern, life-sized statue of Monkey, Pigsy, Sandy and Tripitaka. Monkey carried a fan.

The Japanese couple pointed at the statue as we drove into the car park. 'Son Goku!' the woman said. 'Sun Wukong!' Omar said. 'Monkey!' I said. When we stopped, the couple jumped out of the car and ran towards the statue. They took a whole series of photos of each other in front of Monkey. The wife giggled and posed. They were still at it when Jack and I came back from the caves. They didn't bother looking at the caves. They were just here for Monkey.

Mamet had promised that we would see a karez on our tour. Each karez is part of an ingenious system of underground irrigation channels that carry melting snow from the mountains down to the plains around Turpan. Built hundreds of years ago, they are still the only reason that Turpan's crops survive the heat.

'Standing at a height and looking over the Turfan plain, a traveller will see long lines of earth-works on the barren glacis which give the impression of mounds flung up by gigantic moles,' Mildred wrote. It looks the same today. The mounds are shafts that lead down into the channels so that maintenance work can be done on the karez.

I expected to be shown a hole in the ground, but we drove back in the direction of the town, and down some leafy side streets. Omar pulled up outside a walled property with a ticket gate and the usual souvenir stands. This was Karez Paradise. Inside, multilingual signs and dioramas using repurposed shop mannequins showed us how the karez system was built. Uyghur women in faux-traditional costumes and sparkly headpieces wandered around offering to be photographed with tourists, for a fee. They looked pretty grumpy, which I would have been too, wearing layers of satin in the heat. In fact, I was in much the same mood as the dressed-up Uyghurs. I was so hot that my head hurt, and I was annoyed about having to pay a hefty entrance fee to see a tricked-up theme-park version of something I knew I could have seen for free out on the plains below the Flaming Hills.

Signs and arrows led us underground, where the relief from the heat was instant. We walked alongside a water channel where cutaways and diagrams showed how the system worked.

When we reached the surface, the path led us through gardens and past a long row of souvenir stands that sold Uyghur costumes and booklets about Karez Paradise. The stallholders all called out to us. 'Just look, come here, *you come here!* Come here *now*!' I knew I should just keep walking, or laugh good-naturedly, but the heat and the heckling and being treated like a wallet on legs suddenly felt like more than I could take. I held my hands in front of my face and ran back to the ticket gate.

Jack kept walking. When he reached the gate he shook his head at me. 'All you did was make them laugh at you,' he said. He was annoyed. 'It's just how they make a living, they weren't hurting you.'

'I know,' I said.

We sat quietly for a moment, then Jack pulled a bottle out of his bag. 'I bought you some Future Lemon,' he said. We shared the drink while we waited for the Japanese couple.

When Omar drove us back to town, Mamet was waiting at the hotel. 'Good tour, wasn't it?' he said as soon as we got out of the car. Jack and I had taken a liking to Omar, so we made a deal with Mamet for Omar to take us out the next day. I was keen to see a village outside of Turpan called Tuyoq. Mildred had described it in detail, and had compared it to Tuscany.

According to Mildred, the Muslim shrine at Tuyoq had some unorthodox rituals associated with it. When a young boy was taken there for the first time he was swung back and forth in front of a deep cave inside the shrine, after which he was deliberately pulled back, his forehead was spat on, and blessings were chanted over him. The cave itself was said to house seven men and a dog who had been sleeping for hundreds of years, waiting for all the world to repent and turn to Allah.

I asked Mamet if he had heard of the story and the ritual. 'Oh yes, that's right,' he said. I was almost certain he had no idea what I was talking about.

Jack and I ate fresh noodles at one of the market stalls, where we watched the cook kneading and stretching the dough strings in exactly the way Mildred had described, and we decided that, having done the tourist bus tour, we should add cultural insult to injury and check out the nightly Uyghur dance show held in the courtyard at the Turpan Hotel.

On the way, we stopped at an Internet cafe. One email was from my boyfriend, who said he was taping episodes of the new *Doctor Who* for me. Another was from my mother, who had just received photos of the Dunhuang sand dunes from Jack. 'I couldn't help thinking of a song I've turned to in time of discouragement and dryness – "Let me find you in the desert, 'til these sands are holy ground",' she wrote. 'Did you find the desert promoted reflection?'

I felt a twinge that was either guilt, or irritation, or guilt about feeling irritated, or irritation at myself for feeling guilty, and I decided not to reply straight away.

I looked at the website of Melbourne's *Age* newspaper. The main headlines were about the defection of two Chinese diplomats to Australia, and their claim that there was a Chinese spy network in Australia. I clicked on the links to read the full stories, but each time the link did not work. I tried clicking on some other, unrelated stories, and the links worked fine.

I imagined that the Australian government would be embarrassed by the defection. When it came to China, the Australian government had always been more concerned about trade than human-rights abuses.

I went to the BBC's news page for the Asia-Pacific region. One headline stated: 'Chinese defector accuses Australia'. Underneath the headline was written: 'A fugitive Chinese diplomat says Australian officials refused his asylum request without an interview'. The links to this full story were also broken.

I had been advised that some websites were blocked in China. But from what I could see, even specific stories that might reflect badly on the Chinese government were being targeted. I couldn't imagine how much work would go into screening and censoring news sites from around the world. No doubt it was all automated, but I pictured huge halls with rows and rows of men sitting at computers, tapping keys to sever links.

I wondered if Australia really was crawling with Chinese spies. James and Ange, the English teachers in Xi'an, said that when they visited their London church they did not talk about their Christian activities in China, in case there were spies in the congregation who would report back to Xi'an. They only spoke to small groups of trusted friends who met in people's homes.

When I went to the Chinese embassy in Melbourne to collect my visa, protesters from the Falun Gong sect, which is outlawed in China, approached me. An old woman handed me a leaflet about the mistreatment of Falun Gong practitioners in China, and I thanked her in Chinese. I proudly mentioned this encounter to my Mandarin teacher, Tracey.

'You didn't take the leaflet, did you?' she asked. She said she had heard that the protesters were always being watched. Tracey didn't say who was watching. If you accepted a leaflet, Tracey said, it could cause trouble for you.

I had made a worried face.

'It's probably OK for foreigners,' she said.

Nobody had interrogated me so far.

On the way from the Internet cafe to the Turpan Hotel we passed John's Information Cafe and decided to stop for a drink. Akbar and his friends were at the same table as before, playing cards. As soon as we sat down, Akbar came over to us.

'I hope you enjoyed your tour today… *with Mamet*,' he said. He sounded sour.

'News travels fast around here,' I said.

'Yes,' he said. Jack and I looked at our drinks. Akbar let us feel guilty for a moment.

'So, you want to go somewhere else?' he said brightly. 'Maybe you know about the beautiful village Tuyoq, with grape vines ...'

I said we had already organised to go to Tuyoq the next day.

'With Mamet?' Akbar asked. He shook his head sadly when I nodded, and he turned to go.

'But maybe you can help me with something that Mamet didn't know about,' I said.

Akbar smiled and sat down with us. I pulled out *The Gobi Desert* and explained that it was written by English women who had been to Tuyoq in the 1920s. I wondered if he knew about rituals held at the Tuyoq shrine that were described in the book.

'English women? No,' he said. I said I was sure. He said 'No, there was one Stein and one Le Coq, that's all.'

I showed him the publication date and the photos of Turpan and Tuyoq. He started turning the pages, then he called his friends over, and they slowly looked at all the photos. He recognised places and knew all their alternative names. He was fascinated.

When Akbar turned the page and saw the photo of General Ma, he immediately punched hard at the book and made a pained noise. He obviously recognised him; he wouldn't have had time to read the caption. He looked at me and said 'If this was my book ...' and made to punch it again.

'Why do you hate him?' I asked.

'He came in saying "Follow me, I am Muslim too," but he kills Muslims and invites the Russians in.' Akbar turned to the picture of the Hami khan's advisor, Yolbas. Like the Uyghur men in Hami, he laughed in recognition. He showed Yolbas to his friends, who all smiled.

Another picture showed an ancient-looking tower in the oasis of Sirkup. Akbar looked confused and slowly pronounced the name in the caption. 'Oh, Sirkup!' he said. 'This is all gone now, destroyed.'

'In the Cultural Revolution?' I asked. He nodded. Like other people I spoke to in China, he didn't seem to want to refer directly to the Cultural Revolution. They just called it 'that time'.

Akbar really wanted to buy the book from me. It was the only copy of the Virago edition I had ever found, and I was reluctant to let it go. I explained that it was precious to me, and I copied out all the details for him in the hope that he might be able to find a copy online. I apologised, but said I had to keep this book.

Akbar nodded. 'I understand,' he said. 'I always say I will give anything to my friends except my wife and my books.'

We parted with friendly handshakes and an exchange of email addresses. Akbar didn't laugh at us going to the touristy dance show. 'They're good dancers,' he said.

Down the road at the Turpan Hotel, benches were lined up in the courtyard in front of a backdrop painted with grapevines and the Emin mosque. A small band of Uyghur men wearing matching embroidered shirts were tuning their instruments. The audience was almost entirely made up of middle-aged to elderly tourists from Germany, America and Japan. Most of the male tourists wore brand-new embroidered doppa caps. Some of them looked self-conscious, and kept adjusting the caps. A couple of the women wore sequined headpieces over their grey perms.

The show started just before dusk. Music played from speakers on either side of the backdrop. The music was crackly and distorted, and it occasionally skipped, like an old record. The live band played along with the recorded music, almost inaudibly.

A pretty girl swished out in front of us. She wore a sparkly, swirly yellow dress and lots of make-up, which was a feat in the heat. She carried a microphone and blatantly mimed to the recorded music while five other girls in the same costumes danced around her. This went on for about six more songs. The audience cheered enthusiastically after every song.

Sometimes the girls were joined by two men in pink satin outfits. The men wore high leather boots that were decorated with gold paint, just like Monkey's. The dance steps seemed to combine the graceful hand and head movements of Asian dance with more vigorous spinning and kicking that looked Russian. Even the music seemed to be caught somewhere between Moscow and the deserts of north India.

The recorded music was turned off for the final song, and the live band played alone, which was a big improvement. The dance seemed to be about seduction. The two men performed increasingly elaborate dancing feats to try to win over the girl in the swishiest dress. Then they started dragging up men from the audience, encouraging them to dance for the woman. The tourists looked as if they were having fun, but I felt embarrassed for them. It was like watching my parents dance.

Jack and I were both hot and tired. The dance went on and on, and the female tourists started dancing too. One of them wiggled up against one of the pink-satin Uyghur men. 'I would kill every person in this courtyard for a drop of sweet beer,' Jack said.

Omar drove us through the Flaming Hills again the next morning. There was no plant life, only gravel at the sides of the road. We drove along the top of a steep gorge, and eventually we rounded a corner and saw a patch of vivid green in the distance, below us. This was the vineyard village of Tuyoq.

A car park and ticket office had been built on the edge of the village. The car park was empty. A Chinese woman sold us tickets to enter Tuyoq for 30 yuan each. Clearly the village was some kind of tourist attraction, but we seemed to be the only visitors there.

The dirt roads through the village were just wide enough for the small tractors that we saw parked outside houses. Everything was quiet. The houses were all made from crumbling mud bricks and looked about a million years old; they leaned over the laneways at crazy angles. There was greenery everywhere. A stream gushed through the village. The few people we passed ignored us. Ancient bed frames sat under the trees outside the houses; on some of the beds, old Uyghur men reclined and smoked.

We saw a camel tethered in front of a house. It was very thin. Its hump was bony and its fur was threadbare. The camel glared at us as if it really, really hated us. Jack took its photo.

I felt as if I was wandering through somebody's backyard. 'I hope the locals don't resent people traipsing through and gawking at their camels,' I said. We kept walking around the winding paths until the houses gave way to fields of grape vines. Mildred said Tuyoq was like Tuscany, although I was not sure she had ever actually been there, and I suspect it had changed a lot less than Tuscany had since the 1920s. The paths through the vines were shady, and I could hear the hum of insects. It had been a long time since I had been anywhere this quiet. China had been full of distorted music and raised voices and badly tuned engines. Jack and I walked in silence for a long time.

From the grape fields we could see across to the bare hillside at the other end of the village. Shrines with domed roofs were built into the side of the hill. The top dome was the biggest, and was covered in glazed green tiles. I assumed this was the Muslim shrine the Trio had visited.

We walked back through the village. At the bottom of the hill a Uyghur woman stopped us and indicated that we had to buy another ticket to walk up to the shrine. She pulled a wad of battered-looking tickets out of somewhere in her voluminous skirts. We shrugged and gave her ten yuan.

Every rock and post and pillar on the way up the hill had offering scarves tied around it, like I had seen at Buddhist sacred sites. In *The*

Gobi Desert Mildred wrote that Buddhist customs had grown up around this Muslim shrine. When we reached the green-domed building an old man waved us away from the door. He wasn't unfriendly. He was just explaining that we shouldn't be there. 'Fair enough,' I said to Jack. We moved away and looked out over the village.

On the way down the hill we passed a group of Chinese men walking up. They wore suits and mirrored sunglasses, and they talked loudly. One of the men was shouting into a mobile phone.

'You're worried about people resenting you, but I reckon they'd resent the Chinese tourists just as much,' Jack said. It didn't make me feel much better.

Omar was waiting at the car. He looked at his watch and said something about food. We weren't sure what he meant, but we nodded. We drove back over the Flaming Hills and down a dirt road to another, less photogenic village. Omar manoeuvred the car down a narrow, dusty alleyway and parked. We were at Omar's house. He told us not to tell Mamet.

A girl who looked about nine years old, with a short dress and skinny legs, ran to hug Omar. A toddler ran after her and hung onto Omar's trousers. I'd never seen children more excited to see their dad. He laughed, and tickled and teased them, then he called us into a big, bare room with a raised platform and low table.

A woman wearing a headscarf and loose dress nodded to us and brought us big bowls of tea. She had a gold tooth and dangling earrings. Later, Jack and I argued over whether this was Omar's wife or his mother. Jack thought she was much older than Omar, but I thought she just wore matronly clothes and had spent too much time in the Turpan sun without the benefit of a good moisturiser.

We sat cross-legged around the table. Omar's daughter sat in his lap and giggled at us. Omar's wife, or possibly mother, laid out plates of sultanas and melon slices. She gave us some bread that was as hard as rock. Omar laughed when I tried to eat it, and showed me how to crumble it into my tea and pick it out with chopsticks. Considering how little we could communicate, the whole meal was remarkably relaxed. I don't think we committed any major *faux pas*.

The family lined up to wave when we drove away. I think they were waving to Omar rather than to us. We might have been a bit of a novelty, but he was the man they adored.

On the way back to Turpan we asked if we could see a real karez. 'Not Karez Paradise,' I said. Omar pulled over in the middle of the rocky plain, with the Flaming Hills behind us, and walked us to a hole in the ground. That's all it was. But when he dropped a stone in the hole, it was seconds before we heard a splash. The waterways were a long, long way down.

***

When we returned to Turpan and got back to our hotel room, Jack realised he had left his hat in the car. He has lost his hat all over the world, and he has always got it back again. Once it went halfway across Turkey and back on a bus without him. In Kyrgyzstan he stayed with a family who spoke almost no English. The son spoke entirely in movie quotes, and he called Jack 'Indiana Jones' because of the hat. When they went horse riding and the wind blew the hat off Jack's head, the son rode off to retrieve it. 'I'll be back!' he had shouted as he galloped away.

Jack rang Mamet, who rang Omar. Jack looked out the window and waited for Omar. When he saw him he laughed and told me to look. Omar was sauntering across the street, wearing Jack's Indiana Jones hat. He looked very pleased with himself.

'He's pretending to be Australian,' Jack said. 'It's just like the scene in *Fawlty Towers* where Manuel pretends to be Basil.' Jack said he could imagine Omar wearing the hat and making his friends laugh by saying 'Hello, I am Australian! Hey you! Drive me here! Drive me there! I think I'm so good because I have lots of money!'

While I was packing my bag the next day, just before we caught the bus to Urumqi, I saw a little brown cockroach scurry across the wall. Later, when we were back in the desert and I was watching the Uyghur Kylie Minogue dancing on a television screen at the front of the bus, I realised the cockroach was the only insect I had seen in Turpan.

Chapter Thirteen

The Mountain of God

> Well has it been said by the ancient sages that of all the ways
> to clarity, the shortest is the way you choose for yourself.
> *Monkey* Series 2, 'Who Am I?'

Mildred Cable nearly lost her nose in Urumqi.
    The Trio stayed with CIM missionary George Hunter in Urumqi, the capital of Xinjiang province, from November 1929 to February 1930, and they had never experienced such cold weather. They had to start checking their extremities for frostbite. One day Mildred was crossing a windy courtyard in the snow when a man called out to her: 'Your nose, Madame. Rub it quickly with the snow.'
    The cold must have damaged the skin so much that it had started to darken. She was lucky she didn't end up looking like Michael Jackson; any longer and the nerve endings in her nose would have been permanently damaged and the flesh would have decayed. 'A

drastic rubbing brought the circulation back and not till then would a kind and experienced Siberian woman allow her into a warm room,' the Trio's newsletter said. 'There some vodka was produced, the outward application of which completed the cure without internal treatment.'

Their host would have been horrified at the use of vodka, inside or out. George Hunter was a secretive and highly conservative old Scottish crank who had intentionally chosen the most far-flung part of China to base himself. He was sent by the CIM, but, much like the Trio, he ran his own show.

Hunter wouldn't reveal how many converts he had made, partly through fear that he and the Lord would both look bad if the converts backslid at all. He refused to baptise women or speak with Catholics or celebrate Christmas ('Christ *Mass*!'). When a visiting missionary produced a game of draughts one evening, Hunter shouted 'Do you think I am here to play games?' Another young missionary unpacked a football, but hastily repacked it after experiencing what Mildred called 'withering displeasure' from Hunter.

Hunter believed in an absolutely literal interpretation of every word of the Bible. Mildred gave a good example of why she thought this was a pity. Jesus said that it was easier for a camel to go through the eye of a needle than for a rich man to enter the kingdom of God. Some scholars believe 'camel' is a mistranslation of the word for 'rope', while others think 'needle' was a term for a small opening in a city wall. But George Hunter insisted on preaching about this parable in literal terms, in towns where people often saw camels being stopped at small gates to have their loads removed before they could squeeze through. Mildred wrote:

> If handled a little differently, what an appealing lesson could have been drawn from the word of the Master, but instead the

realistically-minded Chinese would often go out from the service shaking their heads in amazement at the doctrine they heard.

The women were fully aware of Hunter's odd nature. They made it clear in the biography they wrote about him after he died.

George Hunter, from first to last, was reckoned by his fellow missionaries to be a difficult man to live with. He knew no compromise in matters of what he was pleased to call 'principle,' but which others viewed as merely his personal outlook on life ... The young men who, as missionaries, were expected to live in unbroken peace and harmony found George Hunter a difficult member, and it was not a matter of unmixed sorrow when he packed his sleeping-bag and started on some long trek.

And that's the opinion of his *friends*.

In spite of all this, the women respected Hunter, and could see a softer side to him. Mildred may have identified with him because, like her, he had come to China with a broken heart. His childhood sweetheart died before they could be married, and he mourned her for a long time. The one time he returned to Scotland he laid a heart-shaped rock on her unmarked grave.

The first time the Trio visited Hunter, he rode out to meet them in the desert, wearing his usual homespun Chinese clothes. He gave their carter directions to his house in Urumqi, and disappeared again. When the Trio reached his compound he was standing at the doorway wearing a suit, turned-down collar and tie, felt hat and shiny shoes. He believed this was the only appropriate attire in which to receive English women to his home.

You can imagine Eva suppressing laughter, but the women were gracious, and they appreciated the effort he went to. 'The whole episode was charming, as was also the courtly manner in which he bade us welcome to Urumchi,' Mildred wrote.

After Hunter spent a few years alone in Urumqi, an earnest, cheerful young missionary called Percy Mather had joined him. Mather seems to have had the knack of getting along with Hunter, who became very attached to him, although to the last they always addressed each other as 'Mr Hunter' and 'Mr Mather'. When the Trio visited in late 1929 they persuaded the overworked Mather to come back to England with them for a holiday, and he joined them in travelling across Russia and through Europe by train. (The train trip was a thrill for Topsy. She and Eva were caught sneaking off to the dining car together to eat cream cake for breakfast.)

The women were extremely fond of Percy Mather. Mildred and Francesca eventually wrote his biography, as well as Hunter's. Mather died young, in May 1933, from typhoid he contracted when he looked after hundreds of patients at Urumqi's public hospital during an epidemic. A grief-stricken George Hunter built a wall around Mather's grave to keep the wolves away.

The taxi drivers at the Urumqi bus station were the most hard-nosed operators we met in China. None of them would use their meters, and they all asked for at least twenty yuan to take us to our hotel. Two different drivers called to us across the car park, claiming they would use their meter, but after we walked over and took our packs off, they changed their minds and refused. Both times, all the other drivers roared with laughter.

'Let's get out of here,' Jack said. His face was red. We left the car park and walked up the street, while the taxi drivers hooted and slapped their sides behind us.

Further up the street a Uyghur man with a rickety-looking green truck offered to take us for 15 yuan. I gave in, and threw my pack on the back of the truck. Jack said I was too soft, and that I should have held out for five yuan. He was up for a fight after being mocked by the taxi drivers.

Our driver spoke only Russian and Uyghur, so we had about ten words in common. He asked us questions in Russian. I don't think he believed that we couldn't understand him. In the end Jack started randomly answering '*nyet*' and '*da*', which amused the driver no end. '*Da! Nyet!*' he shouted in response, banging on the steering wheel.

I looked out at Urumqi. I had expected it to be a dump, based on the reports of the Trio.

> The town has no beauty, no style, no dignity and no architectural interest. The climate is violent, exaggerated, and at no season pleasant ... The summer heat is even worse than the winter cold [this from a woman who nearly lost her nose to Urumqi's cold], and the dirty, dusty roadways are filled with jaded, unhealthy-looking people.

From our fume-belching truck, Urumqi looked very much like a standard, busy Chinese city, with high-rise buildings and wide streets and green parks. It looked more pleasant than the average town, in fact, and was less stiflingly hot than Turpan. Certainly it had no architectural interest, but that was hardly unusual in China.

We had chosen our hotel pretty much entirely for its name: Peafowl Mansions. 'Foul pee,' we giggled to each other. When we reached the hotel it turned out to be disappointingly nondescript looking, just another high-rise with a shiny lobby. We were assigned a room on the eighth floor, and we got into the elevator. The elevator stopped at the third floor, and the door opened.

Quite unexpectedly, there seemed to be a nightclub on the third floor. We could see through to a dark room with flashing lights and thumping techno music. Han women wearing matching sexy red dresses stood by the door and turned on us with wide, forced smiles. The elevator doors closed again.

Jack and I looked at each other. It was a slightly surreal moment.

The next day we tried to find the Uyghur quarter. Either the layout of the city had changed dramatically within the past year or so, or the map was completely crap. We walked a long way, snatching the map from each other and becoming increasingly hot and snappy. Eventually we happened upon an area that turned out to have gone the same way as the Muslim quarter of Hami.

Apparently the authorities in Urumqi had knocked down most of the old Uyghur market a few years earlier. There was now a Chinese-run, Uyghur-themed tourist trap called Erdaoqiao Market, a building that stretched for a whole block and was filled with stalls piled with overpriced souvenirs and staffed by desperate people who shouted as we walked past. Some of them actually grabbed at us, so eager were they for us to buy sequined hats and curved knives and synthetic pashmina shawls.

In the evening, more by luck than by virtue of having a useable map, we found the block of streets where Urumqi's night food market sets up. We were walking along a main road, just before eight o'clock, when we crossed a sidestreet that was crammed with people pushing charcoal burners and stalls on wheels. They were lined up like horses at a starting gate, ready to run across the street to the market area and get their food stalls going. It was clear that they weren't allowed to cross the street yet.

We waited to see what would happen. At eight on the dot some kind of signal was given, and they were off. They all rushed across in a crowd, jockeying for position, smoke spewing from burners that had already been lit. Cars and buses and donkey carts kept trying to cross against the stalls. The potential for a huge variety of horrible accidents was enormous.

The Mountain of God

Before too long a pall of chilli-flavoured smoke hung over the streets, burning our eyes. We put up with it, because we had to look at everything on offer. Anything that could be skewered had a metal stick through it. There was mutton, of course, and small birds, tripe, liver, fish, prawns and things we couldn't possibly identify. We saw huge bowls full of intestines, and whole roast sheep with the curly-horned skulls sitting on top. Chilli and snails bubbled together in pots, and little crustaceans climbed out of their containers and escaped into other dishes.

Neither of us braved the snails. We sat at a wobbly plastic table and ate skewered meats and drank cold beer. The streets buzzed with a mix of Uyghurs and Han, and probably Kazakhs as well, all of whom seemed to be getting along fine in the shared pursuits of cooking and eating well. Jack and I raised our plastic beer cups together and smiled at each other, blinking back tears brought on by the chilli smoke.

This would have been a nice place to end the Tales of Travels with my Brother, but we had made a last-minute decision to take one more trip together. Instead of going to Kashgar, Jack was going to accompany me to Heaven Lake, a couple of hours east of Urumqi.

As far as I can tell, the Trio skirted the foothills nearby, but never actually made it up to Heaven Lake itself. They wrote about it with awe, however, relaying the rumours they had heard about the beauty of the mountains. It seems to have been off-limits for most travellers in their day.

> Towering above Urumchi is the matchless snowy peak of the Bogdo-Ola, Mount of God. Its lower slopes are clothed with pine forests and carpeted with wild flowers and mountain strawberries, and in its recesses it hides rushing torrents, quiet lakes and dashing waterfalls. There could be no more perfect place for a summer resort, but a personal permit must be obtained from the

Governor by anyone who wishes to go there, and it is therefore only accessible to the favoured few, while the people of Urumchi have to endure the damp stuffy heat of the town all through the summer.

These days, nomadic Kazakh people pitch their big round tent-like yurts in the mountains around Heaven Lake. Guidebooks and websites mentioned a man called Rashit who took in paying visitors. I hoped to find him up there somewhere.

The aim of my journey, inasmuch as I had one, was to see what the Trio had seen, but right from the start I had been drawn to Heaven Lake, a place they had never visited. I imagined that following missionaries across China would make me reflect on my own beliefs. Heaven Lake, under the Mountain of God, sounded like an appropriate place to come to some kind of resolution about my relationship to the faith I had been born into. Both my mother and my publisher had warmed to this suggestion.

Now I confided to Jack that there might be nothing for me to reflect on. I liked the Trio, and I thought their defense of Christianity – and the way they lived it – was pretty admirable. But they hadn't influenced me into a spiritual awakening. I held a cold beer bottle against my hot cheek for a moment, and I tried to explain how I felt to Jack.

'You know how some gay people talk about coming out? How it became impossible to live a lie anymore, even though telling the truth was going to upset their families? It's just about the huge relief of being true to who you are,' I said. 'I used to think that sounded kind of cheesy. But now I get it, because that's exactly how I felt about not being a Christian anymore. I mean, I weighed up all kinds of intellectual arguments for and against, and there are plenty of good ones either way, but in the end it went beyond that. I just wasn't a believer.'

'How do you know what's right and wrong then?' Jack asked. I knew he wasn't criticising me. He was just standing in for my father and playing devil's advocate. 'What would you say if someone asked you where you got your morals from?'

I said I had decided that morals and religious belief could be separate issues, and that morals could be formed by something as basic as just having empathy for other people. I told him about the kind hotel manager in Zhangye and the music-shop woman who gave me tea when I fell down the sewer in Jiuquan. I didn't think they had helped me just because Jesus or Mohammed or Buddha had instructed them to be kind to strangers. 'I muddle through and try not to hurt anyone,' I said. 'I'm not saying that's what everyone should do. But I can't seem to do anything else.'

'So you're not thinking of converting to Buddhism then?' he said. I knew he was joking.

'Hell no,' I said. Even though I had turned out to be more like a hippy than a missionary, I didn't share the average hippy's belief that Buddhism or Hinduism were inherently better, or even more interesting, than Christianity. They all asked you to make an illogical leap of faith and then do as you were told.

Jack paid the kebab man and we walked back to the hotel in the dusk, our stomachs distended. The weather was neither violent nor exaggerated, and everyone around us looked pretty healthy and happy.

Eating out in Urumqi has not always been such a pleasant experience. The Trio recounted stories of meals that turned out to be memorable for reasons unconnected to the quality of the food. The first took place in 1927, when the governor of Turkestan held a banquet in Urumqi and invited a number of men he suspected of plotting against him. After the first drinks were served, Governor Wang left the hall and returned with a soldier.

> He stood behind the chair of one of the instigators of the plot and had him beheaded on the spot, then repeated the action and another conspirator fell dead, after which he resumed his seat, and the ghastly meal proceeded to its close.

Another version of this story has the second victim ducking away from the sword and being only wounded. He is supposed to have run bleeding from the hall with the soldier in pursuit. The rest of the guests sat in horrified silence, listening to the man's screams when the soldier caught up with him. Governor Wang urged them to enjoy the rest of the meal.

Strangely enough, the Trio liked Governor Wang. Mildred said he was stately and dignified. He told the Trio he thought the education of women was essential for China, and he suggested that they could help him set up a women's education program in Urumqi.

It wasn't to be. By the next time the Trio visited Urumqi, karma had caught up with Governor Wang at the second awkward banquet. In 1928 he attended a graduation ceremony that was followed by a feast. The governor's disgruntled Minister of Foreign Affairs, a man called Fan, disguised some of his supporters as students, and one of them shot Governor Wang dead in the middle of the meal.

Mildred claimed that a Chinese proverb was being bandied about the Urumqi bazaars in the weeks before the second banquet: 'He who murders at a feast, at a feast shall his blood be shed.' Those Chinese have some pretty specific proverbs.

Before we went to Heaven Lake, Jack and I put our packs away in the left-luggage room at Peafowl Mansions. Anyone who has carted all their possessions around on their back for months knows the thrill of leaving their pack behind and going away with just an overnight bag.

We ate piles of dumplings for breakfast, at a tiny hole in the wall that seemed to serve nothing else. Then we followed our map across main streets and through shop-filled underpasses to the People's Park. The sun was warm and golden, and Urumqi glowed.

Minibuses were lined up outside the park. All the drivers said they were going to Tian Chi, the Chinese name for Heaven Lake. I started to wonder how busy it would be at the lake, and whether I would be able to reflect on anything at all above the noise of day-tripping Chinese tourists. Jack and I bought a ticket and sat on a bench while our bus filled up. We could hear waltz music playing inside the park. We looked through the railings and saw middle-aged couples ballroom dancing on a raised concrete platform. The dancers looked graceful and serene.

The bus took us through city blocks, then into the shabbier outskirts of town, past motorbike mechanics and toilet-fittings suppliers and lumber yards. Then everything just trailed off, as it did outside every oasis town, into the flat expanse of the Gobi desert, where there is nothing but sand and gravel in every direction.

In the Gobi you're pretty much as far as you can be from the ocean, but there are theories that the desert used to be an inland sea. Mildred wrote about seeing fish fossils and coral remains that explorers from a Swedish expedition found in the desert near Urumqi. She liked the idea of the inland sea, and managed to link it to her dislike of the city.

> Would that the ebb and flow of the great Gobi Ocean might cleanse the streets of unwholesome Urumchi and wash out to sea

the carcasses of street dogs frozen to death in the winter cold and coming to light as the snow slowly disappears.

The speakers at the front of the bus blasted the most popular song in China ever, Celine Dion's fucking 'My Heart Will Go On'. 'That's it,' I said to Jack. 'Let's see how loud this baby will go.' I had loaded a Tom Waits album from my iBook to my MP3 player the night before. I put my earphones in and looked out at the desert and listened to 'A Town with No Cheer', a song about a hot train journey between Melbourne and Adelaide.

The desert wasn't as monotonous as I had first thought. After a few bus and train trips I had started to notice variations in the colours of the rocks; back near Dunhuang the stones were almost black, but here they were pale yellow and sometimes pink. The Trio would have seen all of this, and far more besides. I listened to Tom Waits sing about the V-line train from Melbourne, and I suddenly realised that the Trio must have understood the Gobi desert in the same way that I understood my home town.

I thought about how I could see subtle differences between Melbourne suburbs that would seem identical to a visitor from China. I could distinguish the cultural variations between the cheap, friendly Preston market and the touristy Queen Vic market, between the comfortable 'little Saigon' of Richmond and the poorer Vietnamese shops in Footscray. I could picture the way the architecture changed every few blocks along the beach road between Brighton and Frankston. Sitting on a bus in the Gobi desert, I saw Melbourne clearly, and the rush of love I felt for it made me understand a little better how the Trio must have felt about China and the Gobi.

After nearly two hours the desert started rolling and dipping and then there were hills and bushes, then the bushes turned to deciduous trees, and within about half an hour we were in the Swiss Alps. That's what it looked like, anyway. The road ran next to a stream that was just a trickle of water at the foot of the hills. The further we climbed, the harder and wider the stream gushed. Flocks of fat, shaggy sheep drank at the stream and lay around under the shade of the trees. Green meadows stretched behind the stream.

We reached an asphalt bus-stand area, with souvenir stalls and drink stands and two sets of entrance fees, neither of which had been mentioned to us when we bought our bus ticket. On the far side of the car park we could see the bottom end of a cable car that carried passengers up the steep hill to the lake.

I don't have a very good head for heights.

A couple of young men stood by the bottom of the cable, hustling people into the cars. They positioned Jack and me on either side of the track, and when the next car swung around I took a deep breath and we jumped in and the flimsy gates were slammed shut.

I looked at Jack. 'China doesn't have a very good safety record on ... well, stuff, does it?' I said.

Jack laughed. 'Mum would like this,' he said. Our mother's fear of heights is worse than mine. Ever since he was very young, Jack would search out high places to climb, just to scare her.

We were lifted further from the ground, up a steep fir-lined slope. I concentrated on breathing evenly. Our little car wobbled a bit. 'Look, the trees will break your fall,' Jack said. 'You'll just be horribly injured instead of killed.'

Tiny sheep grazed a long way beneath us. It would have been very peaceful, except that each column holding up the cable had a speaker placed on it, with Chinese pop music blaring out. Jack said the music was to soothe frightened travellers, and he sang along, translating the lyrics for me:

'No, you won't die, it's really very safe
We've never had an accident

Except for that one time, and lightning doesn't strike twice
Well, not very often.'

Near the top of the hill we passed a young Western guy and girl who were walking all the way up. They carried backpacks and wore heavy hiking boots. I assumed they were mad.

When we reached the top of the mountain, more strapping young Chinese men helped us out of the car. We were at the edge of another car park, with another collection of souvenir stalls. A young woman walked towards us, ignoring all the Chinese tourists around us, and spoke to Jack and me. She looked like a Uyghur, only she was wearing tight jeans and had very short hair. She turned out to be Kazakh.

'Do you want to stay in yurts?' she asked us. When I said we wanted to find Rashit's yurt, she smiled and said she was Shirley, Rashit's sister. At least I think that's what she said. I wasn't sure if she had taken a Western name, or if she had a Kazakh name that sounded like Shirley. Maybe she said 'Surely I'm Rashit's sister.'

Shirley said she would take us to the yurts. She led us down a road and we rounded a corner, and there was the lake.

The crowds and touts and abandoned noodle packets and Future Cola bottles could only detract so much from the lake's gorgeousness. A deep blue expanse of water lay in a bowl of grassy hills with snow-covered peaks towering in the background. The sun and breeze were exactly as bright and strong as they should have been. Shirley pointed out the highest mountain. It was Bogeda Feng, the Mountain of God.

We turned our backs on the tourists and followed Shirley along the road and down to a path by the water. We hiked for a long time, and saw only trees and rocks and water. Nobody passed us on the track. Shirley didn't say much.

After about an hour, we rounded another bend and saw five yurts in a clearing by the water. They all looked big enough to sleep about ten people. A couple of the yurts had brightly painted doors and patterned banners wrapped around them, but the others were a plain dirty white. A woman was sitting at a rough wooden table outside one of the yurts. The view from the table was pretty much perfect. Shirley gestured to a hand-painted banner on another yurt, then she disappeared. The banner said SHITS. We looked a bit closer and saw that the banner had slipped a bit at one end, so the capital R and A had become obscured.

We sat down and introduced ourselves to the woman at the table. Maya was French, and she was drinking salty Kazakh tea. 'It's not very nice,' she said. A Kazakh woman appeared from a yurt that we later learned was the kitchen, carrying cups of salty tea for Jack and me.

Maya had been staying with Rashit's clan for a few days. She said they were a nomadic extended family that had pitched yurts here in the summer for generations. In the winter, when the lake froze over, they travelled down to the desert. These days the government asked the family for lots of money for the privilege of staying by the lake, so they set up a couple of extra yurts for paying visitors, and threw extra noodles in the pot for them.

We chatted about our travels, and I told Maya about the Trio. She reeled off the names of early European women travellers she admired: Ella Maillart, Gertrude Bell, Isabella Bird. She said they were free and independent women. 'And they were not religious,' she said, as if that gave them extra points for coolness.

I nodded, but her knee-jerk anti-Christian response kind of annoyed me. I didn't think any of Maya's heroines were going to come out ahead of the Trio if it came to a battle of the right-on lady explorers. They may have been ahead of their time when it came to women's rights, or at least wealthy white women's rights, but some of them could be astoundingly condescending when it came to other races. Gertrude Bell referred to people in a Chinese crowd as 'happy gnomes'. Derogatory nicknames for locals were common – Etta Close called one of her East African porters 'Baboon'. Most of them were rabidly opposed to inter-marriage between races.

Admittedly I liked Ella Maillart, and I knew that in spite of the stories of lesbianism and Eastern spirituality that swirled around her, the Trio loved her books. Platt wrote that a signed copy of Maillart's *Forbidden Journey*, about her travels through Xinjiang, was among the Trio's most treasured possessions. He didn't say whether the women ever met.

'So why is it you like these English women?' Maya asked.

I gave her the stock responses I gave my female colleagues at home, about feminism and independence and educating girls: all the things that made the Trio appear to be ahead of their time and in line with women of our own time, and therefore *right*. I said that today the Trio would be doing something heroic like working for Medicins Sans Frontières or the Red Cross.

We looked at the lake and drank our tea, and I thought that in fact what I admired about the Trio was not so much what they did but the way they did it. I liked the way they told stories. I liked the fact that they laughed at themselves. I admired the way they respected other people's opinions completely but also held on to their own beliefs completely. I was impressed by their physical and moral courage.

'Oh, and I'm so jealous of how fluently they spoke Mandarin,' I said.

Maya laughed. We talked about our difficulties in communicating because of our minimal Mandarin skills, and how it became even more difficult now that we had to switch to Uyghur and Kazakh. I told Maya that Jack and I had been spoiled in India, where almost everyone speaks some English.

'Oh, but Indians, zey speak it wiz soch a ferny accent, I lovv zat!' she said. I knew I'd laugh if I looked at Jack, so I resolutely stared at the lake.

Maya excused herself. She had to pack her bag and walk back to the car park to catch a bus to Urumqi. Jack and I just admired the view. Hundreds of goats trotted down the hill from behind us, bleating and butting into each other. They lined up to drink from the lake. Two Kazakh men rode horses around the goats, rounding them up if they strayed away from the group.

A few cups of tea later, after waving goodbye to Maya, I walked down to the lake and put my bare feet in the water. It was freezing cold. I sat on the rocks by the water's edge and read a chapter of my English translation of *Monkey*. Occasionally a motorboat carrying Chinese tourists roared past. The rest of the time the silence was broken only by the bleating of Rashit's sheep. I'd be bleating too, if I was a sheep tethered to a kitchen yurt in Xinjiang, home of the mutton kebab.

I finished reading a passage where Monkey pisses into a gourd and presents it to a priest as holy water. I looked up and saw that Jack was talking to the young couple we had seen climbing the mountain. I clambered over the rocks and joined them.

John and Sarah were Americans in their early twenties. They were studying in Tianjin, and claimed to be 'cutting class' to travel around Xinjiang. John spoke fluent Mandarin and Russian, and had already picked up some Uyghur.

I asked John what people were saying when they pointed at us and laughed and said something to their friends. I usually picked up '*lao wei*', a slightly derogatory term for foreigner, but I couldn't understand much more than that. John said that people were almost always saying 'Look, they're foreigners! They're so stupid, they can't speak Chinese.' He said these people very rarely seemed to be discomforted if he responded in Mandarin.

I asked if Chinese people were hostile towards Americans. Sarah said no, all the hostility came from other expatriates.

'I was at a bar in Tianjin ...' John said.

'We call it the Cantina because it's like that scene in *Star Wars* where the bar has people from everywhere in the universe,' Sarah said. 'Which sounds really cool, except it's all the creepy people; it's like every country has off-loaded its awful people to this one bar.'

'Anyway,' John said, 'I was buying a drink and this Australian asked me where I was from. I'd never met him or spoken to him before. I said I was from the US and he said "Ah, ya fucking wanker."'

'Oh wow, you met Russell Crowe,' I said.

John and Sarah killed time on the endless Chinese train trips by recalling and singing the lyrics to 1980s sitcoms. We challenged them to perform for us, and they sang the *Perfect Strangers* and *Growing Pains* themes, complete with harmonies and instrumental breaks. We applauded. So did the Kazakh women, who were chopping vegetables by the kitchen yurt.

A man strode down the lakeside path and sat down on a rock outside the closest yurt to us. He introduced himself as Rashit, and called for another pot of tea. He nursed his tea and looked at the lake.

Soon a group of young men emerged from one of the yurts. I wondered what they had been doing. After talking to them later, I realised they had probably been praying.

'Eight Uyghur boys, two American boys,' Rashit said quietly, to nobody in particular, as if he was weighing up the significance of this.

The men started throwing a Frisbee around, laughing and shouting to each other. The Frisbee kept almost landing in the pot of noodles that was boiling on the fire outside the kitchen yurt. The Kazakh women didn't seem to mind.

The two Americans had little hipster goatees. One of them seemed to speak Uyghur, and the Uyghur men spoke some English. After a while one of the Americans sat down to rest, so I walked over and sat on the grass next to him. I introduced myself and asked what he and his friend were doing in Xinjiang.

'We're just talking to folks about Jesus,' he said. He didn't tell me his name. He told me he had worked in Urumqi for a few years, before returning to the US. He and his friend had now been sent on a short visit by their church, to do some teaching among Uyghur Christian men.

I told him I was researching the travels of missionaries who had lived and worked with Uyghur people, and I was keen to find out how many Uyghurs were Christians now.

The American called over one of the Uyghur men. 'He'd know better than me,' he said.

The Uyghur man sat down and shook my hand. I told him my name but he didn't tell me his. I told him I had read that there were only about fifty Uyghur Christians in Xinjiang, and I was wondering if that had changed. He said no, that sounded about right.

'That's in fellowship,' the American added. It was a term I understood. He meant there were about fifty Uyghur Christians who met together regularly for Christian teaching and worship. He said there were many more who had been converted over the years, but who didn't meet regularly with other Christians, sometimes for fear of repercussions from family or authorities.

I remembered a story Ange told me in Xi'an. She said she knew about a Uyghur girl who became a Christian when she was studying in Muslim-dominated Kazakhstan. When she went home to Xinjiang she didn't tell her family about her new faith, but one day when she was working in the fields her father found her Bible among her things. He found her and beat her until he thought she was dead, and left her in the field. She regained consciousness and crawled away, and she was now in hiding.

The American said all the Uyghur Christians met unofficially in people's homes, in what were known as house churches. The Uyghur man laughed when I asked if any Uyghur Christians went to official Three Self Patriotic Movement churches. He said there were plenty of thriving TSPM churches in Urumqi, but that Uyghurs would not be welcome at them. If they turned up they would be asked to leave. He said TSPM churches were only for Han Chinese.

I already knew that there was a gulf between Hui and Uyghur Muslim communities. They had different mosques and customs, and the Hui seemed to have more religious freedom than the Uyghurs. It appeared that the same was true for Christians.

I asked the Uyhgur man about separatism. Did he think there was still a movement for Xinjiang to become independent of China? The man laughed again. He said independence was accepted by almost everybody as a lost cause. Uyghur people resented Chinese government policies, he said, but they knew that with a Han majority in Xinjiang there was nothing they could do to fight it. He said the impetus for separatism all came from Uyghurs living outside China, in places like Germany. He said these people didn't understand the reality. He said China's aggressive reaction to Taiwan's declared independence had been taken by most Uyghurs as a warning about what could happen in Xinjiang.

Of course there were always a few hotheaded Uyghurs who were willing to fight the authorities in smaller ways. The man asked if I had been to the new Erdaoqiao Market in Urumqi. I said I had.

The man said that when the old market was knocked down and the new structure was erected, some Uyghur men were so angry that they hatched a plan to blow up the building. Apparently they got hold of some explosives and were ready to go bombing, but one of the members of the group turned out to be a police spy, and the rest of them were arrested.

'Now tell her your joke about the men on the train,' the American said.

A Swiss man, a Cuban man and a Uyghur man are on a train, the joke goes. The Swiss man opens his bag, pulls out a watch and casually throws it out the window. The others are surprised. 'I can afford to do that, we've got lots of those in my country,' he says. The Cuban responds by pulling a cigar from his pocket and throwing it out the window. 'Well, we have lots of those in my country,' he explains. The Uyghur looks around him and sees a Han Chinese man. He drags him to the window and throws him out. The other men look shocked. The Uyghur says 'We have lots of those in my country'.

In the evening, after we ate our noodles and the sun set over the lake, the Uyghur men built a fire on the rocks right by the water. It flared up and made the whole vista look even more dramatic. The men all sat round the fire and sang Christian songs in English. The songs didn't sound familiar to me, but I had been out of the loop for a couple of years, and fashions in catchy choruses had probably passed me by. One of the Uyghur men played a guitar. Sarah, John, Jack and I watched them from the table.

Later, I pointed out to Jack that Sarah and John didn't make fun of the missionaries the way that many young Australians would have. 'Remember that Safran interview?' I said. We were both fans of Australian TV performer John Safran, who had travelled the world making a comedy series about religion, only to discover that most cultures still take it very seriously. He concluded that Australia – or at least the young, inner-city Australia of his experience – was just about the most secular place on the planet, the only country where religious belief is considered quaint and outmoded and only important to little old ladies and nutjobs.

The air around us became much colder after the sun went down, and we decided to sit by the flames. We walked towards the fire, chatting loudly about TV theme tunes until we were close enough to realise that the group around the fire was silent. Heads were bowed and eyes were closed, and one of the Americans started praying. We sat down by the fire.

The cadences of the American's prayer were startlingly familiar to me. He finished up by saying 'So Lord, I really want to ask you to just bless us Lord, open our eyes Lord to what you have to say to us tonight Lord, we ask in your most precious name Lord.'

Everyone joined him in saying 'Amen'. The American explained that in the afternoon he had talked to the group about what he called the wilderness experience. He said that just as the children of Israel had wandered in the desert for forty years, Christians today experienced times of suffering and dryness and even unbelief. But tonight, he said, he was going to talk about the next phase. Just as the children of Israel had been allowed to enter the Promised Land, we could receive the blessings that God wanted for us.

The metaphor was pretty apt, seeing as we had all reached Heaven Lake after travelling through the desert. I think Mildred would have liked it. The American talked about how much God loved us, about how much he wanted for us, not because we had earned it or deserved it, but just because he loved us.

Whenever the American read a Bible verse he asked one of the Uyghur men to read the same verse in Uyghur. The fire glowed and crackled, and I moved a bit closer.

I thought about all the years when I had tried to believe, and how I kept hoping that I would hear the right sermon or read the right book or someone would have a special word from the Lord for me, and it would all come together, it would feel right, God would speak directly into my situation and I would believe. At one time, sitting by the fire under the Mountain of God and hearing this talk, I might have felt that this was it.

But it was far too late now. The American kept talking and I suddenly knew I'd had enough. The fire was warm and comforting but the stones were hard and my bum was getting numb. I didn't want to listen anymore. 'I'm going to bed,' I said to Jack, not particularly quietly.

I walked away from the fire, up to the yurt, and breathed in the cold air on my own. Someone had lit a candle inside the yurt, and there were enough grubby quilts laid out to keep an army warm. I rolled out a quilt, lay down and went to sleep.

Chapter Fourteen

England

On May 26, 1936, a birthday party for Eva French was celebrated under a patch of trees by a stream in the Gobi desert. She was 67.

Sir Thomas Cook helped Mildred and Francesca light a fire and bake some scones. They used some carefully hoarded baking powder that the English consul-general from Kashgar had given them in Urumqi. They brought out the last lick of honey they had bought at the Russian border, and they spread a clean cloth under the trees.

They suspected it would be their last birthday in China, and they were right. Three months later they were bundled out of the country on government orders.

The women had only been back in China for a year, after spending two years writing and lecturing in England. When they had arrived in Urumqi in 1935, after an overland journey through Europe, they had immediately noticed changes. Nobody could go anywhere without a permit, and Sir Thomas Cook and Brother Chen were in jail in Urumqi on charges of travelling without the correct paperwork. The USSR now had a strong influence in Xinjiang, Japanese troops had started moving into China from the north, and communists were approaching from the south. Soldiers had occupied Jiuquan, and food was scarce. Many of the Trio's friends had died during a typhus epidemic.

During that last year the Trio kept doing what they had always done. They ran literacy classes and looked after sick people and travelled from oasis to oasis with their Bibles. But they knew they didn't have long. Mildred began to suffer badly from insomnia.

When all foreigners were ordered to leave Gansu, the Trio wrote:

> Things tighten more and more, and finally the hard hour has come when we have to tell the Christians that we must leave, for our common-sense warns us that our presence here is a danger to our converts. So long as we are here the Christians will refuse to leave us, and together – foreigner and Chinese Christians are a tempting target.

Early in September 1936, they left Jiuquan for the last time. They were taken in a lorry convoy to Lanzhou, and from there they flew over China for the first time. They looked down on the road to Xi'an that they had travelled by mule cart. 'It lay, a little pale thread below us, and the distance it took us twenty days to cover at three miles an hour, we now covered in two hours, ten minutes.'

They caught a train from Xi'an to Beijing, and then had to decide whether to go back to England by sea or the Trans-Siberian Railway. They chose the train because it was cheaper than the boat, and they bought the cheapest, hardest, third-class seats.

It would be easy to think they were masochists. But the idea of being a good steward of the Lord's money was, and still is, important to most missionaries. When you've seen the kind of poverty much of the world lives in, you can't justify unnecessary expenditures. So you might, for example, dress your child in hardy second-hand cords from the charity shop rather than buying fashionable new acid-washed jeans, even if this makes your child's social life difficult.

Not that I'm bitter.

Not all the foreign missionaries were ordered out of China, at least not straight away. Hundreds of them struggled on through World War II. It wasn't until 1949, when the communists took over the whole country and Mao Zedong declared the People's Republic of China, that all the missionaries were expelled. Many believed the Chinese Christians wouldn't cope without them. In the West, it was feared that Christianity would disappear in China.

In 1949 there were about about three million Catholics and three quarters of a million Protestants in China. In 2006 there were anywhere between 22 million and 90 million Christians in China, depending on who you listened to. The lowest figures are official government numbers, and only include people registered with the Three Self Patriotic Movement and the Catholic Patriotic Association. David Aikman, the former Beijing bureau chief for *Time* magazine, estimated in his 2003 book *Jesus in Beijing* that the number was close to 80 million. He admitted it was hard to know for sure.

Even using the most conservative numbers, Christians make up a significantly larger proportion of Chinese society today than they did when the missionaries left, and the numbers are growing. The vast majority of these Christians have had no contact with foreigners, even if the seeds of the faith had been sown by people like the Trio, generations ago. An indigenous, underground Christian movement called Back to Jerusalem is training hundreds of Chinese missionaries to travel west along the Silk Road through Xinjiang and towards the Middle East.

I think the Trio would have liked the way things turned out.

In 1932 Mildred wrote to friends: 'Somewhere in Dorset, in a village we have never yet seen, is a little stone cottage, which we cannot locate because we have never been there, but it is ours – our own ...'

Willow Cottage was where the women retired when they returned to England for good. There doesn't seem to have been any thought of them not living together. They and Topsy were irrevocably each other's family.

'Retired' is hardly the right word for what the Trio did. They wrote books and lectured and worked for numerous Christian organisations, and they travelled around the world preaching about the importance of missions. After *The Gobi Desert* was published, Mildred and Francesca were awarded the Lawrence of Arabia Medal by the Royal Central Asian Society and the Livingstone medal by the Royal Scottish Geographical Society. The mother of Topsy's beloved Princess Elizabeth, the Queen of England, gave out copies of *The Gobi Desert* as Christmas presents and invited the women to Buckingham Palace to show her their photographs. Topsy made guest appearances at conferences; it sounds as if she was seen as something of a celebrity oddity.

Mildred learned to drive, although she did it badly. The first time Dr Platt came to visit them at Willow Cottage, Mildred picked him up at the train station. She zoomed off and chattered away, pointing out local sites rather than steering the car. 'It was an exciting ride,' Platt wrote.

Topsy was nearly twenty by this time. Soon after the family settled in England, her long plaits were cut off and her hair was put up. That night, when she went to bed, she explained to her mamas that the prayer 'Bless Thy Little Lamb Tonight' was no longer appropriate for her. She was a sheep, she said. She might be small, but she was a woman now.

All the same, Topsy spent most of her time close to home. She loved to garden and cook. Eva spent less time travelling and preaching than the other women; left alone at the cottage, she and Topsy became even closer. Edith Wheeler, a friend of the Trio's, taught Topsy to read, write and use sign language. This helped her communicate better with outsiders, but there was little need to improve things with her mamas. They understood each other already.

By the time World War II broke out, the women were so busy that they bought a flat to live in when they had business in London. Mildred did so much work for the Bible Society that she had an office in its London headquarters.

Ironically, after all their adventures in China, the closest near-death experience they ever had was in the Hampstead flat. In June 1944 a German bomb landed pretty much on top of them. They wrote to friends:

> At 2am we were fast asleep, then suddenly Eva found herself buried in the rubble, to be brought out by the ARP with cuts and bruises. Francesca's head was bruised when the door of her bedroom landed on top of her. Mildred's belongings were scattered. She could find no shoes and had to walk out of her room with bare feet over a mass of broken glass. Edith Wheeler escaped without injury, and Topsy was away attending a wedding, but her empty bedroom collapsed and, indeed, ceased to exist. Some of our neighbours and friends were killed.

Their last overseas trip was to South America in 1951. They went by sea, and wrote about Topsy winning the ship's fancy-dress ball and walking arm in arm with the captain. In the Bible Society's archives in Cambridge, in a folder that contains mostly business correspondence between the society and Mildred, there is a private letter that Mildred wrote to Dr Platt before the ship set sail.

> Whenever I start out on a journey and leave one or other of my beloved companions behind I always wish that I had the courage to speak to you and tell you that in the event of anything unexpected happening to me I look to you as 'next of kin' to go to them and give them what they would need – moral support and friendship. So now I am daring to write it – just burn this if you like, but put my request in your heart.

Then there is Mildred's distinctive signature. She died unexpectedly the next year after a bout of shingles, aged 74, just nine months after the women returned from South America. Dr Platt sent responses to the hundreds of sympathy letters that came to the French sisters through the Bible Society: 'Her mind was crystal clear all the time,' he wrote. Francesca told Platt that she and Eva missed Mildred horribly, but felt her spirit warning them not to be sad. 'The comradeship has left nothing to regret,' she said.

Francesca and Eva died only three weeks apart, in 1960, at Willow Cottage. When Eva became seriously ill, 88-year-old Francesca slept on the floor next to her bed. When a friend questioned this, Francesca retorted 'I've been sleeping on the floor all my life – it's nothing.'

After the two funerals, Edith Wheeler took Topsy away on holiday to Scotland. Topsy was about 40 years old. She was devastated by the losses. Her memory of this time remained clear to the end. In her letters to Patricia East in the 1990s she compulsively detailed the dates and circumstances of each illness, death and funeral.

Dr Platt remembered Mildred's request to look after her family. Just before Edith and Topsy went to Scotland he wrote to Edith, asking after Topsy. She replied:

Topsy is exceedingly sad about leaving the cottage and was rather resentful at first ... She continually asks if I am weak and when I am going to die!! One day when I assured her that I was well and strong she wrote the following and handed it to me. 'When – do not know after waiting short time we both Topsy and Miss Wheeler in heaven? 1962?'

Right from the start, it had been impossible for me to follow the Trio's journeys in anything resembling a chronological order. They continually backtracked and criss-crossed throughout northwest China, and around the whole world for that matter. So it's appropriate enough that I first started looking for the Trio in England, where they spent their final years.

In the ten days between my dinner with Patricia East in Munich and my arrival at the Far East International Hostel in Beijing, I poked around the south of England, visiting libraries and talking to people about the Trio. Patricia warned me that there wasn't much in the archives, and she was right. But it wasn't a wasted trip.

I spent a morning in London, looking at Chinese art at the British Museum. Then I had lunch at the Charing Cross Hotel with a friend of my Australian publisher, an older man who was considering publishing me in England. He wanted to know what kind of publicity I was going to drum up to draw attention to my book.

I wasn't sure what he meant. I wondered if he wanted me to drive a mule cart, or possibly a camel train, through the centre of London.

'I don't know very much about publicity,' I said, tucking into my cheesecake. 'And I'm not especially photogenic or charismatic.' Or skilled at selling myself to publishers, I should have added.

'Oh, all young ladies are photogenic,' he said. 'Of course you're overweight, but I expect you'll lose some of that in China.'

I took a bus to Gloucester to see friends at a missionary training college, where I spent hours below a bookshelf labelled 'China Missions', looking at an eclectic set of literature. The 1901 edition of *Martyred Missionaries* sat next to a 1981 paperback called *God's Smuggler to China* that I remembered reading when I was a child. It was written by the anonymous 'Brother David' with Dan Wooding, whose other books, according to the inside front cover, include *Junkies Are People Too* and *Guerilla for Christ*. The lurid cover art showed an angry Chinese border guard brandishing a Bible he had just discovered in the luggage of a clean-cut white man, presumably Brother David.

The most recent publication on the shelf was a missions report from 2001 called *Operation China*. It described the religious status of each minority group in China. I turned to the Uyghur page and learned that there had been mass executions of Uyghur Christians in Kashgar in 1933, that few Han Christians in Xinjiang were interested in spreading Christianity to the Uyghurs, and that there were about fifty known Uyghur Christians in China, as well as more than four hundred in Kazakhstan.

I travelled on to Guilford and met a woman called Valerie Griffith. Valerie and her husband, Michael, were former missionaries to Japan and Singapore, and Michael had later become head of the Overseas Missionary Fellowship, the organisation that used to be the China Inland Mission. He's still a well-known writer and speaker in the evangelical world.

Valerie knew a lot about CIM history, and had written a book about women missionaries in China in which she devoted two chapters to the Trio. I had emailed her from Australia and told her that I was writing about the Trio. I told her I wasn't an evangelical. Valerie sent me long, generous letters about the Trio and her own trip to China. She said she had not attempted to meet with any Chinese Christians because it could be dangerous for them. She warned me to be careful who I tried to contact in China.

Valerie picked me up from the train station and took me home and fed me salmon with tomato and basil and new potatoes. She drove me around Guilford on a sunny day and pointed out two of Mildred Cable's childhood homes. Then she took me out of town to show me fields of bluebells, because it was springtime, and what visitor to England in springtime doesn't want to see fields of bluebells?

I asked Valerie a lot of questions while we walked through the fields. I thought she might tell me things that I wouldn't find in any writing by or about the Trio. I said that Platt's 1964 biography seemed to be defending the Trio against criticism without quite spelling out what that criticism was. Valerie had some ideas, although she thought personally that the Trio did 'magnificent' work. She had never met the Trio, but she had known older missionaries who had, and she had heard decades of CIM gossip.

Some people never got over the Trio's move from Shanxi to the northwest. They thought the women had abandoned the Christian work in Huozhou. One missionary who went to Huozhou in 1930 told Valerie that there were empty buildings because the Christian work had grown too fast on Western money and then collapsed when the Trio left. After researching the Trio's work, Valerie decided this wasn't really fair. The students had always paid their way, and the school had emptied because the provincial governor wanted to use their educated girls as teachers in new schools, even before the Trio had moved on.

Others thought the Trio were too independent, and should have been more answerable to the CIM. One missionary who worked in

Gansu told Valerie he thought the Trio wanted to keep the area to themselves. 'He felt they had an attitude of "keep off our patch",' she said.

One reason the Trio could set their own rules was because they didn't depend on the CIM for money. The majority of CIM workers were sent an equal share of money donated to the mission every quarter, but the Trio were supported by their own network of family and friends, and by the sale of their books. 'It was acceptable, but it gave them a degree of freedom and independence others didn't have,' Valerie said. It wasn't surprising that this led to some resentment.

The Trio were also criticised for pushing the boundaries of acceptable behaviour for women. Valerie mentioned how Eva and Mildred had served communion to Chinese Christians. In *Something Happened*, they wrote about receiving an angry letter about a lapse in theological practice, which I assumed was about this issue. Their response was only just polite, and boiled down to 'Why don't you come over here and risk your life in the desert, then you can tell us what to do.'

Valerie described Eva and Mildred as 'strong and exceptionally gifted individualists'. She said it was inevitable that people like that would draw criticism. Then she smiled. She said the criticism was probably a healthy balance to the 'adulation and hero-worship' the women received in England.

And finally, the day before I flew to China, I almost met Topsy.

I caught a train from London up to the Midlands, to the town of Leamington Spa, where a woman called Marion Myers met me at the station. Marion's father, Paul Broomhall, had been the Trio's friend and business adviser. He arranged the purchase of Willow Cottage for them while they were still in China.

Paul and his wife, Rosalind, became Topsy's informal guardians after Eva and Francesca died. After her parents died, Marion and her husband, John, took on responsibility for Topsy. They considered her part of their family.

Marion drove me to their house and introduced me to John, who introduced me to their elderly border collies and their ginger cat called Moses ('Because we found him in the bullrushes'). They fed me good bread and real butter and salad and boiled eggs for lunch. Marion had placed a framed picture of the Trio and Topsy on the dining table.

Marion's Broomhall ancestors included a whole dynasty of CIM missionaries, writers and supporters. Her great-great-grandfather Benjamin Broomhall married Hudson Taylor's sister Amelia and led the fight against Britain's opium trade in China (it was finally outlawed as he lay on his deathbed). Her great-uncle Marshall wrote much of *Martyred Missionaries* and her uncle Jim wrote volumes on the history of the CIM. Marion was a counsellor and therapist with an interest in missionaries. She said she had worked with missionaries who had 'experienced emotional breakdown on the field'.

Marion said her father in particular had been very close to Topsy. Topsy always spent Christmas and Easter with the extended family at Penshurst, Paul and Rosalind's home in Sussex. Marion and her siblings had since turned Penshurst into a retreat centre for what she called 'mission and humanitarian workers'.

Marion gave me the background on Topsy's later years. She said Topsy lived at Willow Cottage with Eva and Francesca until well after Mildred's death. Later Topsy and the sisters went to live at Troutstream Hall, a home for retired missionaries in Hertfordshire. She stayed on after Eva and Francesca died.

Topsy lived at Troutstream Hall until 1973, but she became unhappy there after the death of the matron, who knew and understood her. For a couple of years she was shuffled about the place, and she lived with Marion's parents for six months, but in 1975 she moved to Rookstone, a Salvation Army home in London. On January 25, 1998, Marion was called to the home in the middle of the night to be with Topsy, who died peacefully the next day, aged 80 – as far as they knew.

Marion said she had things for me to look at, and more to tell me, but she had a back injury so she had to lie down while she talked. She took me to her bedroom and gave me three cardboard folders. They contained photos, papers and cuttings about the Trio. Marion had collected some of these things from Topsy's room after she died.

Marion lay on the bed while I sat at a low table and looked through the folders. The room was warm and smelled of lavender and dogs. I felt very comfortable, and strangely close to Marion. The two dogs sat at my feet. It had been only seven years since Topsy died, and I realised she would have known these dogs.

Marion was excited about my book. 'I think the Trio were wonderful,' she said, looking up at the roof. She said she was not an evangelical, but she had a strong faith. 'I don't believe – I think I don't believe – that people who haven't heard and die without Christ are damned,' she said. 'I think God's love reaches out to people in every culture and religion.'

I picked up a folder and took out a black-and-white photo of a stone cottage.

'The first time I met the Trio and Topsy I was six,' Marion said. 'We were on our way to Cornwall in the car and we stopped at Willow Cottage. It was very clean, very frugal. Everything was recycled – they probably had newspaper for toilet paper. I remember we had apple pie from the fruit trees in their garden. We were driving on through the night and my brother and I were put to bed in the back seat of the car. Topsy thought this was a great joke. I remember lying all tucked up in the back seat and this Tibetan face looking down on me and laughing and laughing.'

One of the dogs sat up and looked at me and put a paw on my knee. 'Hello,' I said softly. Marion must have heard me.

'Topsy just loved all animals,' she said. 'She loved these dogs, and she loved to go out and feed the ducks.

'She loved Christmas, she loved giving and receiving presents, and she would always send our children presents. It was often a chocolate bar like a Kit Kat, all lovingly wrapped in recycled Christmas paper, but she would have stored it in a drawer next to a box of soap, so it was usually inedible.

'She loved going to the post office. She'd mime the cashier stamping her post office savings book, and that indicated she wanted to go and draw money out. Then she'd take us for a Chinese meal, or go and buy pretty fabric or embroidery silk.' She said Topsy embroidered beautifully, and gave out hand-embroidered tray cloths or mats as presents.

I found a copy of a letter about Topsy that Marion sent to a social worker in 1982, when she was looking for somewhere different for Topsy to live. 'Topsy still maintains a lively interest in other cultures and peoples, in works of art, and in the events of family life, ie birth, marriage and death,' Marion had written. I read this to her. 'What artworks did she like?' I asked.

'Oh, she loved going to galleries, seeing paintings,' Marion said. 'She loved to see Chinese porcelain. The Trio would have taken her to museums. She loved anything Chinese; she used chopsticks and brewed green tea. She was proud of her Chinese heritage.

'She used to make herself beautiful Chinese tops and skirts. She didn't need a pattern to cut them out, and she did all the stitching by hand. She made those intricate Chinese loops to fasten them, so she didn't need buttons or zips. The tops were always voluminous because she kept things inside them – money, rings of keys, letter, tissues and so on. They made her look bigger than she was. She was actually quite small.

'The keys were for her room, and for all the drawers in her room that she kept locked. The drawers were full of things that she hoarded ... all sorts of things, like bits of silk that Mildred had given her. She had so many things and sometimes she would misplace them and she would accuse people of stealing from her.'

Marion paused. 'I really tried to find another place for her,' she said. 'She was too young to be in that kind of home, but the social workers weren't much help. She was a bit of a one-off, so they never knew quite what to do with her.

'It was very sad in a way. I often thought it would have been better if the Trio had prepared her for life without them, maybe getting her into a sheltered flat. But places like that were few and far between in the 50s, and she loved living with the Trio as part of their family. And they told my father they didn't anticipate that Topsy would outlive them. Her life at Willow Cottage had been very mapped out for her, she had her vegetable garden and her jobs and so on. She missed her three mamas terribly.'

Like Marion, I felt sad for Topsy. When I first started reading the Trio's books, I was excited about researching Topsy's life in England. I had expected some kind of happy ending that would symbolise all the good works that the Trio had done. I was surprised at how disappointed I was that she had spent decades in old peoples' homes, never really recovering from her losses. I felt somehow let down that the Trio hadn't properly prepared her for life without them.

'How did Topsy communicate?' I asked.

Marion said that she wrote notes, or mimed, or acted scenes – 'like bumping across the Gobi on a cart'. She tried to speak, but it was indistinct to people who didn't know her. She had communicated effortlessly with the Trio after all their years together. After Edith Wheeler died it seems nobody around her used sign language.

Marion said that, at Rookstone, Topsy didn't get enough opportunities to do the kind of cooking and cleaning jobs that she enjoyed.

'At Troutstream she was appointed as a kind of unofficial housekeeper, she used to help out a lot. At Rookstone they stopped her from doing that. There were hygiene issues – she was like the Trio, she recycled everything, so when she was cleaning up after breakfast and someone had left milk in the bottom of their cereal bowl she would tip it back into the jug.'

I was reminded of Topsy's early years as a beggar, when she would insist on doing jobs for people.

I picked up a scrap of paper. Topsy had written on it: 'Mother Tibet Father Mongolia were married January 1910.' I read this to Marion.

'Ah, she's got them married,' she said. 'She had an innate sense of what was proper, and I think she had some sense of being unwanted and illegitimate, and of needing to hide that.

'When she met people, she always looked to see if they had a wedding ring, and always wanted to know why they weren't married or if they had a boyfriend or anything. She would mime out why she wasn't married – because she couldn't hear the phone, and she'd mime an old-fashioned wind-up phone, which she couldn't answer because she couldn't hear it ringing, and she couldn't hear the doorbell. Although actually she would have been a lovely mother.'

When the French sisters died and left everything to Topsy, English newspapers ran sensational, inaccurate articles about her. 'Sisters leave £16,000 to slave girl who cost 10s' was a typical headline.

Marion said Topsy had several proposals from men who saw the newspaper articles. A man wrote from Holland and said 'You seem like a very nice person, I'd like to marry you.'

'She didn't know quite what to make of it,' Marion said.

'She saw the world in very black and white terms. One thing she always said was that Hitler was evil and Jesus would punish him. When television came in she got quite addicted, she liked the soap operas. She used to tell us who was bad and who was good. At dinner she would talk about the bad man, the cad, and she'd mime how he had a wedding ring but he had gone to bed with someone else.'

I picked up an early photo of the Trio. Topsy had written 'old-fashioned' on the back. I read the words out loud and Marion laughed.

'She loved anything old-fashioned, she would say "old-fashioned" approvingly. She loved romantic films, anything with crinolines. She loved cowboy movies too – I wondered if they reminded her of the Gobi and the bandits.

'If she wanted to say something uncomplimentary about someone, she'd beckon and put her finger to her lips and take you into a corner and write a note about them, she'd write "Topsy no like." Usually she did like people, but she'd tell you if she didn't.'

I laughed. 'Oh, she had an impish sense of humour,' Marion said. 'She and John used to tease each other, they'd have fake boxing matches. She and my father teased each other too.

'She adored my father, I think she saw him as the last link to the Trio. She was very sad when he died. That was in 1995. I made sure she came to the funeral.

'Her whole life was a series of bereavements in some ways. It was when she was stressed, at times of loss, that she accused people of stealing from her.'

Later I looked again at the letter Marion wrote for the social worker. 'One of the sad things is that, in her own terms, she is perhaps justified in feeling that things have been "stolen" from her,' she wrote. 'She knows that the Trio left her all their assets and she would have loved to stay on living at the Willow Cottage, where she had spent many happy years, but it was felt that it was not possible for her to live alone.'

'I used to wonder about them calling her Topsy, that it infantalised her,' Marion said to me. 'But in the end you couldn't have changed it, that was her name.'

Women of the Gobi

I looked at a photo of Topsy in her seventies, wearing an apron over her voluminous top and holding onto a broom. She looked as if she had been disturbed in the middle of her chores. She was smiling.

Epilogue

Shanghai

Before I flew home from China I spent 51 hours on a train from Urumqi to Shanghai. After the dry heat of Xinjiang, the humidity of Shanghai hit me as soon as I stepped off the train. I was back in the tropics.

I stayed in a youth hostel in a sidestreet off the Bund, the riverfront lined with Western-style banks and consulates and trading companies that were built around the turn of the last century. I shared a room with a trio of Swedish girls who looked about twenty years old. They went shopping and came back with bags of pirated DVDs. They drank beer and danced around the room to a tape of Cher's greatest hits, which they played on a Walkman attached to tinny-sounding speakers. It was the only music they had. I plugged in my iBook and encouraged them to choose from the thousand or so songs loaded onto it. The girls scrolled through my whole music collection. Then they switched the Cher tape back on.

On my last night in Shanghai I had dinner with Dan Washburn, the American journalist, and his former Chinese teacher, Liu Yi. It was Yi who had arranged for his friend Paul to take me to Huozhou. When we exchanged emails, Yi had told me he lived at Shanghai University, where he was studying towards his PhD in the sociology of religion in China. It wasn't clear if Yi was any kind of believer, although his mother and grandmother were Christians. His home village, Hao-Yi, was only a few miles from Huozhou.

Dan and I took a taxi to Shanghai University with another journalist, an American called Scott who worked for the New York *Daily News*. Scott was only in China for a week, and spoke no Chinese. Dan had helped hook him up with an interpreter. Scott had a couple of hours to spare and Dan had invited him along to interview Yi.

Yi met us at the university gate. It was an exciting day for him. He had just been told he had been accepted to a university in Hong Kong to continue his PhD studies. We all congratulated him, and Dan declared our dinner would now be a celebration.

The campus was clean and well laid-out and sanitised, like a technology park. There were no rock-band fliers taped to walls. As we walked through the campus, Scott tried to take photos of students without them knowing; he kept posing Dan near his real subjects and pretending to take his photo, while subtly turning the camera onto the students.

The light was starting to fade, as Yi led us to a restaurant on the campus. On the way we passed a line of young men, each of them sitting next to a bike that had a tray full of DVDs attached to the back. Dan said he had just read a report in an American newspaper that Shanghai authorities had cracked down on the trade in pirated DVDs and driven it underground. 'You wonder if the journalist even came here or if they just used the government press release,' he said.

I told him all the travellers at the youth hostel were going home with half a suitcase full of pirated DVDs.

'Of course they are,' he said.

Yi ordered masses of food, including the meatballs called Lion's Heads that his friend Paul had ordered in Huozhou. Scott asked for the name of each dish and wrote it down. The restaurant was noisy and Yi was softly spoken, and Scott kept having to ask Dan to repeat what Yi had said. When Scott stopped talking to eat he had difficulty using his chopsticks.

Scott asked Yi about changes in China, and how they had affected Yi and his family. The first thing Yi spoke about was food. He said that, when he was a child, people in his village mainly ate steamed bread, but now most people ate meat and vegetables. He said everyone was much better off, and all the new factories had created more work.

'But there's a downside to that, isn't there, with the pollution?' Dan prompted.

Yi said yes, the air and rivers in particular were filthy now. He said about four thousand people lived in his village, and he thought that no more than a hundred of them would have attended university. His parents were made to leave school and do agricultural work during the Cultural Revolution. 'My mother had to try to be a student and a farmer at the same time,' he said.

Yi's parents valued education and made him work hard. It was well known that only one of the local high schools had its students accepted into university, so Yi was sent there. He had to travel a long way there and back, and couldn't help out at home as much as he would have liked.

Yi's grandmother was a Christian, but his mother had never been interested in religion. When he was young, Yi was embarrassed about his grandmother's faith. He said children would tease him about her, and peek through the windows to get a glimpse of the strange woman.

When Yi's mother was in her thirties she became ill, and no treatments helped. Some Christians in the village said God would help her, and they encouraged her to go to church. She went, she was prayed for, and her health was restored.

'After that, she turned to God,' Yi said. 'Every morning she gets up and prays for her children.'

Yi said the Christians in his family and village had never had contact with foreigners, and wouldn't think of Christianity as a foreign religion. He said even his grandmother had never met a missionary. 'They think Christianity was born in China,' he said.

Sometimes Yi went to church with his mother, but he pointed out that he had not been baptised. He said he was not a Christian, but he had a sense of something bigger than him that was looking out for him. The news about his move to Hong Kong seemed to have confirmed this for him.

Yi said he was a Communist Party member, which meant he couldn't be a Christian anyway. He had to join the party if he wanted a decent job in the future. 'I can have some belief in my heart, but I can't be a formal church member … I want to be able to support my family, and I'll have to become a dean to ever afford a house in Shanghai.'

Scott asked Yi if he thought China's political system would ever change. 'Yes, maybe in about twenty years,' he said.

Scott had to leave and catch a taxi to the airport, but Dan, Yi and I were still eating. Scott held an American 20-dollar bill out to Dan and said 'Let me pay for dinner.' Yi said no, he insisted that he had invited us out here and he would pay. Dan said meaningfully to Scott, 'It's fine, I'll go outside with you and get you a taxi.' I could see Dan was going to let Scott pay the cashier on the way out.

Scott didn't get it. 'But I want to pay,' he said.

'No, no, I'm paying,' Yi said.

'It's fine, we'll sort it out,' Dan said emphatically to Scott. He pointed his head towards the cashier's desk, using the kind of gesture that a trained sheepdog would understand.

'But ...'

Scott either got it or thought he'd been defeated. He said goodbye effusively to Yi and me. Dan came back after five minutes. Later, when we were leaving, Dan told Yi that Scott had already paid for dinner. Yi seemed to be genuinely disappointed. 'You helped him by talking to him,' Dan said.

We walked to Yi's dorm. He wanted to give me a paper about women missionaries in China that had been presented at a symposium in Shanghai a few weeks earlier. I could hear a live rock band playing in one of the buildings nearby.

Yi kept returning to the topic of his going to Hong Kong to study. He said he would be able to publish papers there. He was clearly a reticent, serious man, but he almost skipped down the street when he talked about Hong Kong.

Yi left us in the lobby of his building and went upstairs to get me the papers. 'You should do a PhD about these women you're researching,' he said when he returned. 'Come and study in Hong Kong, we can be colleagues.'

I asked him if he was putting himself in danger by talking so openly with foreigners. I said I would give him a pseudonym if he wanted one. He laughed out loud.

'Your book is being published in Australia,' he said. 'Who's going to read it?'

Bibliography

Aikman, David, *Jesus in Beijing*, Regnery, Washington, 2003
Amnesty International, 'Uighurs Fleeing Persecution as China Wages its 'War on Terror', 2004, http://web.amnesty.org/library/index/engasa170212004 [1 July 2006]
Benson, Linda, 'Missionaries with Attitude: A Woman's Mission in Northwestern China,' in *International Bulletin of Missionary Research*, October 2005
Birkett, Dea, *Spinsters Abroad*, Basil Blackwell, 1989
Broomhall, Marshall, *Martyred Missionaries of the China Inland Mission*, London, 1901
Brown, Callum, *The Death of Christian Britain*, Routledge, 2001
Cable, A. Mildred, *The Fulfilment of a Dream of Pastor Hsi*, Morgan & Scott, London, 1917

Bibliography

Cable, Mildred, and French, Francesca, *Dispatches from North-West Kansu*, Hodder & Stoughton, London, 1925
——*The Red Lama*, Paternoster Press, London, 1927
——*A Parable of Jade*, Paternoster Press, London, 1927
——*Through Jade Gate & Central Asia*, Hodder & Stoughton, London, 1927
——*Something Happened*, Hodder & Stoughton, London, 1933
——*A Desert Journal*, Hodder & Stoughton, London, 1934
——*Ambassadors for Christ*, Hodder & Stoughton, London, 1935
——*The Making of a Pioneer*, Hodder & Stoughton, London, 1935
——*The Story of Topsy*, Hodder & Stoughton, London, 1937
——*Grace, Child of the Gobi*, Hodder & Stoughton, London, 1938
——*Towards Spiritual Maturity*, Hodder & Stoughton, London, 1939
——*The Gobi Desert*, Hodder & Stoughton, London, 1942
——*China, Her Life & Her People*, Hodder & Stoughton, London, 1946
——*The Book Which Demands a Verdict*, Hodder & Stoughton, London, 1946
——*George Hunter, Apostle of Turkestan*, Hodder & Stoughton, London, 1948
——*Journey with a Purpose*, Hodder & Stoughton, London, 1950
——*Wall of Spears*, Hodder & Stoughton, London, 1951
——*Why Not for the World?*, Hodder & Stoughton, London, 1952
Cheng-en, Wu, *Monkey*, Allen & Unwin, 1942
Crossman, Eileen, *Mountain Rain: A New Biography of James O. Fraser*, OMF, Sevenoaks, 1982
Fleming, Peter, *News from Tartary: A Journey from Peking to Kashmir*, Jonathan Cape, London, 1936
——*The Siege at Peking*, Rupert Hart-Davis, London, 1959
Griffith, Valerie, *Not Less Than Everything*, OMF/Monarch Books, 2005

Hattaway, Paul, *Back to Jerusalem*, Piquant, Carlisle, 2003
Hopkirk, Peter, *Foreign Devils on the Silk Road: The Search for Lost Cities and the Treasures of Chinese Central Asia*, John Murray, Oxford, 1980
Maillart, Ella, *Forbidden Journey: From Peking to Kashmir*, Holt, 1937
Man, John, *Genghis Khan: Life, Death, and Resurrection*, Thomas Dunne Books, 2005
Palmer, Martin, *The Jesus Sutras: Rediscovering the Lost Religion of Taoist Christianity*, Piatkus, London, 2001
Platt, W.J., *Three Women*, Hodder & Stoughton, London, 1964
Polo, Marco, *The Travels of Marco Polo*, Boni & Liveright, 1923
Neville-Hadley, Peter, *China: The Silk Routes*, Cadogen, London, 1997
Seth, Vikram, *From Heaven Lake: Travels Through Sinkiang and Tibet*, Chatto & Windus, London, 1983
Steer, Roger, *J. Hudson Taylor, A Man in Christ*, OMF, 1990
Walker, Annabel, *Aurel Stein, Pioneer of the Silk Road*, John Murray, London, 1995
Warner, Marina, *Introduction to The Gobi Desert*, Virago Press, London, 1984